John Gillies

The History of ancient Greece

It's Colonies and Conquests

John Gillies

The History of ancient Greece
It's Colonies and Conquests

ISBN/EAN: 9783741127007

Manufactured in Europe, USA, Canada, Australia, Japa

Cover: Foto ©ninafisch / pixelio.de

Manufactured and distributed by brebook publishing software (www.brebook.com)

John Gillies

The History of ancient Greece

THE HISTORY
OF
ANCIENT GREECE,

ITS COLONIES, AND CONQUESTS;

From the Earliest Accounts till the
Division of the Macedonian Empire in the East.

INCLUDING THE HISTORY OF
LITERATURE, PHILOSOPHY, AND THE FINE ARTS.

By JOHN GILLIES, LL. D. F. A. S.

Εκ μη τοιγε της ἀπαντων προς ἀλληλα συμπλοκης και παραθεσεως,
ετι δε ὁμοιοτητος και διαφορας, μονως ἀν τις δυναιτο και διανοια
καταντησαι, ἁμα και το χρησιμον και το τερπνον ἐκ της ἱστοριας
λαβειν.   POLYBIUS, L. l. c. v.

BASIL:

Printed for J. J. TOURNEISEN; and J. L. LEGRAND.

MDCCXC.

CONTENTS

OF THE

THIRD VOLUME.

CHAP. XVII.

Physical Calamities conspire with the Evils of War. — Athenian Expedition into Ætolia. — Victories of Demosthenes. — He fortifies Pylus. — Blocks up the Spartans in Sphacteria. — The Spartans solicit Peace. — Artifices and Imprudence of Cleon. — His unmerited Success. — Ridiculed by Aristophanes. — Athenian Conquests. — Battle of Delium. — Commotions in Thrace. — Expedition of Brasidas. — Truce for a Year. — The War renewed. — Battle of Amphipolis. — Peace of Nicias. — Dissatisfaction of the Spartan Allies. Page 1

CHAP. XVIII.

Discontents fomented by the Corinthians. — The Argive Alliance. — To which Athens accedes. — Birth and Education of Alcibiades. — His Friendship with Socrates. — His character — And Views — Which are favored by the State of Greece. — He deceives the Spartan Ambassadors. — Renewal of the Peloponnesian War. — Battle of Mantinea. — Tumults in Argos. — Massacre of the Scioneans. — Cruel Conquest of Melos. 40.

CHAP. XIX.

Alcibiades promotes the Sicilian Expedition. — Revolutions in that Island. — Embassy to Athens. — Extravagant Views of Alcibiades. — Opposed by Nicias. — The Athenians prepare to invade Sicily. — Their Armament beheld with Suspicion by the Italian States. — Deliberations concerning the Mode of carrying on the War. — Alcibiades takes Catana by Stratagem. — His Intrigues in Messene. — He is unseasonably recalled to Athens. — Charged with Treason and Impiety. — Escapes to Sparta. — Nicias determines to attack Syracuse. — Description of that City. — The Athenians prevail in a Battle. — Return to Catana and Naxos. Page 67

CHAP. XX.

Preparations for the ensuing Campaign. — The Athenians begin the Siege with Vigor. — Distress and Sedition in Syracuse. — Arrival of Gylippus — who defeats the Athenians. — Transactions in Greece. — A second Armament arrives at Syracuse. — Its first Operations successful. — The Athenians defeated. — Prepare to raise the Siege. — Naval Engagement in the Great Harbour. — Despondency of the Athenians. — Stratagem of Hermocrates. — The Athenians raise their camp. — Melancholy Firmness of Nicias. — Demosthenes capitulates. — Nicias surrenders. — Cruel Treatment of the Athenian Captives. — Singular Exception. 104

CHAP. XXI.

Consequences of the Athenian Misfortunes in Sicily. — Formidable Confederacy against Athens. — Peculiar Resources of free Governments. — Naval Operations. — Battle of Miletus. — Intrigues of Alcibiades. — The

CONTENTS.

Athenian Democracy subverted.—Tyrannical Government of the Four Hundred.— Battle of Eretria.— Democracy re-established in Athens. — Naval Success of the Athenians.— Triumphant Return of Alcibiades.— The Eleusinian Mysteries — and Plynteria. Page 147

CHAP. XXII.

Character of Lysander. — His Conference with Cyrus. - He defeats the Athenian Fleet. — Disgrace of Alcibiades. — Lysander succeeded by Callicratidas. — His Transactions with the Persians — with the Spartan Allies. — Battle of Arginussæ. — Trial of the Athenian Admirals. — Eteonicus checks a Mutiny of the Peloponnesian Troops. — Lysander resumes the Command. — Battle of Ægos Potamos. — Spartan Empire in Asia. — Siege and Surrender of Athens. — Humiliation of the Athenians. 198

CHAP XXIII.

Rapacity and Cruelty of the Spartan Government. — The Thirty Tyrants in Athens. — Persecution of Lysias and his Family. — Theramenes opposes the Tyrants. — Sanguinary Speech of Critias. — Death of Theramenes. — Persecution and Death of Alcibiades. — Thrasybulus seizes Phyle — Defeats the Tyrants. — Memorable Speech of Thrasybulus. — Oath of Amnesty — was faithfully observed. 242

CHAP. XXIV.

Accusation of Socrates. — Artifices of his Accusers. — His Defence. — Condemnation. — Address to the Judges. — His Conversation in Prison — and Death. — Transient Persecution of his Disciples. — Writings of Cebes — Æschines. — State of Philosophy. — Of the Fine Arts. — Of Literature. — Herodotus — Thucydides — Xenophon. — Transition to the public Transactions of Greece. — The Spartans invade Elis. — The Messenians driven from Greece. — History of Cyrene — Of Sicily. — War with Carthage. — Siege of Agrigentum. — Reign of Dionysius. — Sicily the first Province of Rome.   Page 271

CHAP. XXV.

Death of Darius Nothus. — Cyrus disputes the Succession with his elder Brother Artaxerxes. — Character of Cyrus. — State of Lower Asia under his administration. — His Strength and Resources. — His Expedition into Upper Asia. — Descries the vast army of his Brother. — Battle of Canaxa. — Death of Cyrus. — His Grecian Auxiliaries victorious. — Their Treaty with Tissaphernes. — Perfidious Assassination of the Grecian Generals. — Artaxerxes sends to the Greeks to demand their Arms. — Conference on that Subject.   323

CHAP. XXVI.

Consternation of the Greeks. — Manly Advice of Xenophon. — Their Retreat. — Difficulties attending it — Surmounted by their Skill and Perseverance. — Their Sufferings among the Carduchian Mountains. — They traverse Armenia. — First behold the Sea from Mount Theches. — Defeat the Colchians. — Description of the southern Shore of the Euxine. — Transactions with the Greek Colonies there. — The Greeks arrive at Byzantium. — Enter into the Service of Seuthes. — His History. — Conjunct Expeditions of the Greeks and Thracians. — The Greeks return to the Service of their Country.   354

THE

THE HISTORY OF GREECE.

CHAP. XVII.

Physical Calamities conspire with the Evils of War. — Athenian Expedition into Ætolia. — Victories of Demosthenes. — He fortifies Pylus. — Blocks up the Spartans in Sphacteria. — The Spartans solicit Peace. — Artifices and Imprudence of Cleon. — His unmerited Success. — Ridiculed by Aristophanes. — Athenian Conquests. — Battle of Delium. — Commotions in Thrace. — Expedition of Brasidas. — Truce for a Year. — The War renewed. — Battle of Amphipolis. — Peace of Nicias. — Dissatisfaction of the Spartan Allies.

IT would be agreeable to diversify the dark and melancholy scenes of the Peloponnesian war; by introducing occurrences and transactions of a different and more pleasing kind. But such, unfortunately, is the settled gloom of our present

Vol. III. B

THE HISTORY OF GREECE

CHAP.
XVII.
evils of war.
Olymp.
lxxxviii. 2.
A. C. 427.

subject, that the episodes commonly reflect the same color with the principal action. The miserable period now under our review, and already distinguished by revolt and sedition, was still farther deformed by a return of the pestilence, and by innumerable earthquakes. The disease carried off five thousand Athenian troops, and a great but uncertain number of other citizens. It raged, during a twelvemonth, with unabating violence; many remedies were employed, but all equally ineffectual. The poison at length spent its force, and the malady disappeared by a slow and insensible progress, similar to that observed in the Levant, and other parts of the world, which are still liable to be visited by this dreadful calamity[1]. The earthquakes alarmed Attica and Bœotia, but proved most destructive in the neighbouring isles. The dreadful concussions of the land were accompanied, or perhaps produced, by a violent agitation of the sea. The reflux of the waves overwhelmed the flourishing city of Orobia, on the western coast of Euboea. Similar disasters happened in the small islands of Atalanta and Peperathus. Nor did these alarming events terminate the afflictions of the Greeks; for Nature, as if she had delighted to produce at one period every thing most awful, poured forth a torrent of fire from Mount Ætna, which demolished the industrious labors of the Cataneans. A dreadful eruption had happened fifty years before this period; and the present was the third, and most memorable, by which Sicily

Olymp.
lxxxviii. 3.
A. C. 426.

[1] Voyage de Tournefort, vol. II. Discourse on the Plague, in the Phil. Transf. vol. xlv.

had been agitated and inflamed, since the coasts of that island were adorned by Grecian colonies[s].

CHAP. XVII.

Expedition of Demosthenes to Ætolia. Olymp. lxxxviii. 4. A.C. 425.

If the Peloponnesian war had not been carried on with an animosity unknown to the mildness of modern times, the long sufferings of the contending parties would have disposed them eagerly to desire the blessings of tranquillity. But such virulent passions rankled in Athens and Sparta, that while calamities were equally balanced, and the capitals of both republics were secure, no combination of adverse circumstances seemed sufficient to determine either side to purchase peace by the smallest diminution of honor. Yet to this necessity, Sparta in the following year was reduced by a train of events, equally sudden and singular. Demosthenes, a general of merit and enterprise, commanded the Athenian forces at Naupactus. This town, as related above, had been bestowed on the unfortunate Messenians; by whose assistance, together with that of the Athenian allies in Acarnania, Cephallenia, and Zacynthus, Demosthenes undertook to reduce the hostile provinces of Ætolia, Ambracia, and Leucadia. But the operations necessary for this purpose were obstructed by the jealousies and dissensions which prevailed among the confederates; each state insisting, that the whole force of the war should be immediately directed against its particular enemies.

The allied army, thus distracted by contrariety, and weakened by defection, performed nothing decisive against Leucadia or Ambracia. In Ætolia

Misunderstanding among the Athenian allies.

[s] Thucydid. p. 250.

CHAP. XVII.

they were extremely unfortunate. The Messenians, who were continually harassed by the natives of that barbarous province, persuaded Demosthenes that it would be easy to over-run their country, before the inhabitants, who lived in scattered villages, widely separated from each other, could collect their force, or attempt resistance. In pursuance of this advice, Demosthenes entered Ætolia, took and plundered the towns, and drove the inhabitants before him. During several days he marched unresisted; but having proceeded to Ægitium, the principal, or rather only city in the province, he found that his design had by no means escaped the notice of the enemy. Ægitium is situate among lofty mountains, and about ten miles distant from the Corinthian gulf. Among these intricate, and almost inaccessible heights the flower of the Ætolian nation were posted. Even the most distant tribes had come up, before the confederate army entered their borders.

Singular mode of battle.

Ægitium was stormed; but the inhabitants escaped to their countrymen concealed among the mountains. While the Athenians and their allies pursued them, the Ætolians rushed, in separate bodies, from different eminences, and checked the pursuers with their darts and javelins. Having discharged their missile weapons, they retired, being light-armed, and incapable to resist the impression of pikemen. New detachments continually poured forth from the mountains, and in all directions annoyed the confederates. The latter lost no ground, as long as their archers had darts, and were able to use them. But when the greatest part of their light troops were wounded or slain, the heavy-armed men began to give way. They still, however, maintained their order; and the battle long continued, in alternate pursuits and retreats, the Ætolians always flying before the enemy as soon as they had discharged their javelins. But at length the confederates were exhausted by so many repeated charges, and totally defeated by opponents who durst not wait their approach.

Unfortunate issue of the expedition.

Their conductors through this intricate country had all perished. They mistook their road to the sea. The enemy were light-armed, and in their own territories. The pursuit, therefore, was unusually destructive. Many fell into caverns, or tumbled headlong from precipices. A large party wandered into an impervious wood, which being set on fire by the enemy, consumed them in its flames. A miserable remnant returned to Naupactus, afflicted by the loss of their companions, and highly mortified at being defeated by Barbarians, alike ignorant of the rules of war, and of the laws of civil society, who spoke an unknown dialect, and fed on raw flesh[1].

Demosthenes defends Naupactus, &c.

This disaster deterred Demosthenes from returning to Athens, till fortune gave him an opportunity to retrieve the honor of his arms. The Ætolians and Ambraciots, the most formidable enemies of the republic on that western coast of Greece, solicited and obtained assistance from Lacedæmon and Corinth, vigorously attacked the towns of Naupactus and Amphilochian Argos, and

[1] Thucydid. p. 232, et seqq.

6 THE HISTORY OF GREECE:

CHAP. XVII.

threatened to reduce the whole province of Acarnania, in which the latter was situated. The vigilance and activity of Demosthenes not only saved these important cities, but obtained the most signal advantages over the assailants. With profound military skill he divided the strength of the enemy, and, by a well-conducted stratagem, totally defeated the Ambraciots among the heights of Idomené. A strong detachment of that brave nation had advanced the preceding day to Olpæ, a place fortified by the Acarnanians, and the seat of their courts of justice. Demosthenes obliged them to retreat with considerable loss, and intercepted their return homeward. Meanwhile the collected force of the Ambraciots marched to support their detachment, with whose misfortunes they were totally unacquainted. Apprized of this design, Demosthenes beset the passes, and seized the most advantageous posts on their route. With the remainder of his force he advanced to attack them in front. They had already proceeded to Idomené, and encamped on the lowest ridge of that mountain[a].

Defeats the Ætolians and Ambraciots.

Surprises their camp.

Demosthenes placed his Messenians in the van, and commanded them, as they marched along, to discourse in their Doric dialect. This circumstance, as the morning was yet in its dawn, effectually prevented the advanced guards from suspecting them to be enemies. Demosthenes then rushed forward with the Messenians and Acarnanians. The Ambraciots were yet in their beds. The camp was no sooner assaulted, than the rout began. Many were slain on the spot; the rest fled amain; but the

[a] Thucydid. p. 244, et seqq.

THE HISTORY OF GREECE. 7

passes were beset, and the pursuers light-armed. Some ran to the sea, and beheld a new object of terror, in some Athenian ships then cruising on the coast. In this complication of calamities, they plunged into the water, and swam to the hostile squadron, chusing rather to be destroyed by the Athenians, than by the enemies from whom they had escaped.

On the following day, the victors, who remained at Idomené, stripping the dead, and erecting a trophy, were addressed by a herald sent on the part of the detachment who had so much suffered in its retreat from Olpæ. This herald knew nothing of the fresh disaster that had befallen his countrymen. Observing the arms of the Ambraciots, he was astonished at their number. The victors perceiving his surprise, asked him, before he explained his commission, "What he judged to be the amount of the slain"? "Not more than two hundred, replied the herald. The demander then said, "It should seem otherwise, for there are the arms of more than a thousand men." The herald rejoined, "They cannot then belong to our party." The other replied, "They must, if you fought yesterday at Idomené," "We fought no where yesterday; we suffered the day before, in our retreat from Olpæ." "But we fought yesterday against these Ambraciots, who were marching to your relief." When the herald heard this, he burst into a groan, and went abruptly off, without further explaining his commission[1].

[1] Thucydid. p. 244, et seqq.

CHAP. XVII.
Demosthenes sails to the Peloponnesus.
Olymp. lxxxviii. 4.
A. C. 425.

Emotions of the Messenians at the sight of their native shores.

The Athenians and Messenians fortify Pylus.

These important successes enabled Demosthenes to return with honor to Athens. The term of his military command had expired; but his mind could not brook inactivity. He therefore solicited permission to accompany, as a volunteer, the armament which sailed to Corcyra, the success of which has already been related, with leave to employ the Messenians, whom he carried along with him, on the coast of Peloponnesus, should any opportunity occur there, for promoting the public service. While the fleet slowly coasted along the southern shores of that peninsula, the Messenians viewed, with mingled joy and sorrow, the long lost, but still beloved, seats of their ancestors. They regretted, in particular, the decay of ancient Pylus; the royal residence of their admired Nestor, whose youth had been adorned by valor, and his age renowned for wisdom. Their immortal resentment against Sparta was inflamed by beholding the ruins of Messené. A thousand ideas and sentiments, which time had obliterated, revived at the sight of their native shores.

When the tumult of their emotions subsided, they explained their feelings to Demosthenes, and to each other. He suggested, or at least warmly approved, the design of landing, and rebuilding Pylus, which had been abandoned by the Spartans, though it enjoyed a convenient harbour, and was strongly fortified by nature. Demosthenes proposed this measure to Eurymedon and Sophocles, who answered him with the insolence congenial to their character, "That there were many barren capes on the coast of Peloponnesus, which those

THE HISTORY OF GREECE.

might fortify who wished to entail an useless expense on their country." He next applied to the several captains of the fleet, and even to the inferior officers, but without better success, although he assured them that the place abounded in wood and stone, with which a wall, sufficient for defence might speedily be completed. He had desisted from farther entreaties, when a fortunate storm drove the whole fleet towards the Pylian harbour. This circumstance enabled him to renew his instances with greater force, alleging that the events of fortune confirmed the expedience of the undertaking. At length the sailors and soldiers, weary of idleness (for the weather prevented them from putting to sea), began the work of their own accord, and carried it on with such vigor and activity, that in six days the place was strongly fortified on every side[c]. The Athenian fleet then proceeded to Corcyra, Demosthenes retaining only five ships to guard this new acquisition.

The Spartans were no sooner apprized of this daring measure, than they withdrew their army from its annual incursion into Attica, and recalled their fleet from Corcyra. The citizens, residing at home, immediately flew to arms, and marched towards Pylus, which was only fifty miles distant from their capital. They found the new fortress so well prepared for defence, that nothing could be undertaken against it with any prospect of success, until their whole forces had assembled. This occasioned but a short delay; after which Pylus was vigorously assaulted by sea and land. The

CHAP. XVII.

The Spartans attempt to dislodge them.

[c] Thucydid. p. 216, et seqq.

CHAP.
XVII.

walls were weakest towards the harbour; the entrance of which, however, was so narrow, that only two ships could sail into it abreast. Here the attack was most furious, and the resistance most obstinate.

Gallantry of Brasidas.

Demosthenes encouraged his troops by his voice and arm. The gallant Brasidas, a man destined to act such an illustrious part in the following scenes of the war, called out to the Lacedæmonian pilots to drive against the beach; and exhorted them, by the destruction of their ships, to save the honor of their country. He farther recommended this boldness by his example; but, in performing it, received a wound which rendered him insensible. His body dropped into the sea, seemingly deprived of life, but was recovered by the affectionate zeal of his attendants. When his senses returned, he perceived the loss of his shield, a matter highly punishable by the Spartan laws, if the shield of Brasidas had not been lost with more glory than ever shield was defended'.

About four hundred Spartans blocked up in Sphacteria.

During three days, Demosthenes, with very unequal strength, resisted the enemy; when the approach of the Athenian fleet from Corcyra, which he had apprized of his danger, terminated the incredible labors of his exhausted garrison. A naval engagement ensued, in which the Lacedæmonians were defeated. But neither this defeat, nor the loss of five ships, nor the total dispersion of their fleet, nor the unexpected relief of Pylus, gave them so much uneasiness, as an event principally occasioned by their own imprudence. The island

' Thucydid. p. 218.

of Sphacteria, scarce two miles in circumference, barren, woody, and uninhabited, lies before the harbour of Pylus. In this island the Spartans had posted four hundred and twenty heavy-armed men, with a much greater proportion of Helots, not reflecting that the Athenians, as soon as they had resumed the command of the neighbouring sea, must have these forces at their devotion. This circumstance occurred not to the Spartans till after their defeat; and then affected them the more deeply, because the troops blocked up in the island belonged to the first families of the republic.

Advice of this misfortune was immediately sent to the capital. The annual magistrates, attended by a deputation of the senate, hastened to examine matters on the spot. The evil appeared to be incapable of remedy; and of such importance was this body of Spartans to the community, that all present agreed in the necessity of soliciting a truce, until ambassadors were sent to Athens to treat of a general peace. The Athenians granted a suspension of hostilities, on condition that the Spartans, as a pledge of their sincerity, surrendered their whole fleet (consisting of about sixty vessels) into the harbour of Pylus. Even this mortifying proposal was accepted. Twenty days were consumed in the embassy; during which time the troops intercepted in Sphacteria were supplied with a stated proportion of meal, meat, and wine[a], that of the

CHAP. XVII.

Consternation in Sparta.

[a] Thucydides does not ascertain the quantity of meat. He says, two chœnixes of meal, and two cotyls of wine; that is, two pints of meal, and one pint of wine English measure, a very small allowance; but the Athenians were afraid lest the besieged might hoard their provisions, if allowed more for daily support; which, if the negociation

freemen amounting to double the quantity allowed to the slaves.

When the Spartan ambassadors were admitted to an audience at Athens, they artfully apologized for the intended length of their discourses. In all their transactions with the Greeks, they had hitherto affected the dignified brevity [*] inspired by conscious pre-eminence: "Yet on the present occasion, they allowed that it was necessary to explain, at some length, the advantages which would result to all Greece, and particularly to Athens herself, if the latter accepted the treaty and alliance, the free gifts of unfeigned friendship, spontaneously offered by Sparta. They pretended not to conceal or extenuate the greatness of their misfortune; but the Athenians ought also to remember the vicissitudes of war. It was full time to embrace a hearty reconcilement, and to terminate the calamities of their common country. The war had as yet been carried on with more emulation than hatred, neither party had been reduced to extremity, nor had any incurable evil been yet inflicted or suffered. Terms of agreement, if accepted in the moment of victory, would redound to the glory of Athens; if rejected, would ascertain, who were the authors of the war, and to whom the public calamities ought thenceforth to be imputed; since it was well known, that if Athens and Sparta were unanimous, no power in Greece would venture to dispute their commands [10]."

failed, would enable them to hold out the place longer, than they could otherwise have done.

[*] Imperatoria brevitas. TACITUS.
[10] Thucyd. p. 262, et seqq.

The meek spirit of this discourse only discovered to the Athenians the full extent of their good fortune, of which they determined completely to avail themselves. Instigated by the violence of Cleon, they answered the ambassadors with great haughtiness; demanding, as preliminaries to the treaty, that the Spartans in Sphacteria should be sent to Athens; and that several places of great importance, belonging to the Spartans or their allies, should be delivered into their hands. These lofty pretensions, which were by no means justified by military success, appeared totally inadmissible to the ambassadors, who returned in disgust to the Spartan camp.

Nothing, it was evident, could be expected from the moderation of Athens; but it was expected from her justice, that she would restore the fleet, which had been surrendered as a pledge of the treaty. Even this was, on various pretences, denied[n]. Both parties, therefore, prepared for hostilities; the Athenians to maintain their arrogance, the Spartans to avenge it.

The former employed the operation of famine, as the readiest and least dangerous mode of reducing the soldiers in Sphacteria. The Athenian fleet, now greatly augmented, carefully guarded the island night and day. But notwithstanding their utmost vigilance, small vessels availed themselves

[n] The Athenians objected, "an incursion towards their borders during the suspension of hostilities, και αλλα εν εγκληματα," and other matters of little moment, says Thucydides, with his usual impartiality, p. 266.

CHAP.
XVII.

of storms and darkness to throw provisions into the place; a service undertaken by slaves from the promise of liberty; and by freemen, from the prospect of great pecuniary rewards. The Athenians redoubled their diligence, and often intercepted these victuallers; but they found it more difficult to interrupt the expert divers, who, plunging deep under water, dragged after them bottles of leather, filled with honey and flour. The blockade was thus fruitlessly protracted several weeks. Demosthenes was averse to attack an island difficult of access, covered with wood, destitute of roads, and defended on the side of Pylus by a natural fortification, strengthened by art. Meanwhile the Athenians began to suffer inconveniences in their turn. Their garrison in Pylus was closely pressed by the enemy; there was but one source of fresh water, and that scanty, in the place; provisions grew scarce: the barrenness of the neighbouring coast afforded no supply: while they besieged the Spartans, they themselves experienced the hardships of a siege.

Artifices and impudence of Cleon.

When their situation was reported at Athens, the assembly fell into commotion: many clamored against Demosthenes; several accused Cleon. The artful demagogue, whose opposition had chiefly prevented an advantageous peace with Sparta, affected to disbelieve the intelligence, and advised sending men of approved confidence to Pylus, in order to detect the imposture. The populace called aloud, "that Cleon himself should undertake that commission." But the dissembler dreaded to

THE HISTORY OF GREECE. 13

become the dupe of his own artifice. He perceived, that if he went to Pylus, he must, at his return, either acknowledge the truth of the report, and thus be subjected to immediate shame, or fabricate false intelligence, and thus be exposed to future punishment. He therefore eluded his own proposal, by declaring, "that it ill became the dignity of Athens to stoop to a formal and tedious examination; and that, whatever were the state of the armament, if the commanders acted like men, they might take Sphacteria in a few days: that if he had the honor to be general, he would sail to the island with a small body of light infantry, and take it at the first onset."

These sarcastic observations were chiefly directed against Nicias, one of the generals actually present in the assembly; a man of a virtuous, but timid disposition; endowed with much p[ru]d[en]ce, and little enterprise; possessed of moderate abilities, and immoderate riches; a zealous partisan of aristocracy, and an avowed enemy to Cleon, whom he regarded as the worst enemy of his country.

A person of this character could not be much inclined to engage in the hazardous expedition to Sphacteria. When the Athenians, with the usual licentiousness that prevailed in their assemblies, called out to Cleon, "that if the enterprise appeared so easy, it would better suit the extent of his abilities;" Nicias rose up, and immediately offered to cede to him the command. Cleon at first accepted it, thinking Nicias's proposal merely a feint; but when the latter appeared in earnest,

16   THE HISTORY OF GREECE.

CHAP.
XVII.

his adverſary drew back, alleging, "that Nicias, not Cleon, was general." The Athenians, with the malicious pleaſantry natural to the multitude, preſſed Cleon the cloſer, the more eagerly he receded. He was at length overcome by their importunity, but not forſaken by his impudence[11]. Advancing to the middle of the aſſembly, he declared, "that he was not afraid of the Lacedæmonians; and engaged, in twenty days, to bring the Spartans as priſoners to Athens, or to die in the attempt[12]." This heroic language excited laughter among the multitude; the wiſe rejoiced in thinking, that they muſt obtain one of two advantages, either the deſtruction of a turbulent demagogue (which they rather hoped), or the capture of the Spartans in Sphacteria.

Boaſtful promiſe of the latter;

which is performed by accident. Olymp. lxxxviii. 4. A. C. 425.

The latter event was haſtened by an accident; while ſome ſoldiers were preparing their victuals, the wood was ſet on fire, and long burned unperceived, till a briſk gale ariſing, the conflagration raged with ſuch violence, as threatened to conſume the iſland. This unforeſeen diſaſter diſcloſed the ſtrength and poſition of the Spartans; and Demoſthenes was actually preparing to attack them, when Cleon, with his light-armed troops, arrived in the camp. The iſland was invaded during night; the advanced guards were taken or ſlain. At the dawn, the Athenians made a deſcent from

[11] Thucydid. p. 271.

[12] Ἢ ϲωϲω αυταϲπουϲ, or, "kill them on the ſpot." A little alteration in the text will give the meaning which I preferred as moſt agreeable to what follows; but the other tranſlation better ſuits the boaſtful character of Cleon.

ſeventy

THE HISTORY OF GREECE. 17

seventy ships. The main body of the enemy retired to the strong post opposite to Pylus, harassed in their march by showers of arrows, stones, and darts, involved in the ashes of the burnt wood, which, mounting widely into the air, on all sides intercepted their sight, and increased the gloom of battle. The Spartans, closely embodied, and presenting a dreadful front to the assailants, made good their retreat. Having occupied the destined post, they boldly defended it wherever the enemy approached, for the nature of the ground hindered it from being surrounded. The Athenians used their utmost efforts to repel and overcome them; and during the greatest part of the day, both parties obstinately persevered in their purpose, under the painful pressures of battle, thirst, and a burning sun. At length the Messenians, whose ardor had been signally distinguished in every part of this enterprise, discovered an unknown path leading to the eminence which defended the Lacedæmonian rear. The Spartans were thus encompassed on all sides, and reduced to a similar situation to that of their illustrious countrymen who fell at Thermopylæ.

CHAP. XVII.

Nor did their commanders disgrace the country of Leonidas. Their general, Epitades, was slain. Hippagretes was dying of his wounds. Styphon, the third in command, still exhorted them to persevere. But Demosthenes and Cleon, desirous rather to carry them prisoners to Athens, than to put them to death, invited them, by the loud proclamation of a herald, to lay down their arms.

The Spartans in Sphacteria carried prisoners to Athens.

VOL. III.   C

18   THE HISTORY OF GREECE.

CHAP.
XVII.

The greater part dropped their shields, and waved their hands, in token of compliance. A conference followed between Demosthenes and Cleon on one side, and Styphon on the other. Styphon desired leave to send over to the Lacedæmonians on the continent for advice. Several messages passed between them; in the last of which it was said, "the Lacedæmonians permit you to consult your own utility, provided you submit to nothing base:" in consequence of which determination, they surrendered their arms and their persons. They were conducted to Athens, within the time assigned by Cleon; having held out fifty-two days after the expiration of the truce, during which time they had been so sparing of the provisions conveyed to them by the extraordinary means above-mentioned, that, when the place was taken, they had still some thing in reserve [14].

Humiliation of Sparta.

The Athenians withdrew their fleet, leaving a strong garrison in Pylus, which was soon reinforced by an enterprising body of Messenians from Naupactus. The Messenians, though possessed of no more than one barren cape on their native and once happy coast, resumed their inveterate hatred against Sparta, whose territories they continually infested by incursions, or harassed by alarms. This species of war, destructive in itself, was rendered still more dangerous by the revolts of the Helots, attracted by every motive of affection towards their ancient kinsmen, and animated by every principle of resentment against their tyrannical masters. Meanwhile the

[14] Thucydid. p. 271—279.

THE HISTORY OF GREECE. 19

Athenian fleet renewed and multiplied their ravages on the coast of Peloponnesus. Reduced to extremity by such proceedings, the Spartans sent to Athens repeated overtures of accommodation. But the good fortune of the Athenians had only nourished their ambition. At the instigation of Cleon, they dismissed the Spartan ambassadors more insolently than ever[11]. Such was their deference to the opinion of this arrogant demagogue; at the same time that, with the most inconsistent levity, they listened with pleasure to the plays of Aristophanes, which lashed the character and administration of Cleon with the boldest severity of satire, sharpened by the edge of the most poignant ridicule.

The taking of Pylus, the triumphant return of Cleon, a notorious coward transformed by caprice and accident into a brave and successful commander, were topics well suiting the comic vein of Aristophanes. The imperious demagogue had deserved the personal resentment of the poet, by denying the legitimacy of his birth[12], and thereby contesting his title to vote in the assembly. On former occasions, Aristophanes had stigmatized the incapacity and insolence of Cleon, together with his perfidious selfishness in embroiling the affairs of the republic. In the comedy[13] first represented in the seventh year of the war, he attacks him in the moment of victory, when fortune had rendered

[11] Aristoph. Equit. v. 794. [12] Vit. anonym. Aristoph.
[13] The ἱππεῖς.

C 2

CHAP. XVII.

Account of his comedy, entitled, the Knights.

him the idol of a licentious multitude, when no comedian was so daring as to play his character, and no painter so bold as to design his mask [18].

Aristophanes, therefore, appeared for the first time on the stage, only disguising his own face, the better to represent the part of Cleon. In this ludicrous piece, which seems to have been celebrated even beyond its merit, the people of Athens are described under the allegory of a capricious old dotard, whose credulity, abused by a malicious slave lately admitted into his house [19], persecutes and torments his faithful old servants. Demosthenes bitterly complains, that, intending to gratify the palate of the old man, he had brought a delicate morsel from Pylus; but that it had been stolen by Cleon, and by him served up to their common master. After lamenting, with his companion Nicias, the hardships of their condition, they hold counsel together, and contrive various expedients for putting an end to their common calamities. The desponding Nicias proposes drinking bull's blood, after the example of Themistocles; Demosthenes, with more courage, advises a hearty draught of wine. Finding Cleon asleep, they seize the opportunity not only to purloin this liquor, but to rifle his pockets, in which they discover some ancient oracles, typically representing the succession of Athenian magistrates. Towards the end of the prophecy, it was said, that the dragon

[18] Τω το καλος τας αυτω οψις φιλει
Των χειροτεχνων ισασαι. Equitem, v. 231.
[19] Νεωνητον κακον, "the new-bought mischief."

THE HISTORY OF GREECE. 21

should overcome the devouring vulture. The rapacious avarice of Cleon corresponded to the type of the vulture; and the dragon darkly shadowed out Agoracritus, an eminent maker of puddings and sausages, the shape and contents of which alluded to the figure and food of that terrible serpent. Nicias and Demosthenes hail this favorite of fortune, as the destined master of the republic. Agoracritus alleges in vain, that he is totally unacquainted with political affairs, ignorant of every liberal art, and has hardly learned to read. They reply, by announcing to him the oracle, and by proving that his pretended imperfections better qualified him to conduct the government of Athens. This office required none of the talents, the want of which he lamented. He matched Cleon in impudence, and surpassed him in strength of lungs. His profession had taught him to squeeze, to amass, to bruise, to embroil, and to confound; and long experience had rendered him accomplished in all the frauds and chicane of the market[10]. He might therefore boldly enter the lists with Cleon, being assured of assistance from the whole body of Athenian knights[11]. Agoracritus, thus encouraged, prepares for encountering his adversary. The contest, long doubtful, is maintained in a style of the lowest buffoonery, always ludicrous, often indecent. The old dotard, or rather the Athenians whom he represents,

CHAP. XVII.

[10] The same word in Greek denotes the market and the forum. Indeed the same place usually served for both.
[11] The ἱππεῖς, or Equites, the second rank of citizens at Athens, who detested Cleon, and from whom the play takes its name.

C 3

CHAP. XVII.

finally acknowledge their paſt errors; and regret being ſo long deceived by an upſtart ſlave, through whoſe obſtinacy in continuing the war, they had been cooped up within the walls of an unwholeſome city, and hindered from enjoying their beautiful fields and happy rural amuſements. Agoracritus ſeizes this favorable moment to produce two ancient treaties with the Lacedæmonians, perſonified by two beautiful women, whom he had found cloſely mewed up in the houſe of Cleon. Of theſe females the old Athenian becomes ſuddenly enamoured, and they retire together to the country.

The Athenians take Cythera. Olymp. lxxxix. 1. A. C. 424.

The people of Athens permitted, and even approved, the licentious boldneſs of Ariſtophanes; but neither the ſtrength of reaſon, nor the ſharpneſs of ſatire, could reſiſt the impetuoſity of their ambition. The war was rendered popular by ſucceſs; they prepared for carrying it on with redoubled vigor. The firſt operations of the enſuing ſummer gratified their utmoſt hopes. The principal diviſion of the fleet, conducted by the prudence of Nicias, took the fertile and populous iſland of Cythera, ſtretching from the ſouthern promontory of Laconia towards the Cretan ſea, and long enriched by the commerce of Egypt and Libya. The Lacedæmonian garriſon, as well as the Spartan magiſtrates in the iſland, ſurrendered priſoners of war. The more dangerous part of the inhabitants were removed to the Athenian iſles; the remainder were ſubjected to an annual tribute of eight hundred pounds ſterling; an Athenian garriſon took poſſeſſion of the fortreſs.

THE HISTORY OF GREECE.

Soon after this important conquest, the arms of Demosthenes and Hippocrates reduced the town of Nicæa, the principal sea-port of the Megareans; and the Athenian fleet ravaged with impunity several maritime cities on the eastern coast of Peloponnesus. Thyrea was condemned to a harder fate. This city, together with the surrounding district, had been granted, by the compassion of Sparta, to the miserable natives of Ægina, who (as above mentioned) had been driven from their once powerful island by the cruelty of Athens. This cruelty still continued to pursue them. Their newly-raised walls were taken by assault; their houses burned; and the inhabitants, without distinction, put to the sword.

Hitherto all the enterprises of the Athenians were crowned with success. Fortune first deserted them in Bœotia. During several months their generals, Demosthenes and Hippocrates, availing themselves of the political factions of that country, had been carrying on secret intrigues with Chæronea, Siphæ, and Orchomenus, places abounding in declared partisans of democracy, and eternally hostile to the ambition of Thebes. The insurgents had agreed to take arms, in order to betray the western parts of Bœotia to Demosthenes, who sailed with forty gallies from Naupactus; while Hippocrates, at the head of seven thousand heavy-armed Athenians, and a much greater proportion of light-armed auxiliaries, invaded the eastern frontier of that province. It was expected, that, before the Thebans could bring a sufficient force into

CHAP. XVII. Reduce Nicæa, and ravage Peloponnesus.

Endeavour to produce a revolution in Bœotia.

CHAP. XVII.

the field, the invaders and insurgents, advancing from opposite extremities of the country, might unite in the centre, and perhaps subdue Thebes itself, the most powerful, as well as most zealous, ally of Sparta.

Their plan too complicated for execution.

This plan, though concerted with much ability, was found too complicated for execution. Demosthenes steered towards Siphæ, before his coadjutor was ready to take the field; some mistake, it is said, having happened about the time appointed for action; and the whole contrivance was betrayed by Nicomachus, a Phocian, to the Spartans, and by them communicated to the Bœotians. The cities which meditated revolt were thus secured, before Demosthenes appeared at Siphæ, and before Hippocrates had even marched from Attica.

They are defeated in the battle of Delium. Olymp. lxxxix. 1. A. C. 424.

The latter at length entered the eastern frontier of Bœotia; and, as the principal design had miscarried, contented himself with taking and fortifying Delium, a place sacred to Apollo. Having garrisoned this post, he prepared for returning home. But while his army still lay in the neighbourhood of Delium, the Thebans, encouraged by Pagondas, a brave and skilful leader, marched with great rapidity from Tanagra, in order to intercept his retreat. Their forces amounted to eighteen thousand; the Athenians were little less numerous. An engagement ensued, which national emulation rendered bloody and obstinate. Before the battle, Pagondas had detached a small squadron of horse, with orders to ride up after the commencement of the action. This stratagem

THE HISTORY OF GREECE.

was decisive. The Athenians, terrified at the sight of a reinforcement, which their fears magnified into a new army, were thrown into disorder, and put to flight. Approaching darkness saved them from total destruction. They escaped disgracefully into Attica, after leaving in the field of battle a thousand pikemen, with their commander Hippocrates.

The victorious army immediately formed the siege of Delium, which was taken by means of a machine first contrived for that purpose. Several parts of the fortification, which had been raised in great haste, consisted chiefly of wood. The besiegers therefore, joining together a number of large beams, formed a huge mast, perforated in the middle; to one of its extremities they appended a prodigious mass of pitch and sulphur; and to the other a bellows, which, when this unusual instrument of destruction was raised above the wooden rampart, immediately threw the whole into flames. The Athenian garrison, diminished by death or desertion to two hundred men, surrendered prisoners of war[11].

The Athenians had scarcely time to lament their losses in Bœotia, when they received intelligence of a calamity in another quarter, equally unexpected, and still more alarming. This event is the more remarkable, because it naturally arose out of the preceding prosperity of Athens, and the past misfortunes of Sparta. The uninterrupted

[11] Thucyd. p. 304—326.

CHAP. XVII.

train of success which attended the arms of Nicias and Demosthenes in the eighth year of the war, alarmed the citizens of Olynthus and other places of the Chalcidicé, which having embraced the earliest opportunity of revolting from the Athenians, justly dreaded the vengeance of an incensed and victorious people. Every southerly wind threatened them with the approach of an Athenian fleet. Their apprehensions were not less painful on the side of Thessaly. The slightest movement in that country terrified them with the apprehensions of an Athenian army, which, victorious in the south, should advance to punish its northern enemies. But as none of these dreaded dangers were realized, the inhabitants of the Chalcidicé gradually resumed courage, put their towns in a posture of defence, and craved assistance from their Peloponnesian allies. At the same time Perdiccas, king of Macedon, who regarded the Athenians as his ancient and natural enemies, and the rapacious invaders of his coast, sent money into the south of Greece, for the purpose of hiring soldiers, whom he intended to employ in resisting the encroachments of that ambitious people, as well as in subduing the Elymeans, Lyncestæ, and other barbarous tribes, not yet incorporated in the Macedonian kingdom.

Fomented by the Spartans.

Such were the enemies, whose activity the good fortune of Athens had roused; while the calamities of Sparta prompted her to supply the reinforcement of troops, which both Perdiccas and the Chalcidians demanded. During the seventh and eighth years of the war, that republic fatally experienced the truth of Pericles's maxim, "that those who command the sea, may also become masters at land." The Athenian fleets domineered over the coast of Peloponnesus. It was impossible to foresee what places would be the next objects of their continual descents. The maritime parts were successively laid waste, and finally abandoned by the inhabitants, who found resistance ineffectual and useless. These misfortunes were increased by the frequent desertion of the Helots to the neighbouring garrisons in Pylus and Cythera, and by the dread of a general insurrection among those numerous and unhappy victims of Spartan tyranny. To prevent this evil, the Spartans had recourse to such expedients as excite astonishment and horror. They commanded the Helots to chuse two thousand of their bravest and most meritorious youths, who, by the general consent of their companions, deserved the crown of liberty; and when invested with this perfidious ornament, the unsuspecting freemen had paraded the streets, and sacrificed in the temples, exulting in their late emancipation, these new members of the community gradually disappeared from the sight of men, nor was it ever known by what means they had been destroyed. But the veil of mystery, which concealed that dark and bloody stratagem, prevented neither the resentment of the slaves, nor the just suspicion of their masters. The latter were eager to embrace any measure that might deliver their country from its dangerous domestic foes. With much satisfaction, therefore, they sent seven hundred Helots to the standard of Brasidas, whose merit had recommended him to Perdiccas and the Chalcidians, as the general best qualified to manage the Macedonian war. About a thousand soldiers were levied in the neighbouring cities of Peloponnesus. Several Spartans cheerfully accompanied a leader whom they admired. With this inconsiderable force Brasidas, towards the beginning of autumn, undertook an expedition highly important in its consequences, and conducted with consummate prudence and bravery [11].

Having traversed the friendly countries of Bœotia and Phocis, he arrived at the foot of Mount Oëta, and penetrated through the narrow defiles confined between that steep and woody range of hills, and the boisterous waves of the Malian gulf. The fight of Thermopylæ animated the enthusiasm of the Spartans, and encouraged them to force their way through the hostile plains of Thessaly; a country actually torn by domestic discord, but always friendly to the Athenians. The celerity of Brasidas anticipated the slow opposition of a divided enemy. Having reached the Macedonian town of Dium, he joined forces with Perdiccas, who proposed directing the first operations of the combined army against Arribæus, the king or leader of the barbarous Lynceslæ. But even this Barbarian knew the valor of the Spartans, and the equity of Brasidas. To the decision of the

[11] Thucyd. p. 804.

Grecian general he offered to submit the differences between Perdiccas and himself, and engaged to abide by the award, however unfavorable to his interest. The Spartan listened to a proposal extremely reasonable in itself, though altogether inconsistent with the ambitious views of Perdiccas, who disdained to accept as a judge the man whom he paid as an auxiliary. Brasidas, on the other hand declined in firm but decent terms, to employ his valor against those who implored his justice. The generals thus separated in mutual disgust; and Perdiccas thenceforth reduced his contribution of subsidy from a moiety to a third; but even that was extorted from his fears, not bestowed by his munificence.

Brasidas hastened to join the Chalcidians, by whom he was received with a degree of joy suitable to the impatience with which he had been expected. Amidst the general defection of their neighbours, the towns of Acanthus and Stagirus still maintained their allegiance to Athens. Brasidas appeared before the gates of Acanthus, while the peaceful inhabitants were preparing for the labors of the vintage. He sent a messenger, craving leave to enter the place, and to address the assembly. The Acanthians were divided in opinion; but the majority, fearing to expose their ripe fields and vineyards to the resentment of his army, agreed to admit the general alone and unattended, and impartially to weigh whatever he proposed for their deliberation. Brasidas, though a Spartan, was an able speaker. He observed to the Acanthians,

CHAP. XVII.

His transactions with the Acanthians.

CHAP. XVII.

convened in full assembly, "that, in compliance with the generous resolution of Sparta, he had undertaken, and finally accomplished, a long and dangerous journey, to deliver them from the tyranny of Athenian magistrates and garrisons, and to restore them, what the common oppressors of Greece had so long withheld, the independent government of their own equitable laws. This was the object, which, amidst all the calamities of war, the Spartans had ever kept in view; this was the purpose, which, before his departure from home, the principal magistrates had sworn unanimously to maintain. *That* freedom and independence', which formed the domestic happiness of Sparta, his countrymen were ambitious to communicate to all their allies. But if the Acanthians refused to share the general benefit, they must not complain of experiencing the unhappy effects of their obstinacy. The arms of Sparta would compel those whom her arguments had failed to persuade. Nor could this be blamed as injustice; first, because the resources with which the Acanthians furnished Athens, under the ignominious name of tribute, served to rivet the chains of Greece; and secondly, because the example of a people, so wealthy and flourishing, and long renowned for their penetration and sagacity, might influence the resolutions of neighbouring states, and deter them from concurring with the measures necessary to promote the public welfare and security."

His merit and success.

This judicious discourse, enforced by the terror of the Spartan army, engaged the Acanthians to

THE HISTORY OF GREECE. 31

accept the friendship of Brasidas. Stagirus, another city on the Strymonic gulf, readily followed the example, and opened its gates to the deliverer. During the ensuing winter, the measures of the Spartan general were conducted with equal ability and enterprise. His successful operations against the inland towns facilitated the surrender of such places, as, by their maritime or insular situation, were most exposed to the vengeance of Athens, and therefore most averse to revolt. His moderate use of victory ensured the good-will of the vanquished. The various parts of a plan, thus artfully combined, mutually assisted each other; the success of one undertaking contributed to that of the next which followed it; and, at length, without any considerable miscarriage, he had rendered himself master of most places in the peninsulas of Acta, Sithonia, and Pallené.

The loss of Amphipolis was that which most deeply afflicted the Athenians: a rich and populous city, beautifully situate on a small but well cultivated island, surrounded by the river Strymon, the banks of which supplied excellent timber, and other materials of naval strength. By possessing this town, the Spartans now commanded both branches of the river, and might thus pass, without interruption, to the Athenian colonies, or subjects, on the coast of Thrace; seize, or plunder, the gold mines opposite to the isle of Thasos; and ravage the fertile fields of the Thracian Chersonesus. The conquest of a place so essential to the enemy, had exercised the courage, the eloquence,

CHAP. XVII.

and the dexterity of Brasidas. He formed a conspiracy with the malecontents in the place, skilfully disposed his army before the walls, harangued the assembly of the people. A most seasonable promptitude distinguished all his measures; yet the Athenian Eucleus, who commanded the garrison, found time to send a vessel to Thasos, requesting immediate and effectual relief.

notwithstanding the activity of Thucydides the historian;

The Athenians had committed the government of that island, as well as the direction of the mines on the opposite continent, to the celebrated historian of a war, in which he was a meritorious, though unfortunate, actor. Without a moment's delay, Thucydides put to sea with seven gallies, and arrived in the mouth of the Strymon the same day on which his assistance had been demanded. But it was already too late to save Amphipolis[24]. The Spartan general, who had exact information of all the measures of the besieged, well knew the importance of anticipating the arrival of Thucydides, whose name was highly respected by the Greek colonies in Thrace, and whose influence was considerable among the native Barbarians. Brasidas, therefore, proposed such a capitulation to the Amphipolitans as it seemed imprudent to refuse. They were to be released from the tribute which they had hitherto paid the Athenians; to enjoy the utmost degree of political independence, not inconsistent with the alliance of Sparta; even the Athenian garrison, if they continued in the place, were to be entitled to all the rights of citizens; and such

[24] Thucydid. p. 812.

persons

persons as chose to leave it, were granted a reasonable time to remove their families and their property. The last condition was embraced by the Athenians, and their more determined partisans. They retired to the neighbouring town of Eion, situate near the sea, on the northern branch of the Strymon; a place secured against every hostile assault by the skill and activity of Thucydides.

Towards the end of winter, the full extent of Brasidas's success was made known at Athens. The assembly was in commotion; and the populace were the more enraged at their losses, as it now appeared so easy to have prevented them, either by guarding the narrow defiles which led to their Macedonian possessions, or by sending their fleet with a seasonable reinforcement to their feeble garrisons in those parts. Their own neglect had occasioned the public disgrace; but with the usual injustice and absurdity accompanying popular discontents, they exculpated themselves, and banished their generals. Thucydides was involved in this cruel sentence. An armament was sent to Macedon; and new commanders were named to oppose Brasidas.

But the designs of that commander, who had begun to build vessels on the Strymon, and aspired at nothing less than succeeding to the authority, without exercising the oppression, of Athens, over those extensive shores, were more successfully opposed by the envy of the Spartan magistrates. The pride of the nobility was wounded by the glory of an expedition, in which they had no share; and

CHAP.
XVII.
their selfishness, while it obstinately prevented the supplies necessary to complete the plan of Brasidas, was eager to reap the profit of his past success. The restoration of their kinsmen taken at Sphacteria formed the object of their fondest wish; and they expected that the Athenians might listen to a proposal for that purpose, in order to recover the places which they had lost, and to check the fortunate career of a prudent and enterprising general. The Athenians readily entered into these views; it was determined that matters of such importance should be discussed with leisure and impartiality; a truce was therefore agreed on for a year between the contending republics.

Olymp. lxxxix. 2.
A. C. 423.

This transaction was concluded in the ninth summer of the war. It was totally unexpected by Brasidas, who received the voluntary submission of Scioné and Menda, two places of considerable importance in the peninsula of Pallené; of the former, indeed, before he was acquainted with the suspension of hostilities; but of the latter, even after he was apprized of that treaty.

The war renewed.
O'ymp. lxxxix. 3.
A. C. 422.

While the active valor of Brasidas prevented the confirmation of peace, the conscious worthlessness of Cleon promoted the renewal, or rather the continuance, of war. The glory of Athens was the perpetual theme of his discourse. He exhorted his countrymen to punish the perfidy of Sparta, in abetting the insolent revolt of Menda and Scioné; and to employ his own skill and bravery, which had been so successfully exerted on the coast of Peloponnesus, to repair their declining fortune in

Macedonia. The Athenians listened to the specious advice of this turbulent declaimer, who, in the ensuing spring, sailed to the Macedonian coast with a fleet of thirty gallies, twelve hundred citizens, heavy-armed, a squadron of three hundred horse, and a powerful body of light-armed auxiliaries. The surrender of Menda and Torona, whose inhabitants were treated with every excess of cruelty, encouraged him to attack Amphipolis. With this design, having collected his forces at Eion, he waited the arrival of some Macedonian troops, promised by Perdiccas, who having quarrelled with the Spartan general, deceitfully flattered the hopes of his antagonist.

The army of Cleon contained the flower of the Athenian youth, whose ardent valor disdained a precarious dependence on Barbarian aid. They accused the cowardice of their leader, which was only equalled by his incapacity, and lamented their own hard fate in being subjected to the authority of a man so unworthy to command them. The impatient temper of an arrogant demagogue was ill fitted to endure these seditious complaints. He hastily led his troops before the place, without previously examining the strength of the walls, the situation of the ground, the number or disposition of the enemy. Brasidas, meanwhile, had taken proper measures to avail himself of the known imprudence of his adversary. A considerable body of men had been concealed in the woody mountain Cerdylium, which overhangs Amphipolis. The greater part of the army were drawn up, ready for

CHAP. XVII.

action, at the several gates of the city. Clearidas, who commanded there, had orders to rush forth at a given signal, while Brasidas in person, conducting a select band of intrepid followers, watched the first opportunity for attack. The plan, contrived with so much skill, was executed with equal dexterity and precision. Confounded with the rapidity of such an unexpected and complicated charge, the enemy fled amain, abandoning their shields, and exposing their naked backs to the swords and spears of the pursuers. The forces on either side amounted to about three thousand; six hundred Athenians fell victims to the folly of Cleon, who, though foremost in the flight, was arrested by the hand of a Myrcinian targeteer.

Death of Cleon.

Death and honors of Brasidas.

His death might appease the manes of his unfortunate countrymen; but nothing could alleviate the sorrow of the victors for the loss of their admired Brasidas, who received a mortal wound while he advanced to the attack. He was conveyed alive to Amphipolis, and enjoyed the consolation of his last victory, in which only seven men had perished on the Spartan side. The sad magnificence of his funeral was adorned by the splendor of military honors; but what was still more honorable to Brasidas, he was sincerely lamented by the grateful tears of numerous communities, who regarded his virtues and abilities as the surest pledges of their own happiness and security. The citizens of Amphipolis paid an extraordinary tribute to his memory. Having demolished every monument of their ancient leaders and patriots, they erected the statue of Brasidas in the most conspicuous square of the city, appointed annual games to be celebrated at his tomb, and sacrificed to his revered shade, as to the great hero and original founder of their community[11].

CHAP. XVII.

Peace of Nicias. Olymp. lxxxix 4. A. C. 421.

The battle of Amphipolis removed the principal obstacles to peace. There was not any Spartan general qualified to accomplish the designs of Brasidas. The Athenians, dejected by defeat, and humbled by disgrace, wanted the bold imposing eloquence of Cleon, to disguise their weakness, and varnish their misfortunes. With the disheartened remains of an enfeebled armament, they despaired of recovering their Macedonian possessions; and the greater part returned home, well disposed for an accommodation with the enemy. These dispositions were confirmed by the pacific temper of Nicias, who had succeeded to the influence of Cleon, and who fortunately discovered in the moderation of Pleistoanax, king of Sparta, a coadjutor extremely solicitous to promote his views. During winter, several friendly conferences were held between the commissioners of the two republics; and, towards the commencement of the ensuing spring, a treaty of peace, and soon afterwards a defensive alliance, for fifty years, was ratified by the kings and ephori of Sparta on the one side, and by the archons and generals of Athens on the other. In consequence of this negociation, which was intended to comprehend the respective allies of the contracting powers, all places and prisoners, taken in

[11] Thucydid. p. 307.

the course of the war, were to be mutually restored; the revolted cities in Macedon were specified by name; but it was regulated that the Athenians should not require from them any higher revenue than that apportioned by the justice of Aristides[w].

Distribution of the Lacedæmonian allies.

In all their transactions, the Greeks were ever prodigal of promises, but backward in performance; and, amidst the continual rotation of authority, magistrates easily found excuses for violating the conditions granted by their predecessors. The known principles of republican inconstancy, ever ready to vibrate between excessive animosity and immoderate friendship, might likewise suggest a reason for converting the treaty of peace into a contract of alliance. But this measure, in the present case, was the effect of necessity. Athens and Sparta might make mutual restitution, because their respective interests required it. But no motive of interest engaged the former power to restore Nicæa to the Megareans, or the towns of Solium and Anactorium to Corinth. The Thebans, shortly before the peace, had seized the Athenian fortress of Panactum, situate on the frontier of Bœotia. They were still masters of Platæa. Elated by their signal victory at Delium, they could not be supposed willing to abandon their conquests, or even much inclined to peace. It was still less to be expected that the Macedonian cities should, for the convenience of Sparta, submit to the severe yoke

[w] Thucydid. p. 354. et seqq.

of Athens, from which they had recently been delivered; nor could it be hoped that even the inferior states of Peloponnesus should tamely lay down their arms, without obtaining any of those advantages with which they had been long flattered by their Spartan allies.

CHAP. XVIII.

Difcontents fomented by the Corinthians. — The Argive Alliance. — To which Athens accedes. — Birth and Education of Alcibiades. — His Friendship with Socrates. — His character — And Views — Which are favored by the State of Greece. — He deceives the Spartan Ambaffadors. — Renewal of the Peloponnefian War. — Battle of Mantinæa. — Tumults in Argos. — Maffacre of the Scionæans. — Cruel Conqueft of Melos.

CHAP. XVIII.
Difcontents fomented by the Corinthians.

THE voluptuous, yet turbulent citizens of Corinth, enjoy the odious diftinction of renewing a war which their intrigues and animofities had firft kindled. Under pretence of having taken an oath never to abandon the Macedonian cities, they declined being parties in the general treaty of peace. The alliance between Athens and Sparta, in which it was ftipulated, that thefe contracting powers fhould be entitled to make fuch alterations in the treaty as circumftances might require, the Corinthians affected, with fome reafon, to confider as a confpiracy againft the common liberties of Greece[1]. Fired with this idea, they haftened to Argos, in order to animate that republic with the fame paffions which rankled in their own breafts. Having

[1] The clauſe was worded in fuch a manner as might naturally excite alarm: Προσθεῖναι και ἀφελεῖν ὅτι ἂν ΑΜΦΟΙΝ τοῖν πολέοιν δοκῇ Thucydid. l. v. p. 354.

roused the ambition of the *magistrates*, they
artfully reminded the *people* of the glory of Agamemnon, recalled to the Argives their ancient and
just pre-eminence in the Peloponnesus, and conjured them to maintain the honor of that illustrious peninsula, which had been so shamefully abandoned by the pusillanimity, or betrayed by the
selfishness, of Sparta.

The Argives wanted neither power nor inclination to assume that important office. During the
Peloponnesian war, they had observed the principles
of a prudent neutrality, equally favorable to their
populousness and their wealth. Their protection
was courted by Mantinæa, the most powerful city
in Arcadia, which had recently conquered some
villages in its neighbourhood, to which Sparta laid
claim. The Elians, long hostile to Sparta, eagerly
promoted the Argive alliance, which was farther
strengthened by the speedy accession of the Macedonian allies, whose inhabitants were not more flattered by the kind zeal of Corinth, than provoked
by the cruel indifference of Sparta. Thebes and
Megara were equally offended with their Lacedæmonian allies, and equally inclined to war. But a
rigid aristocracy prevailed in those states, whose
ambitious magistrates, trembling for their personal
authority, and that of their families, declined entering into confederacy with free democratical republics [a].

But this democratical association soon acquired
an accession still more important, and received into

[a] Thucyd. L. v. p. 371.

its bosom the fountain of liberty itself; even the republic of Athens. This extraordinary event happened in the year following the negociation between Athens and Sparta. It was effected by means extremely remote from the experience of modern times; means which it is incumbent on us to explain, lest the political transactions of Greece should appear too fluctuating and capricious to afford a proper subject for history.

Birth and education of Alcibiades.

Amidst the factious turbulence of senates and assemblies, no measure could be adopted by one party, without being condemned by another. Many Athenians disapproved the peace of Nicias[1]; but the general blaze of opposition was eclipsed by the splendor of one man, who, on this occasion, first displayed those singular but unhappy talents, which proved fatal to himself and to his country. Alcibiades had not yet reached his thirtieth year, the age required by the wisdom of Solon for being entitled to speak in the assembly. But every advantageous circumstance of birth and fortune, talents natural and acquired, accomplishments of mind and body, pleaded an exception in favor of this extraordinary character, which, producing at once flowers and fruit, united with the blooming vivacity of youth, the ripened wisdom of experience[2]. His father, the rich and generous Clinias, derived his extraction from the heroic

---

[1] The Greeks sometimes distinguished treaties by the names of those who made them; the peace of Cimon; the peace of Nicias; and, as we shall see hereafter, the peace of Antalcidas.
[2] Plut. et Nepos in Alcibiad.

Ajax, and had distinguished his own valor and patriotism in the glorious scenes of the Persian war. In the female line, the son of Clinias was allied to the eloquence and magnanimity of Pericles, who, as his nearest surviving kinsman, was intrusted with the care of his minority. But the statesman, who governed with undivided sway the affairs of Athens and of Greece, could not bestow much attention on this important domestic task. The tender years of Alcibiades were committed to the illiberal discipline of mercenary preceptors; his youth and inexperience were beset by the destructive adulation of servile flatterers,— until the young Athenian, having begun to relish the poems of Homer, the admiration of which is congenial to every great mind, learned from thence to despise the pedantry of the one, and to detest the meanness of the other [a].

CHAP. XVIII.

From Homer Alcibiades early imbibed that ambition for excellence which is the great lesson of the immortal bard. Having attained the verge of manhood, he readily distinguished, among the crowd of rhetoricians and sophists, the superior merit of Socrates, who, rejecting all factitious and abstruse studies, confined his speculations to matters of real importance and utility; who, having never travelled to Egypt and the East in search of *mysterious* knowledge, reasoned with an Attic perspicuity and freedom; and who, being unbiassed by the system of any master, and always master of himself, thought,

His early attachment to Socrates.

[a] Plut. in Alcibiad.

CHAP. XVIII.

Their mutual obligations and friendship.

spoke, and acted with equal independence and dignity. An amiable and most instructive writer, the disciple and friend of Socrates, has left an admirable panegyric of the uniform temperance, the unshaken probity, the diffusive benevolence invariably displayed in his virtuous life of seventy years[a]. His distinguishing excellences are justly appreciated by Xenophon, a scholar worthy of his master[b]; but the youthful levity of Alcibiades (for youth is seldom capable of estimating the highest of all merits, the undeviating tenor of an innocent and useful life) was chiefly delighted with the splendor of particular actions. The eloquence, rather than the innocence of Socrates, excited his admiration. He was charmed with that inimitable raillery, that clear comprehensive logic, which baffled the most acute disputants of the Athenian schools[c]; that erect independence of mind, which disdained the insolence of power, the pride of wealth, and the vanity of popular fame, was well fitted to attract the congenial esteem of Alcibiades, who aspired beyond the beaten paths of vulgar greatness; nor could the gallant youth be less affected by the invincible intrepidity of Socrates, when, quitting the shade of speculation, and covered with the helm and cuirass, he grasped the massy spear, and justified, by his strenuous exertion in the field of battle, the useful lessons of his philosophy[d].

Socrates in his turn (since it is easier for a wise man to correct the errors of reason than to conquer

[a] Xenoph. Memorabil. Socrat.
[b] See particularly Xenoph. Apolog. Socrat.   [c] Plato, passim.
[d] Xenoph. Memorab. Socrat. pp. 442. 804. 818.

THE HISTORY OF GREECE. 45

the delusions of sentiment) was deeply affected with the beauty of Alcibiades[14]; a beauty depending, not on the transient flower of youth, and the seductive delicacy of effeminate graces, but on the ineffable harmony of a form which realized the sublime conceptions of Homer and Phidias concerning their fabulous divinities, and which shone in the autumn of life with undiminished effulgence[15]. The affection of Socrates, though infinitely removed from impurity, resembled rather the ardor of love than the calm moderation of friendship. The sage, whose company was courted by his other disciples, himself courted the company of Alcibiades; and when the ungrateful youth sometimes escaped to his licentious companions, the philosopher pursued him with the eagerness of a father or master, anxious to recover a fugitive son or slave[16]. At the battle of Potidæa he saved the life of his pupil, and in order to gratify the love of military glory, which already animated his youthful bosom, the sage obtained for Alcibiades the prize of valor, which the universal consent of the Athenians thought due to himself. At the fatal engagement of Delium, Alcibiades, it is said, had an opportunity of returning the more substantial favor, by saving the precious life of Socrates[15]; and it may

CHAP. XVIII.

[14] Vid. Xenoph. and Plato, passim. Socrates often acknowledges the danger of beauty, and its power over himself; but loses no opportunity to caution his disciples against the shameful passions, and abominable vices, which flow from this impure source. Vid. Memorab. Socrat. l. ii. passim, et l. v. c. iii. Sympos. c. iv. p. 264.
[15] Plut. in Alcibiad. [15] Plut. ibid.
[16] Strabo, p. 330. et Plut. in Alcibiad.

46 THE HISTORY OF GREECE.

CHAP. XVIII.

well be supposed that an interchange of such important favors would straiten the bands of their mutual friendship, during which the powers of reason and fancy were directed, with unabating diligence, to improve the understanding, and excite the virtue of Alcibiades.

Deceitful character of Alcibiades.

But this favorite youth labored under a defect, which could not be compensated by the highest birth, the most splendid fortune, the noblest endowments of mind and body, and even the inestimable friendship of Socrates. He wanted an honest[16] heart. This we are warranted to affirm on the authority of contemporary writers, who acknowledge, that first admiration, and then interest, was the foundation of his attachment to the illustrious sage, by whose instruction he expected to become, not a good, but an able, man. Some inclination to virtue he might, in such company, perhaps feel, but more probably feign; and the nicest discernment might mistake the real character of a man, who could adopt, at pleasure, the most opposite manners; and who, as will appear from the subsequent events of his various life, could surpass the splendid magnificence of Athens, or the rigid frugality of Sparta; could conform, as interest required, to the laborious exercises of the Thebans, or to the voluptuous indolence of Ionia; assume the soft effeminacy of an Eastern prince, or rival the sturdy vices of the drunken Thracians[17].

[16] Lysias cont. Alcibiad. et Xenoph. Memorab. Socrat. l. l. p. 715.
[17] Nepos in Alcibiad.

THE HISTORY OF GREECE. 47

The first specimen of his political conduct discovered the extraordinary resources of his versatile mind. He opposed the peace of Nicias, as the work of a rival, whom he wished to disgrace. His ambition longed for war, and the Spartans deserved his resentment, having, in all their transactions with Athens, testified the utmost respect for Nicias, while they were at no pains to conceal their want of regard for himself, though his family had been long connected with their republic by an intercourse of hospitality, and he had endeavoured to strengthen that connexion by his personal good offices to the Lacedæmonians taken in Sphacteria. To gratify at once his resentment, his ambition, and his jealousy, he determined to renew the war with Sparta; a design by no means difficult at the present juncture.

CHAP. XVIII.
His views

In compliance with the peace of Nicias, the Spartans withdrew their troops from Amphipolis; but they could restore neither that city, nor the neighbouring places in Macedon, to the dominion of Athens. The Athenians, agreeably to the treaty, allowed the captives taken in Sphacteria to meet the longing embraces of their kinsmen and friends; but good policy forbade their surrendering Pylus, until the enemy had performed some of the conditions stipulated in return. Mutual unwillingness, or inability, to comply with the articles of peace, sowed the seeds of animosity, which found a favorable soil in both republics. The authority of those magistrates, who supported the pacific measures of Nicias and Pleistoanax, had expired. The

Favored by the state of Greece. Olymp. xc. 1. A. C. 422.

CHAP. XVIII.

Spartan youth wished, by new hostilities, to cancel the memory of a war, which had been carried on without profit, and terminated with dishonor. But the wiser part perceived that better success could not be expected while the Athenians possessed Pylus. In their eagerness to recover that fortress, they renewed their alliance with the Thebans, from whom they received Panactum, which they hoped to exchange for Pylus; forgetting, in this transaction, an important clause in their treaty with Athens, "that neither of the contracting powers should, without mutual communication and consent, conclude any new alliance." The Thebans rejoiced in the prospect of embroiling the affairs of Athens and Sparta; and the Corinthians, guided by the same hostile views, readily concurred with the Thebans, and openly re-entered into the Lacedæmonian confederacy [16].

He outwits the Spartan ambassadors.
Olymp. 12. 1.
A. C. 420.

Having concluded this negociation, the Spartans, who yielded to none in the art of dissembling, dispatched ambassadors to Athens, excusing what they termed an apparent infringement of the treaty, and requesting that state to accept Panactum (which had been carefully dismantled) in exchange for Pylus. The senate of Athens heard their proposal without suspicion, especially as they declared themselves invested with full powers to embrace every reasonable plan of present accommodation and permanent friendship. It now remained for the ambassadors to propose their demand in the

[16] Thucydid. L. v. passim.

popular

popular assembly, which, they had reason to hope, might be deceived still more easily than the senate. But in this expectation they were disappointed by a contrivance of Alcibiades, no less singular than audacious. Having invited the ambassadors to an entertainment, during which he talked of their republic with more than his wonted respect, and testified the utmost solicitude for the success of their negociation, he observed to them, that one circumstance gave him much concern, their having mentioned full powers. They must beware of repeating that error in the assembly, because the natural rapacity of the populace, apprized of that circumstance, would not fail to insist on such conditions as the honor of Sparta could not possibly comply with. 'If they concealed the extent of their commission, the declaring of which could only serve to indicate timidity on the one side, and to provoke insolence on the other, he pledged himself to obtain the recovery of Pylus, and the gratification of their utmost hopes. On this occasion the Spartans injudiciously confided in a man, who had been irritated by the former neglect and ingratitude of their country. When they appeared next day in the assembly, Alcibiades demanded, with a loud voice, the object and extent of their commission. According to the concerted plan, they denied their having full powers. The artful Athenian, affecting a transport of indignation, arraigned the audacity and baseness of a people by whom his own unsuspecting temper had been egregiously abused. "But yesterday they declared their full powers in the senate;

they denied to-day what yesterday they displayed with ostentation. Such (I now perceive it) is the usual duplicity of their republic. It is thus they have restored Amphipolis. It is thus, Athenians! they have restored the neighbouring towns in Macedon: it is thus they have, indeed, put you in possession of Panactum, but with demolished walls; and after concluding an alliance with Athens, ratified by solemn oath, most treacherously and daringly infringed it, by entering into a league with Thebes, your determined and inveterate enemy. Can you still, men of Athens! tamely submit to such indignities? Do you not expel such traitors (pointing to the ambassadors) from your presence, and from your city?" This extraordinary harangue totally disconcerted the Spartans. Had their confusion allowed them to extenuate their fault by declaring the truth, the least reflection must have suggested, that Alcibiades would represent their simple story as a new turn of ingenious artifice. They retired abruptly from the assembly[19]; Nicias, and the other partisans of Sparta, shared their disgrace; and the Athenians were soon afterwards persuaded by Alcibiades to embrace the Argive alliance[20].

It might be expected, that the weight of such a powerful confederacy should have speedily crushed the debility of Sparta, already exhausted by the

[19] Thucyd. mentions the shock of an earthquake, which occasioned the dissolution of that assembly, before coming to any conclusion.
[20] Thucydid. l. v. p. 374, et seqq. Plut. in Alcibiad.

former war. But the military operations of Greece depended less on the relative strength of contending powers, than on the alternate preponderance of domestic factions. In the year following the treaty, the Athenians sent a small body of troops to assist their Peloponnesian allies in the reduction of Epidaurus, Tegea, and other hostile cities in Argolis and Arcadia. Yet in the ensuing year, when the Spartans, dreading the loss of some cities, and the defection of others, made a vigorous effort to retrieve their authority in Peloponnesus, the Athenians alone discovered little inclination, and exerted no activity, to obstruct their measures for that purpose. Pleistoanax being a partisan of the peace of Nicias, the Spartans intrusted the command to Agis, his more warlike colleague. All Lacedæmonians of the military age were summoned to the field. The dangerous expedient of arming the Helots was adopted on this important emergency. The Spartan allies showed unusual ardor in their cause. The Thebans sent ten thousand foot, and one thousand horsemen [19]; the Corinthians two thousand heavy-armed men; the Megarians almost an equal number; the ancient cities of Pallené and Sicyon in Achaia gave a powerful and ready assistance; while the small, but generous republic of Phlius, whose territory, bordering on Argolis, was appointed for the

[19] They had, however, but five hundred horses; ἱππεῖς πεντακοσίοις καὶ ἀμίπποις ἴσοις. Perhaps the ἄμιπποι, those not provided with horses, served as attendants on the horsemen. The mixing of light infantry with the cavalry was frequent in later times; but of this hereafter.

CHAP.
XVIII.

The Spartan and Argive armies face each other, but part without engaging. Olymp. 90. 3. A. C. 418.

rendez-vous of the confederates, took the field with the whole body of citizens and slaves capable of bearing arms [10].

The Argives observed the approaching storm, and prepared to resist it. The Eleans and Mantineans joined them; and although the Athenians were long expected in vain, the Argives did not lose courage, but boldly took the field to oppose the invaders. The skilful movements of king Agis intercepted their return to Argos; the high grounds above them were occupied by the Corinthians and Phliasians; their retreat towards Nemea was cut off by the Bœotians and Megarians. A battle seemed inevitable in the winding vale of Argos; but it is easier to admire, than explain, the subsequent conduct of either army. Whether the Argive commanders [11] were disconcerted by the judicious position of the enemy, or that compassion touched their minds on perceiving such numerous bodies of men, chiefly natives of the same peninsula, sprung from the same blood, and speaking the same Doric tongue, prepared to embrue their parricidal hands in kindred blood; or that, being secretly partisans of aristocracy [12], they were unwilling to come to extremities with Sparta; it is certain, that instead of joining battle, they entered

[10] Thucydid. l. v. p. 384, et seqq.

[11] Or rather Thrasyllus, who was one of five generals, but who seems to have enjoyed some pre-eminence over his colleagues. Perhaps it was his turn to command.

[12] Alciphron, who, with Thrasyllus, was the principal agent in this affair, was the "προξενος Λακεδαιμονιων," "the public host of the Lacedæmonians. Thucydid. p. 386.

into conference, with the Lacedæmonian king. In consequence of this unexpected measure, a truce was concluded between the chiefs, without the concurrence or knowledge of the officers or troops in either army. The Argives, Thrasyllus and Alciphron, engaged that their countrymen should give complete satisfaction for the injuries of which they were accused; and king Agis, whose authority, by the Spartan laws, was absolute in the field, led off his obsequious army.

Whatever might be the cause of this measure, it occasioned (after the first pause of silent astonishment) universal discontent, followed by loud and licentious clamors. The Spartans complained, " That, after assembling such a body of men as had scarcely ever been collected in Peloponnesus, whose attachment to their cause was ardent, whose numbers and courage were invincible, and after surrounding their enemies on every side, and depriving them of every resource, the glorious hope, or rather certainty, of the most complete and important victory, should have been sacrificed, in one moment, by the caprice, the cowardice, or the corruption of their general." The Argives lamented, " That their numerous enemies, whom they had a fair opportunity of engaging in their own country, should have been allowed to escape from their hands by a hasty and ill-judged composition." Nor did they confine their resentment to vain complaints. The most daring or most seditious attacked the houses of Thrasyllus and Alciphron. The rest soon joined in the tumult. The

CHAP.
XVIII.

Alcibiades persuades the Argives to break the truce.
Olymp. xc. 3.
A. C. 418.

effects of the generals were plundered or confiscated; and their lives were saved, with difficulty, by the respected sanctuary of Argive Juno.

Though the Greeks, and indeed the ancients in general, seldom employed resident ambassadors in foreign states, Alcibiades was then invested with that character at Argos. His activity would not fail to promote the popular tumult, in which his own and the Athenian interest was concerned. On a future occasion he boasted, that, chiefly at his instigation, the Argives and their allies were persuaded to break the truce; a measure greatly facilitated by the long-expected arrival of the Athenian transports, conveying a reinforcement of twelve hundred soldiers, and a body of three hundred cavalry. Encouraged by this event, the Argives, regardless of the truce, attacked the ancient and wealthy city of Orchomenus in Arcadia, which, after a feeble resistance, submitted to their arms. They next proceeded to lay siege to the neighbouring town of Tegea, a design extremely contrary to the inclination of the Eleans, who were eager to chastise the inhabitants of Lepreum, a district on their own frontier. The Argives, however, paid no regard to their demands; and the Eleans, offended by this instance of contempt, returned home in disgust.

The Spartans take the field.

The Lacedæmonians learned with indignation the submission of Orchomenus, the siege of Tegea, and the open infraction of the treaty. They had formerly murmured against the imprudent or perfidious measures of king Agis; but when they felt

THE HISTORY OF GREECE.

the effects of his misconduct, their resentment became outrageous. In the first emotions of their animosity, they determined to destroy his house, and to subject him to a fine of several thousand pounds sterling, which, in all probability, he would have been unable to pay. But his eloquence and address appeased the general clamor; and, as the anger of popular assemblies is easily converted into pity, he was again taken into favor. His known talents for war recommended him to the command of the army; and he assured his countrymen, that his future services should speedily wipe off the stain from his character. The Spartans, however, first elected on this occasion ten counsellors to attend their kings in the field, to restrain their too precipitate resolves, and control their too absolute authority.

CHAP. XVIII.

Having taken this precaution, the necessity of which seemed justified by recent experience, they summoned the assistance of their allies, whose ardor to renew hostilities was equal to their own. They proceeded with a numerous army (though inferior to that formerly collected, as their confederates beyond the Isthmus had not yet time to join them), and marched directly to the town of Mantinæa, expecting either to take that place, or to oblige the enemy to defend it, by withdrawing their troops from the siege of Tegea. The approach of the Argives prevented the surprise of Mantinæa; and both armies, whose ambition or resentment had been so lately disappointed of an opportunity to

Battle of Mantinæa.

CHAP.
XVIII.
Military
orations.

display their valor or their fury, eagerly prepared for an engagement.

According to ancient custom, the leaders of the several nations addressed their respective troops. The Mantinæans were animated "by the sight of their city, for the defence of which, as well as for the safety of their wives and children, they were exhorted valiantly to contend. The event of the battle must determine the important alternative of dominion and servitude; dominion which they had lately assumed over various cities in Arcadia, and servitude, which they had already suffered under the cruel tyranny of Sparta." The Argives were reminded "of their ancient pre-eminence in Peloponnesus, which they had recently recovered, and which their honor was now called to maintain. They were reminded of the long and bloody wars which they had formerly carried on, in order to repel the usurpation of a powerful and ambitious neighbour. This was the same enemy who actually provoked their arms, and gave them an opportunity of revenging, in one day, the accumulated injustice of many centuries." The Athenians heard, and repeated, "That it was glorious to march at the head of gallant and faithful allies, and to show themselves deserving of their hereditary renown. They yielded to none in bravery; their power was unrivalled; and when they had overcome the Lacedæmonians, even in the Peloponnesus, their dominion would be more extensive and secure."

The Spartans briefly exhorted their followers, and each other, "to exert that innate valor which had ever animated their breasts, and which could receive no additional force from a tedious display of useless words." Thus saying, they marched with a slow and firm step, regulated by the sound of the flute, to meet the impetuous onset" of the Argives and Athenians. Above a thousand of the former, chosen from the flower of the noblest youth of Argos, had been employed, since the first dissensions occasioned by the peace of Nicias, in the constant exercise of arms, in order to maintain the honorable pretensions of their country. They behaved with signal bravery. The Athenians were not wanting to their ancient fame. The Mantinæans strenuously defended every thing most dear to them. But the allied army had been considerably weakened by the desertion of the Eleans; and the martial enthusiasm of king Agis, seconded by the persevering valor of the Spartans", decided the

[side note: CHAP. XVIII. The Spartans victorious.]

" The admirable verses of Milton, who was a diligent reader of Thucydides, are the best commentary on this battle.

Anon they move
In perfect phalanx to the Dorian mood
Of flutes and soft recorders, such as rais'd
To height of noblest temper heroes old,
Arming to battle; and instead of rage,
Deliberate valor breath'd firm and unmov'd, &c.

Par. Lost, b. I.

" If the text is not corrupt, the words of Thucydides are very remarkable : Ἀλλὰ μαλιστα δὴ κατα παντα τῇ ἐκπειρίᾳ Λακεδαιμονιοι ἐλασσωθεντες, τῇ ἀνδρείᾳ ἐδειξαν οὐχ ἥσσον περιγενόμενοι, p. 394. "Thus the Lacedæmonians, exceedingly inferior as they appeared on this occasion to the enemy in military skill, showed themselves as much superior to them in true manly courage." It appears from the

CHAP. XVIII.

Tumults in Argos.

fortune of the battle. The allies were repulsed, broken, thrown into disorder, and put to flight. The Spartans, unwilling to irritate their despair, or superstitiously observing an ancient maxim, which enjoined them "to make a bridge for a flying enemy," did not continue the pursuit, but speedily returned home to celebrate the Carnean festival, rejoicing in having restored the lustre of their arms, and recovered their authority in the Peloponnesus.

This, in fact, proved the immediate consequence of a battle, which was not so bloody as might have been expected, the vanquished having lost *eleven*, and the victors only *three*, hundred. But the revolutions of Greece chiefly depended on the fluctuating politics of domestic factions. The Spartans had a numerous party in Argos itself, who, emboldened by the recent victory of their friends, immediately took arms, abolished the popular government, destroyed the partisans of Athens, abjured the league with that state, and entered into a new confederacy with Sparta. This event happened a

description of the battle, that the Lacedæmonians were defective, not in skill, but in discipline. In approaching the enemy, their right wing extended too far, which frequently happened from the desire of every soldier to cover his unarmed side by the shield of the next person on his right. In consequence of this tendency, the Lacedæmonian left wing was over-reached by the enemy's right. Agis ordered the Skirites and Brasidians to wheel from their places on the right, and lengthen the front of the left wing: commanding the battalions of Hipponoidas and Aristocles to fill up the vacuity occasioned by this movement. But these generals absolutely refused to obey orders, and were afterwards banished Sparta on that account. Thucydid. p. 393, et seqq.

few weeks after the engagement, and towards the
close of the fourteenth winter of the Peloponnesian war. During the two following years, Argos
paid dearly for a moment of transient splendor,
having undergone three bloody revolutions, which
renewed the atrocities of Corcyrean sedition. The
contest ended, as in Corcyra, in favor of the
Athenians and democracy.

CHAP.
XVIII.

The affairs of the Peloponnesus had long occupied, without engrossing, the attention of Athens.
The year preceding her alliance with Argos, the
Athenians reduced the rebellious city of Scioné,
in the peninsula of Pallené, against which their
resentment had been provoked to the utmost fury,
because the Scioneans, though inhabiting a country
almost surrounded by the sea, had defied the
naval power of Athens, and, amidst the misfortunes of that state, revolted to her enemies. The
citizens of Scioné became the victims of a revenge
equally cruel and imprudent. The males, above
the age of puberty, were put to the sword; the
women and children dragged into servitude; the
name and honors of the city extinguished for
ever; and the territory planted with a new colony,
consisting chiefly of Platæan exiles. These atrocious cruelties alarmed the terror, exasperated the
resentment, and invigorated the resistance, of the
neighbouring republics. Their defence was undertaken by Perdiccas, king of Macedon, whom
the Athenians therefore interdicted the use of the
Grecian seas. But that ambitious people made so
little progress in reducing the Macedonian coast,

Massacre
of the
Scioneans.

CHAP.
XVIII.

that they finally defifted from this defign, contenting themselves with guarding thofe places which ftill preferved their allegiance, with re-eftablifhing domeftic order, and with collecting the cuftomary tribute from their numerous colonies and dependences

The Athenians attack Melos, Olymp. 91. 1.
A. C. 416.

The productive induftry diffufed through all branches of the community, the equality of private fortune, the abfence of habitual luxury, together with the natural advantages of their foil and climate, enabled the Greeks to flourifh amidft furious and bloody wars. After a fhort period of tranquillity, their exuberant population overflowed, and was obliged to difcharge itfelf in foreign colonies or conquefts. Such a period Athens enjoyed for five years after the peace of Nicias as the Macedonian and Argive wars only employed her activity, without exhaufting her ftrength. The neceffity of exerting her fuperfluous vigor in fome ufeful and honorable defign, was fatally experienced, in the year following, by the unfortunate ifland of Melos, one of the largeft of the Cyclades, lying directly oppofite to the Cape of Malea, the fouthern promontory of Laconia.

Defcription of that ifland.

This beautiful ifland, fixty miles in circumference, of a circular form, of an agreeable temperature, and affording, in peculiar perfection[11], the ufual productions of a fine climate, had early invited

[11] The ifland of Melos is every where impregnated with iron, bitumen, fulphur, and other minerals. It is defcribed by Tournefort as a great laboratory. Its fubterranean fires are fuppofed to give peculiar force and flavor to its wines and fruits.

THE HISTORY OF GREECE. 61

the colonization of the Spartans; and the happy settlement had enjoyed political independence for seven hundred years. The strength and importance of the capital, which had the same name with the island, may be understood by the armament, of thirty ships, and near three thousand soldiers, which the Athenians brought against it. Before they commenced hostilities, either by attacking the city, or by ravaging the country, they sent ambassadors to the Melians, in order to persuade them to surrender, without incurring the danger or the punishment of an unequal, and probably a fruitless, resistance. The cautious islanders, well acquainted with the eloquence and address of the enemy with whom they had to contend, denied them the permission to speak before the public assembly, but appointed a deputation of the magistrates, to hear and examine their demands. The Athenian ambassadors were received in the senate-house, where a most important and interesting conference was held [n], which, while it engages our compassion for the unhappy victims of ambition, explains the prevailing sentiments and opinions of the Greeks in matters of war and government, and illustrates the daring injustice of the Athenian republic. The ambassadors began the dialogue, by observing, "That since the distrust of the Melians, probably arising from the conscious weakness of their cause, had refused them the liberty of speaking, in a continued oration, to the assembly of the people, they should use that mode of conference which seemed

CHAP. XVIII.

Conference between the commissioners of Athens and Melos.

[n] Thucydid. l. v. p. 400, et seqq.

CHAP.
XVIII.
most agreeable to the inclinations of their adversaries, and patiently listen to the objection which might occur to any part of their discourse." *Melians.* "The proposal is just and reasonable; but you have come hither with an armed force, which renders you judges in your own cause. Though vanquished in debate, you may still conquer by arms; but if we yield in argument, we must submit to slavery." *Athenians* "If you intend to talk of matters foreign to the subject, we have done." *M.* "It is surely excusable for those, whose all is at stake, to turn themselves on every side, and to suggest their suspicions and their doubts. But let the conference be carried on in the manner which you have proposed." *A.* "And, on both sides, let all superfluous arguments be omitted; either that *we*, having repelled and conquered the Persians, are entitled to govern the Greeks; or that *you*, being a colony of Lacedæmon, are entitled to independence. Let us speak like men of sense and experience, who know that the equal rules of justice are observed only by men of an equal condition; but that it belongs to the strong to command, and to the weak to obey; because such is the interest of both." *M.* "How can our interest and yours coincide?" *A.* "By submission, you will save your lives; and by preserving you, we will increase our own power." *M* "Consider (for this also must be mentioned, since disregarding *justice*, you are governed only by *utility*) that your unprovoked invasion of the Melians will rouse the resentment of all Greece; will render all

neutral states your enemies; and, if ever your empire should decline, (as what human grandeur is not subject to decay?) will expose you to a dreadful and just punishment." *A.* "The continuance of our empire is the care of fortune and the gods; the little that man can do to preserve it, we will not neglect. The liberty of Melos offends the pride of the neighbouring isles, and stirs them to rebellion. The interest of our present power must prevail over the apprehension of future danger." *M.* "While the Athenians are thus prepared to incur danger for the preservation of empire, and their subject islands to defy death for the hopes of freedom, would it not be the basest and most infamous cowardice in us, who have long enjoyed liberty, to decline any toil or danger for maintaining the most valuable and the most glorious of all human possessions?" *A.* "We are not come hither to dispute the prize of valor, but to offer terms of safety." *M.* "The event of war is uncertain; there is some hope in resistance, none in submission. *A.* "Flattering hope often deceives the prosperous and the powerful, but always destroys the weak and unfortunate, who, disregarding natural means of preservation, have recourse to idle dreams of the fancy, to omens, oracles, divination, and all the fallacious illusions of a vain superstition." *M.* "We know that it will be difficult for the Melians to contend with the strength and fortune of Athens: yet we trust that the gods will support the justice of our cause; and that the Lacedæmonians, from whom we are descended, moved by a sense of honor, will defend their own blood." *A.* "Believe not that Athens will be forsaken by the gods. Ambition is implanted in man. The wisdom of providence, not an Athenian decree, has established the inevitable law, that the strong should govern the weak. As to the assistance of the Lacedæmonians, we sincerely congratulate your happy ignorance of their principles. Whatever equity prevails in their domestic institutions, they have but one rule respecting their neighbours, which is, to regulate all their transactions with them by their own convenience." *M.* "It is chiefly that consideration which affords us hope, that they will not forsake an island which they have planted, lest they should be regarded as traitors, than which nothing could be more unfavorable to their interest, especially since Melos, lying in the neighbourhood of their own territories, would be a dangerous possession in the hands of an enemy." *A.* "The timid caution of the Lacedæmonians seldom takes the field, even against their inveterate enemies in the Peloponnesus, unless when their standard is attended by numerous allies. It is not to be imagined that, for the safety of a colony, they will alone cross the Cretan sea, to contend with the superior navy of Athens." *M.* "Should the Lacedæmonians be averse to sail, they can transport others in their stead; and the extent of the Cretan sea may elude the vigilance of your ships; or should that probability fail, the Lacedæmonians may attack your subjects on the continent, and accomplish the designs of the warlike Brasidas.

Brasidas." *A.* "You are determined, it seems, to learn, by fatal experience, that fear never compelled the Athenians to desist from their designs; especially never to raise the siege of any place which they had once invested. For during the whole of this long conference, you have not mentioned a single particular capable of affording any just ground of confidence. Deceived by the splendor of words, you talk of honor and independence, rejecting the offers of a powerful state, whose arms you are unable to resist, and whose protection you might obtain at the expense of a moderate tribute. Lest shame should have any share in this dangerous behaviour, we shall leave you to consult privately, only reminding you once more, that your present deliberations involve the fate of your country."

CHAP. XVIII.

The Athenian ambassadors retired; and shortly afterwards, the Melians recalled them, and "declared their unanimous resolution not to betray, in one unlucky hour, the liberty which they had maintained for seven hundred years; depending on the vigorous assistance of their Lacedæmonian kinsmen, and trusting especially in that divine providence which had hitherto most wonderfully preserved them amidst the general convulsions of Greece. But they entreated the Athenians to accept their offers of neutrality, and to abstain from unprovoked violence." The ambassadors prepared for returning to the camp, leaving the commissioners with a sarcastic threat, "That of all men, in such a delicate situation, the Melians alone

Magnanimity of the Melians.

Conquest of Melos, and cruel treatment of the Inhabitants.

CHAP.
XVIII.

thought the future more certain than the paſt, and would grievouſly ſuffer for their folly, in preferring to the propoſals of certain and immediate ſafety, the deceitfulneſs of hope, the inſtability of fortune, and the vain proſpect of Lacedæmonian aid." The Athenians, irritated by oppoſition, inveſted, without delay, the capital of Melos, which was blocked up for ſeveral months by ſea and land. The beſieged, after ſuffering cruelly by famine, made ſeveral deſperate ſallies, ſeized the Athenian magazines, and deſtroyed part of their works. But towards the end of winter, their reſiſtance was defeated by the vigorous efforts of the enemy, combined with domeſtic treaſon. The males above the age of fourteen ſhared the unhappy fate of the Scioneans. The women and children were ſubjected to perpetual ſervitude, and five hundred new inhabitants, drawn from the neighbouring colonies of Athens, were ſent to occupy the vacant lands, which had been cultivated and adorned for ſeven centuries by the labor of the exterminated Melians[17].

[17] Thucydid. l. v. p. 410. ad fin.

CHAP. XIX.

Alcibiades promotes the Sicilian Expedition. — Revolutions in that Island. — Embassy to Athens. — Extravagant Views of Alcibiades. — Opposed by Nicias. — The Athenians prepare to invade Sicily. — Their Armament beheld with Suspicion by the Italian States. — Deliberations concerning the Mode of carrying on the War. — Alcibiades takes Catana by Stratagem. — His Intrigues in Messené. — He is unseasonably recalled to Athens. — Charged with Treason and Impiety. — Escapes to Sparta. — Nicias determines to attack Syracuse. — Description of that City. — The Athenians prevail in a Battle. — Return to Catana and Naxos.

THE inhuman massacre of the Melians has been ascribed by an instructive, though often inaccurate biographer[1], to the unfeeling pride of Alcibiades. But more ancient and authentic writers[2], whose silence seems to exculpate the son of Clinias from this atrocious accusation, represent him as the principal author of the expedition against Sicily; an expedition not more unjust in its principle than fatal in its consequences.

The salutary union between the princes of Syracuse and Agrigentum triumphed, as we had

[1] Plut. in Alcib.
[2] Thucyd. l. v. Lysias Orat. cont. Alcib.

68 THE HISTORY OF GREECE.

CHAP. XIX.

occasion to relate, over the ambition and resources of Carthage. Sicily flourished under the virtuous administration of Gelon[a] and Theron; but its tranquillity was disturbed by the dissensions of their immediate successors. Hieron king of Syracuse proved victorious in a long and bloody war, during which the incapacity and misfortunes of his rival Thrasideus emboldened the resentment of his subjects, already provoked by his injustice and cruelty[b]. He escaped the popular fury, but fell a victim to his own despair, and the Agrigentines, having expelled the family of an odious tyrant, instituted a republican form of policy.

Reign of Hieron in Syracuse.

The false, cruel, and avaricious Hieron (for such at least he is described[c] in the first years of his reign) probably received little benefit from the dangerous influence of prosperity. But his mind was not incapable of reflection; and, in the course of a long sickness and confinement, he discovered the emptiness of such objects as kings are taught to admire, and had recourse to the solid pleasures of the mind. By conversing with Grecian philosophers, he learned the most important of all lessons, that of conversing with himself; a conversation which none but the most virtuous or the most vicious of men can long and frequently maintain, without deriving from it essential profit. With the improvement of his understanding, the sentiments of Hieron improved; his character and manners underwent a total change; and the latter

---

[a] See vol. II. p. 170.   [c] Diodor. l. xi. c. lx. et seqq.
[b] Diodor. Sic. l. xi. c. lxvi.

years of his reign adorn the history of Sicily, and the age in which he lived [f]. The poets Simonides, Æschylus, and Bacchilides, frequented his court, and admired the greatness of his mind, rather than of his fortune. The sublime genius of Pindar has celebrated the magnificent generosity of his illustrious patron. And in an age when writing was the picture of conversation, because men talked as they needed not have been ashamed to write, the impartial disciple of Socrates, who had nothing to hope or to fear from the ashes of a king of Sicily, has represented Hieron, in the Dialogue entitled from his name [g], as a model of wisdom and virtue.

CHAP. XIX.

It is a mortifying reflection that the inimitable qualities of a virtuous prince should naturally encourage the sloth, or irritate the vices, of a degenerate successor. The glorious reign of Hieron was followed by the bloody tyranny of Thrasybulus; a wretch who, disgracing the throne and human nature, was expelled from Sicily by the just indignation of his subjects. Resentment is more permanent than gratitude. The Syracusans forgot the fame of Gelon; they forgot the recent merit of Hieron; and, that they might never be again subjected to a tyrant like Thrasybulus, exchanged the odious power of kings for the dangerous fury of democracy [h].

The tyranny of Thrasybulus, and establishment of democracy. Olymp. lxxviii. 3. A. C. 466.

The inferior cities having successively imitated the example of Agrigentum and Syracuse, the

Effects of that revolution.

[f] Ælian. l. ix. c. vii.   [g] Xenophont. Hieron.
[h] Aristot. de Repub. l. v. c. xii.

F 3

CHAP. XIX.

Grecian colonies in Sicily experienced the disorders of that tumultuous liberty which had so long prevailed in the mother-country. Distracted by internal discord, and harassed by external hostility, they had neither leisure nor inclination to attend to the politics of Greece. The republic of Syracuse, which was alone capable of interposing with effect, in the quarrels of that country, imitated, instead of opposing, the ambition of Athens. Most of the Dorian settlements had become confederates, or rather tributaries, to the Syracusans; and towards the commencement of the Peloponnesian war, that aspiring people, though torn by domestic factions, strenuously exerted their valor against the Ionic settlements of Leontium, Catana, and Naxos.

Dissensions in Sicily, in which the Athenians interfere. Olymp. lxxxviii. 3. A. C. 426.

While these unhappy islanders struggled with the turbulence of a government more stormy than the whirlpools of Scylla and Charybdis, they likewise enjoyed, however, the peculiar advantages of democracy; which, of all political constitutions, presents the widest scope to the exercise of superior talents, and has always been the most productive in great men. The active fermentation of popular assemblies had given the eloquence of a Gorgias to Leontium, and the abilities of a Hermocrates to Syracuse. In the sixth year of the Peloponnesian war, the former came to Athens to solicit the protection of that republic against the unjust usurpation of the Sicilian capital. His arguments convinced the judgment, and the brilliant harmony of his style transported the sensibility, of the Athenians.

They immediately dispatched twenty ships of war to the assistance of their Ionic brethren. Two years afterwards a similar request was made, and as readily complied with; and the Athenians seemed disposed to engage with vigor in the war, when the foresight of Hermocrates, alarmed by the intrusion of these ambitious strangers, promoted a general congress of the states of Sicily.

This convention was held at the central town of Gela; it was attended by the plenipotentiaries of all the Doric and Ionic cities. Hermocrates represented Syracuse; and illustrious as that republic was, his conduct proved him worthy its highest honors. While the representatives of other states dwelt on their particular grievances, and urged their separate interests, Hermocrates regarded and enforced only the general interest of Sicily. His arguments finally prevailed, and all parties were engaged to terminate their domestic contests, lest the whole island should fall a prey to a foreign power*.

But a plan of union, so seasonable and salutary, depended on the transient influence of a single man, while the principles of discord were innumerable and permanent. Within a few years after this event, Leontium was taken and destroyed, its inhabitants reduced to the wretched condition of exiles, and its confederates, the Egesteans, closely besieged by the conjunct arms of Selinus and Syracuse. The unfortunate communities again sent an embassy to Athens, pleading the rights of

Thucyd. p. 290.

CHAP. XIX.

consanguinity, and addressing not only the passions but the interest of their powerful allies. "The Athenians," they insisted, "were bound by every principle of sound policy to repress the growing greatness of Syracuse, which must otherwise become a formidable accession to the Peloponnesian league; and now was the time for undertaking that enterprise, while their Ionian kinsmen in Sicily were still capable of exerting some vigor in their own defence." In order to enforce these arguments, the ambassadors of Egesta or Segesta gave an ostentatious, and even a very false, description of the wealth of their republic; which, according to their account, was capable of furnishing the whole expense of the war. Their fellow-citizens at home carried on the deception by a most unjustifiable artifice, displaying to the Athenian commissioners sent to confer with them, the borrowed riches of their neighbours, and raising, by extraordinary expedients, the sum of sixty talents of silver, to maintain, for a month, an Athenian fleet of sixty sail, as if they had purposed monthly to repeat this large subsidy, which at once exhausted their faculties [10].

with which the Athenians imprudently comply.

The arguments of their Sicilian allies were doubtless entitled to considerable weight with the Athenians; yet various reasons might have dissuaded that ambitious people from undertaking, at the present juncture, an expedition against the powerful republic of Syracuse. The cloud of war, which Pericles saw advancing with rapid motion from the

[10] Thucydid. p. 444.

Peloponnesus, had been at length dispelled by the valor and fortune of the Athenians; not, however, before the arms of Brasidas had shaken their empire to the foundation. The same storm might be again collected, if the Athenians removed their armies from home, especially if they were unfortunate abroad, since the wounded pride of Sparta would eagerly seize the first opportunity of revenge. The rebellion of the Macedonian cities was still unsubdued, and it would be highly imprudent and dangerous, before recovering the allegiance of these ancient possessions, to attempt the acquisition of new territories. Should the Athenian expedition against Sicily be crowned with the most flattering success, it would still be difficult, nay, impossible, to preserve such a distant and extensive conquest; but should this ambitious design fail in the execution, as there was too good reason to apprehend, the misfortunes of the Athenians, whose greatness was the object both of terror and of envy, would encourage the rebellious spirit of their subjects and allies, excite the latent animosity of the Peloponnesians, and reinforce their ancient enemies by the resentment and hostility of Syracuse and her confederates, justly provoked by the daring invasion of their island.

These prudential considerations were unable to cool the ardor of the Athenian assembly, inflamed by the breath of their favorite Alcibiades. It is a just and profound observation of Machiavel, that the real powers of government are often contracted to a narrower point in republics than in

CHAP.
XIX.

monarchies; an observation which that sagacious statesman had learned from the experience of his native city, and which he might have confirmed by the history of the Greeks, whose political measures, and even whose national character, depended on the transient influence of a few individuals. Under the direction of Aristides and Themistocles, the Athenians displayed the soundest policy, adorned by unshaken probity, and by heroic valor. Cimon inspired the generous ambition which animated his own breast: a dignified grandeur and magnanimous firmness distinguished the long administration, I had almost said reign, of Pericles. The son of Clinias succeeded to the power and authority, without succeeding to the virtues of those great men, whom his pride disdained to imitate. Regardless of order and decency, with a licentious magnificence most offensive to the spirit of republican equality, he blended a certain elegance of manners, which not only repelled censure, but attracted applause. Thus dispensed from observing the established formalities of private life, he expected that the glory of his administration might soar above the ordinary dictates of political prudence[11]. Though he preferred what was useful to what was virtuous, he preferred what was brilliant to what was useful, and, disdaining the common gifts of valor and fortune, aspired at objects extraordinary and unattainable. The recovery of the Athenian possessions, and the re-establishment of an empire,

[11] See Plut. in Alcibiad. Hoerat. de Pave above all, the animated picture in Plato's Republic (l. viii. cap. ea. et seqq.), of which Alcibiades, doubtless, was the original.

already too extensive, might have satisfied the ambition of a bold and active statesman. But the extravagant hopes of Alcibiades expatiated in a wider field. The acquisition of Sicily itself he regarded only as a necessary introduction to farther and more important conquests. The intermediate situation of that beautiful and fertile island opened, on the one hand, an easy communication with the eastern front of Italy, which, from Brundusium to the Sicilian frith, was adorned by populous and flourishing cities; and on the other, afforded a short and safe passage to the northern shores of Africa, which, for many ages, had been cultivated and enriched by the united labors of the Greeks and Carthaginians. In his waking or sleeping dreams, Alcibiades grasped the wide extent of those distant possessions, by the resources of which he expected finally to subdue the pertinacious spirit, and obstinate resistance, of the Peloponnesians. Thus secure at home, and sovereign of the sea, Athens might incorporate with her own the troops of the conquered provinces, and maintain an unshaken dominion over the most delightful portion of the earth, while her fortunate citizens, delivered from all laborious and mercenary cares, would be supported by the contributions of subject nations, and enabled to display, in their full extent, that taste for splendor and magnificence, that greatness of soul and superiority of genius, which justly entitled them to the empire of the world [19].

[19] Isocrat. de Pace. Andocid. Orat. III. p. 269. et Aristoph. Vesp. ver. 616.

Allured by these extravagant, but flattering prospects of grandeur, the Athenians, in two successive assemblies, held at the short interval of five days, agreed to the resolution of making war against Sicily, and of raising such naval and military force as seemed necessary for carrying it on with vigor and success. While they still deliberated on the latter object, the virtuous Nicias, who had been named with Alcibiades and Lamachus to the command of the projected armament, omitted nothing that prudence could suggest, and patriotism enforce, to deter his countrymen from such a dangerous and fatal design. On this memorable occasion, he threw aside his usual timidity, and divested himself of that rigid regard for established forms, which was natural to his age and character. Though the assembly was convened to determine the proportion of supplies and troops, and the means of collecting them with the greatest expedition and facility, he ventured, contrary to ancient custom, to propose a different subject of debate; affirming, " That the interest of Athens was concerned, not in providing the preparations for the Sicilian invasion, but in re-examining the expedience of the war. The assembly ought not to be moved by the arguments and entreaties of the persecuted Egestæans, and fugitive Leontines, whom resentment had taught to exaggerate, and misery to deceive. Nor ought the vain phantom of glory and ambition to engage Athens in a design perhaps altogether impracticable, and, in the present juncture, peculiarly unseasonable; since it would be madness to excite the flames of a new war, before the ashes of the old were extinguished. The pleas of danger and self-defence were in the highest degree frivolous; for, should the dreaded power of Syracuse be extended over the whole of Sicily, the Athenians would have nothing to apprehend: this event would rather increase their security. In the actual state of the island, particular cities might be persuaded by fear, or interest, to court the protection of the Peloponnesian confederacy; but the victorious Syracuse would disdain to follow the standard of Sparta. Should the former republic, by an effort of uncommon generosity, subject the partial dictates of her pride to the general safety and honor of the Dorian name, sound policy, however, would still prevent her from endangering the precarious empire which she had obtained over her neighbours, by strengthening the confederacy of Peloponnesus, of which the avowed design was to give liberty and independence to the Grecian cities. Should all remote views of policy be disregarded, yet immediate fear would deter the Syracusans from provoking the resentment of Athens, the effects of which they had not as yet experienced, but which, being unknown, must appear the more formidable. It was evident, therefore, that the Sicilian expedition might be omitted without danger; but if this enterprise, which had been hastily resolved on, were injudiciously executed, or if any of those misfortunes should happen, which are but too frequent in war, the Athenians would be exposed not only to danger, but to disgrace and

CHAP.
XII.

His discourse answered by Alcibiades.

ruin. The result of such an important deliberation ought not to be committed to the rash decision of youthful levity; which viewed the Sicilian war, as it did every other object, through the delusive medium of hope, vanity, and ambition; and, totally disregarding the expense and danger to be incurred by the republic, considered only the profits of military command, which might repair the wreck of exhausted fortunes, and supply a new fund for the indulgence of extravagant and licentious pleasures. He had in his eye a youth of that description, the principal author of the expedition, who was surrounded by a numerous band of adherents, determined to applaud his discourse and to promote his measures. It became the wisdom and dignity of the assembly to resist with firmness that juvenile conspiracy. In such a dangerous crisis, it was the duty of the president to dispense with ordinary forms, and to act, not merely as the instrument, but as the physician of a diseased republic. The question ought to be debated a second time; and the Athenians ought to rescind the decree against Sicily, which had passed without sufficient examination, in the absence of several aged and respectable counsellors ''".

This discourse immediately called up Alcibiades, who, presuming on his credit with the assembly, acknowledged, " That he had aspired to the

'' Thucydid. l. vi. p. 417, et seqq. The Sicilian expedition is uninterruptedly related through the remainder of the sixth and seventh books of Thucydides. The collateral authority of Diodorus, Plutarch, and the orators, is of little importance.

command in Sicily, and that he thought himself justly entitled to that honor. The extravagance of which he was accused, had redounded to the profit of his country; since his magnificence at the Olympic games, however it might be traduced by an abusive epithet, had extended the glory of Athens, and deserved the admiration of Greece. His youth and inexperience had effected what the policy of the wisest statesmen had often attempted in vain. A powerful confederacy had been formed against Sparta, even in the bosom of the Peloponnesus; and the terror of a domestic foe would long prevent the enmity of that rival state from interrupting the progress of Athenian grandeur. In an expedition, evidently directed to this glorious end, expense and danger ought not to be regarded, since wealth was usefully sacrificed to purchase victory and renown; and power was only to be preserved by seizing every favorable opportunity to increase it. To the undertaking which he advised, no reasonable objection could be made; its expense would be furnished by the Egistæans, and other confederates; and the danger could not be great, as Sicily, however extensive and populous, was inhabited by a promiscuous crowd of various nations, without arms or discipline, devoid of patriotism, and incapable of union [10]".

The assembly murmured applause, confirmed their former decree, and testified for the war greater alacrity than before. Nicias perceived the violence

[10] Thucydid. p. 422—426.

CHAP. XIX.

of the popular current; still, however, he made one ineffectual effort to resist its force. "The success of an invader," he observed, "commonly depended on the weight and rapidity of his first unexpected impression, which confirmed the confidence of his friends, and excited dismay and terror in his enemies. If the expedition into Sicily must be undertaken in defiance of every difficulty and danger, it ought therefore to be carried into execution with the utmost vigor. The Athenians might thus secure the assistance of Naxos and Catana, which were connected by affinity with the Egestæans and Leontines. But there remained seven cities, and those far more powerful, with which they must prepare to contend; particularly Selinus and Syracuse, places well provided with ships, magazines, cavalry, archers, heavy-armed troops, and every object and resource most useful in defensive war. An armament simply naval would not be sufficient to cope with such a strength. Five thousand pikemen, with a proportional number of archers and cavalry, could not render the invasion successful. After arriving in Sicily, the towns must be besieged or stormed; workmen, with all sorts of machines and implements, must be collected for those purposes, and transported to an island from which, in the four winter-months, a messenger could scarcely return to Athens. This necessary train, which would greatly encumber the fleet and army, must be subsisted in a hostile country. Besides an hundred gallies, a great number of tenders and victuallers would be required for

the

the expedition. To collect such an immense mass of war, demanded, doubtless, astonishing ardor and perseverance; but if the Athenians intended to employ a smaller force, he must, in justice to his country and himself, decline accepting the command, since nothing less than what he had described could promise a hope of victory, or prevent the certainty of defeat [11].

CHAP. XIX.

The last attempt of Nicias to dissuade his countrymen from this fatal enterprise, by magnifying the difficulty of its execution, produced an opposite effect. The obstacles, which were unable to conquer, only animated the courage of the assembly; and it was determined, that the generals should be invested with full authority to raise such sums of money, and to levy such a body of troops, as might ensure success to their arms. The domestic strength of the Athenians was unequal to the greatness of the undertaking: proper agents were dispatched to demand an extraordinary contribution from their dependent states, as well as to summon the reluctant assistance of their more warlike allies. These auxiliary squadrons were ordered to sail to Corcyra, in which rendezvous the Athenians, towards the middle of summer, were ready to join their confederates.

The Athenians prepare for invading Sicily. Olymp. xci. 2. A. C. 415.

The magnitude of the preparations increased the hopes and the ardor of all ranks of men in the republic. The old expected that nothing could resist such a numerous and well-equipped armament.

The magnitude of their preparations.

[11] Thucydid. p. 427—429.

82 THE HISTORY OF GREECE.

CHAP. XIX.

The young eagerly seized an occasion to gratify their curiosity and love of knowledge in a distant navigation, and to share the honors of such a glorious enterprise. The rich exulted in displaying their magnificence; the poor rejoiced in the immediate assurance of pay sufficient to relieve their present wants[14], and in the prospect of obtaining by their arms the materials of future ease and happiness. Instead of finding any difficulty to complete the levies, the great difficulty consisted in deciding the preference of valor and merit among those who solicited to serve; and the whole complement of forces, to be employed by sea and land, consisted of chosen men[17].

The general alacrity to embark.

Amidst the general alacrity felt, or at least expressed, by people of all descriptions (for the dread of incurring public censure made several express what they did not feel,) Socrates[18] alone ventured openly and boldly to condemn the expedition, and to predict the future calamities of his country. But the authority of a sage was incapable to check the course of that enthusiasm, which had not been interrupted by the anniversary,

[14] The most expert and able seamen received a drachma (seven pence three farthings) as daily pay, besides donatives from their respective captains. Thucydid. et Plut.

[17] Thucydid. p. 430—433.

[18] Plutarch joins Meton the astrologer with Socrates. But the story of Meton, who pretended madness, burned his house, and entreated the Athenians, that, amidst his domestic misfortunes, he might not be deprived of the comfort of his only son, is inconsistent with the narrative of Thucydides, which proves, that instead of compelling reluctance, there was occasion to repress forwardness, to embark.

THE HISTORY OF GREECE.

festival of Adonis, an ancient and melancholy rite, which inauspiciously returned a few days preceding the embarkation. During this dreary ceremony, the streets of Athens were crowded with spectres clothed in funereal robes; the spacious domes and temples resounded with lugubrious cries; while the Grecian matrons, marching in slow procession, tore their dishevelled hair, beat their naked bosoms, and lamented in mournful strains the untimely death of the lover, and beloved favorite, of Venus [b].

When the appointed day arrived, the whole inhabitants of Athens, whether citizens or strangers, assembled early in the Piræus, to admire the greatest spectacle ever beheld in a Grecian harbour. An hundred gallies were adorned with all the splendor of naval pomp: the troops destined to embark, vied with each other in the elegance of their dress, and the brightness of their arms: the alacrity painted in every face, and the magnificence displayed with profusion in every part of the equipage, represented a triumphal show, rather than the stern image of war. But the solidity and greatness of the armament proved that it was intended for use, not for ostentation. Amidst this glare of external pageantry which accompanied the adventurous youth, their friends and kinsmen could not suppress a few parting tears, when they considered the length of the voyage, the dangers of the sea, and the uncertainty of beholding again the

[b] Plut. in Nic. et Alcibiad.

CHAP. XIX.

dearest pledges of their affections. But these partial expressions of grief were speedily interrupted by the animating sounds of the trumpet, which issued at once from an hundred ships, and provoked sympathetic acclamations from the shore. The captains then offered solemn prayers to the gods, which were answered by corresponding vows from the spectators: the customary libations were poured out in goblets of gold and silver; and, after the triumphant Pæan had-been sung in full chorus, the whole fleet at once set sail, and contended for the prize of naval skill and celerity, until they reached the lofty shores of Ægina, from whence they enjoyed a prosperous navigation to the rendezvous of their confederates at Corcyra [20].

A review-ed at Corcyra.

At Corcyra the commanders reviewed the strength of the armament, which consisted of an hundred and thirty-four ships of war, with a proportional number of transports and tenders. The heavy-armed troops, exceeding five thousand, were attended with a sufficient body of slingers and archers. The army, abundantly provided in every other article, was extremely deficient in horses, which amounted to no more than thirty. But, at a moderate computation, we may estimate the whole military and naval strength, including slaves and servants, at twenty thousand men.

The Athenians fall along the coast of Italy.

With this powerful host, had the Athenians at once surprised and assailed the unprepared security of Syracuse, the expedition, however adventurous

[20] Thucydid. L. vi. p. 432, et seq 19. Plut. in Nicia. Diodor. l. xiii. p. 332.

and imprudent, might, perhaps, have been crowned
with fuccefs. But the timid mariners of Greece
would have trembled at the propofal of trufting
fuch a numerous fleet on the broad expanfe of the
Ionian fea. They determined to crofs the narroweft paffage between Italy and Sicily, after coafting along the eaftern fhores of the former, until
they reached the Strait of Meffina. That this defign might be executed with the greater fafety,
they difpatched three light veffels to examine the
difpofition of the Italian cities, and to folicit admiffion into their harbours. The greateft part of
Magna Græcia had, indeed, been peopled by Dorians, naturally hoftile to Athens. But from one
Italian city the Athenians had reafon to expect a
very favorable reception. The effeminate Sybaris
had been demolifhed, as related above[11], by the
warlike inhabitants of Crotona, about the time
that the Athenians, growing more powerful than
their neighbours, began to feize every opportunity
to extend their colonies and their dominion. Governed by fuch principles, they could not long
overlook the happy fituation of Sybaris, near to
which they early formed an eftablifhment that
affumed the name of Thurium, from a falubrious
fountain of frefh water[12]; and the colony was increafed by a numerous fupply of emigrants, who,
under Athenian leaders, failed from Greece thirteen years before the Peloponnefian war[13].

[11] Vol. II. p. 169.
[12] Ὁρμησθέν ἀπὸ τῆς κρήνης βοτίου. Diodor. l. xii. p. 291.
[13] Suid. ad voc. Lyhat.

CHAP. XIX.

Are regarded with suspicion by the Italian cities.

The armament at Corcyra, whatever jealousy its power might create in other cities, was entitled to the gratitude of Thurium; presuming on which, the commanders, without waiting the return of the advice-boats, ordered the fleet to proceed, in three divisions, to the Italian coast. But neither the ties of consanguinity, nor the duties acknowledged by colonies towards their parent state, could prevail on the suspicious Thurians to open their gates, or even to furnish a market, to their Athenian ancestors. The towns of Tarentum and Locris prohibited them the use of their harbours, and refused to supply them with water; and they coasted the whole extent of the shore, from the promontory of Iapygium to that of Rhegium, before any one city would allow them to purchase the commodities for which they had immediate use. The magistrates of Rhegium granted this favor, but they granted nothing more; notwithstanding the earnest solicitations of Alcibiades and his colleagues, who exhorted them, as a colony of Eubœa, to assist their brethren of Leontium, whose republic the Athenians had determined to re-establish and to defend [10].

Rhegium alone supplies them with a market.

They are informed of the state of the Egestæans.

While the armament continued at Rhegium, they were informed by vessels which had been purposely dispatched from Corcyra, that the Egestæans, notwithstanding the boasted accounts lately given of their riches, possessed only thirty talents in their treasury. This disagreeable intelligence, together

[10] Thucydid. p. 443.

with the disappointment of assistance from any Italian city, occasioned a council of war, to consider what measures ought to be pursued in the Sicilian expedition. It was the opinion of Nicias, "that the Egestæans ought to be furnished with that proportion of ships only, the charges of which they were able to defray; and that the Athenian fleet having settled, either by arms or by persuasion, the quarrels between them and their neighbours, should return to their own harbours, after sailing along the coast of Sicily, and displaying to the inhabitants of that island both their inclination and their power to protect the weakness of their allies."

Alcibiades declared, "That it would be shameful and ignominious to dissolve such a powerful armament, without performing some exploit worthy the renown of the republic; that, by the prospect of immediate and effectual support, the inferior cities might easily be alienated from their reluctant confederacy with Selinus and Syracuse; after which, the war ought to be carried on with the utmost vigor against those republics, unless they re-established the Leontines in their territory, and gave complete satisfaction to the injured Egestæans."

Lamachus not only approved the active counsels of Alcibiades, but proposed a measure still more enterprising. "The Athenians ought not to waste time in unimportant objects. Instead of striking at the extremities, they ought to assault at once the heart and strength of the enemy. If they immediately attacked Syracuse, it would not only be the first, but the last city, which they would have occasion to besiege. Nor could the attempt fail, if undertaken without delay, before the Syracusans had time to recollect themselves, and to provide for their own defence; and while the Athenian troops, as yet undaunted by any check, enjoyed unbroken courage and blooming hopes."

Is rejected. This advice, which does equal honor to the spirit and good sense of Lamachus, was rejected by the timidity of Nicias, and probably by the vanity of Alcibiades. The latter perceived a flattering opportunity of exhausting all the resources of his eloquence and intrigue to get possession of the dependent cities, before he illustrated the glory of his arms in the siege of Syracuse. The fleet sailed from Rhegium to execute *his* plan, which was adopted by his colleagues, as forming the middle between the extremes of their respective opinions. A considerable detachment was sent to examine the preparations and the strength of Syracuse, and to proclaim liberty, and offer protection, to all the captives and strangers confined within its walls.

Alcibiades takes Catana by stratagem. With another detachment Alcibiades sailed to Naxos, and persuaded the inhabitants to accept the alliance of Athens. The remainder of the armament proceeded to Catana, which refused to admit the ships into the harbour, or the troops into the city. But on the arrival of Alcibiades, the Cataneans allowed him to address the assembly, and propose his demands. The artful Athenian transported the populace, and even the magistrates themselves, by the charms of his eloquence; the citizens flocked from every quarter, to hear a discourse which was purposely protracted for several hours; the soldiers forsook their posts; and the enemy, who had prepared to avail themselves of this negligence, burst through the unguarded gates, and became masters of the city. Those of the Cataneans who were most attached to the interest of Syracuse, fortunately escaped death by the celerity of their flight. The rest accepted the proffered friendship of the Athenians. This success would probably have been followed by the surrender of Messené, which Alcibiades had filled with distrust and sedition. But when the plot was ripe for execution[º], the man who had contrived, and who alone could conduct it, was disqualified from serving his country. The arrival of the Saluminian galley recalled Alcibiades to Athens, that he might stand trial for his life.

It would be improper to suspend the course of an interesting narrative, by describing the causes and circumstances of this unexpected event, if they were not immediately connected with the subsequent history of the Sicilian expedition, and with the future fortune of the Athenians, who, after engaging, by the advice of one man, in the most

[º] Thucydides says, "When Alcibiades knew he should be banished, he betrayed his accomplices to the party favorable to Syracuse, who immediately put their adversaries to death." Thucydid. p. 452. We shall see hereafter, still more fatal consequences of his resentment against his country. But nothing can more strongly attest the turpitude of his character.

CHAP.
XIX.

The cause of his recal.

romantic schemes of conquest which the madness of ambition had ever dared to entertain, injudiciously arrested the activity of that man in the execution of such extraordinary designs, as could only be accomplished by the wonderful resources of his singular and eccentric genius. It happened, that on the night preceding the intended navigation to Sicily, all the statues of Mercury, which had been erected in the Athenian streets as the boundaries of different edifices and tenements, were thrown down, broken, and defaced. One only image of the god, of uncommon size and beauty, was saved from the general wreck; it was afterwards called the statue of Andocides, as it stood before the house of the Athenian orator of that name. This daring insult was first ascribed to the wicked artifices of the Corinthians, who, it was supposed, might employ such an abominable and sacrilegious contrivance, to deter the Athenian armament from sailing against their colony and kinsmen of Syracuse. But the enemies of Alcibiades availed themselves of the impious levity " of his character, to direct the popular storm against the head of their detested foe. On the evidence of slaves, he was

" Democritus, the chief promoter of the Atomic philosophy, was younger than Anaxagoras, and elder than Socrates. His scholars, Diagoras and Protagoras, propagated his wild system at Athens towards the commencement of the Peloponnesian war. Whether Alcibiades embraced the barren doctrines of that miserable sect, or adhered to the divine philosophy of his master Socrates, or, more probably, fluctuated between them, he must, in all cases alike, have been obnoxious to the suspicion of impiety. Comp. Strabo, l. xiv. p. 703. Sext. Empirio. l. ix. §§. Laert, l. ii. in Democrit. Socrat. et Protag.

accused of having treated, with rude familiarity; other adored images of the gods; and Theffalus, the degenerate fon of the magnanimous Cimon, impeached him of impiety towards the goddesses Ceres and Proferpine, whofe awful ceremonies he had polluted and profaned; affuming, though uninitiated, the name and robes of the high-prieft, calling Polytion (in whofe houfe this dreadful fcene had been reprefented), the torch-bearer, Theodorus the herald, and his other licentious companions the facred brethren and holy minifters of thofe myfterious rites [17].

Such an atrocious accufation alarmed the terrors of the Athenians; one affembly was fummoned after another; and the panic became the more general, when it was underftood that, during the fame night in which the ftatues had been mutilated, a body of Peloponnefian troops had marched towards the Ifthmus of Corinth. In the confufed imagination of the vulgar, it was poffible to unite the incompatible interefts of fuperftition and of freedom; and they were perfuaded by Androcles, and other artful demagogues, that the profanation of the myfteries, the defacing of the ftatues of Mercury, the movement of the Peloponnefian troops, all announced a confpiracy to demolifh the eftablifhed form of popular government, the fafety of which had, ever fince the expulfion of the Pififtratidæ, formed an object of univerfal and moft anxious folicitude.

C H A P. XIX.

He is charged with impiety and treafon. Olymp. xci. 2. A. C. 415.

[47] Plutarch, in Alcibiad.

CHAP.
XIX.
The artifices of his enemies.

Alcibiades defended himself, with his usual eloquence and address, against the malignity of a charge, unsupported by any adequate evidence. The soldiers and sailors, whose eagerness already grasped the conquest of Sicily, interceded for the deliverance of their commander, whom they regarded as the soul of that glorious enterprise. A thousand Argives and Mantineans, who had inlisted, on this occasion, under the Athenian banners, declared their unwillingness to sail, unless they were accompanied by Alcibiades, whose valor and abilities alone had determined them to engage in such an important, but dangerous service. This powerful combination in his favor disappointed the present hopes, without disconcerting the future measures, of his enemies. They perceived that, were he brought to an immediate trial, it would be impossible to obtain sentence against him; but that were his person and influence removed to a distance from Athens, every thing might be hoped from the weakness, inconstancy, and credulity of the populace. It was therefore determined by this perfidious cabal, that such orators as had hitherto disguised, under the mask of friendship or admiration, their envy and hatred of Alcibiades, should declare in full assembly, "that it would be inconsistent with the clearest dictates of prudence and propriety, to involve in the tedious formalities of a judicial procedure, a citizen who had been elected general by the unanimous suffrage of his country, and whose presence was eagerly demanded by the affectionate ardor of his troops. The charges against him deserved, doubtless, to be seriously examined; but the present was not a proper time for such an investigation, which must blunt the courage of his followers, and interrupt the service of the republic. Let him sail, therefore, for Sicily, and at his return home he will either vindicate his innocence, or suffer the punishment of his guilt." Alcibiades perceived the poison concealed under this affected lenity, and testified his reluctance to leave behind him such abundant materials for the malice of informers. But his petition for an immediate trial was rejected by the assembly. He therefore set sail, probably flattering himself, that by the glory and success of his arms, he would silence the clamors, and defeat the machinations, of his accusers.

But this expectation was unfortunately disappointed. In a republican government, it is not more easy to excite, than it is difficult to appease, the fermentation of public discontents, especially if occasioned by any real or pretended diminution of freedom. The removal of Alcibiades gave full scope to the ebullitions of popular frenzy. The Athenians were continually assembled to inquire into the violation of the statues. Many respectable citizens were seized on suspicion, because they had, on former occasions, discovered principles hostile to the wild extravagance of democracy. Others were imprisoned on the evidence of Teucer, an obscure stranger, and Diopeithes, a calumnious demagogue. The violence of the public disorder opened a door to private vengeance. Every

CHAP.
XIX.

individual was desirous to see his personal enemies among the number of state-criminals, and his resentment was invited falsely to accuse them, by an injudicious decree of the assembly, offering high rewards to those who should denounce the guilty, and even to the guilty themselves, who should denounce their associates.

Alcibiades escapes to Sparta. Olymp. xci. 2. A. C. 415.

Among the persons who had been seized on suspicion, was the crafty and intriguing Timæus, and the profligate and impious Andocides, the same whose statue of Mercury had escaped the general mutilation. The known character of these men naturally marked them out as peculiar victims of popular fury. As they were confined in the same prison, they had an opportunity of communicating their apprehensions, and of contriving means of safety. Timæus persuaded his friend (for the ties of common danger create between knaves a temporary friendship), that it would be weakness to die by a false accusation, when he might save himself by a lie. Andocides turned informer. The prisoners whom he named were banished or put to death; the rest were set at liberty. The absent, among whom was Alcibiades, were recalled to stand trial. But they did not obey the summons sent them by the Salaminian galley. The wanderings and misfortunes of more obscure names are unknown. Alcibiades escaped to Thurium, and afterwards to Argos; and when he understood that the Athenians had set a price on his head, he finally took refuge in Sparta; where his active genius seized the first opportunity to advise and to promote those fatal measures, which, while they gratified his private resentment, occasioned the ruin of his country[1].

The removal of Alcibiades soon appeared in the languid operations of the Athenian armament. The cautious timidity of Nicias, supported by wealth, eloquence, and authority, gained an absolute ascendant over the more warlike and enterprising character of Lamachus, whose poverty exposed him to contempt. Instead of making a bold impression on Selinus or Syracuse, Nicias contented himself with taking possession of the inconsiderable colony of Hyccara. He ravaged, or laid under contribution, some places of smaller note, and obtained thirty talents from the Egestæans, which, added to the sale of the booty, furnished about thirty thousand pounds sterling[20], a sum that might be usefully employed in the prosecution of an expensive war. But this advantage did not compensate for the courage inspired into the Syracusans by delay, and for the dishonor sustained by the Athenian troops, in their unsuccessful attempts against Hybla and Himera, as well as for their dejection at being confined, during the greatest part

---

[1] Plut. in Alcibiad. et Isocrates, and Lysias, in the Orations for and against the son of Alcibiades. Several facts and circumstances are differently represented in the orations of Andocides; but that orator was a party concerned.

[20] Thirty talents from the Egestæans, amount to   L 5,813
The sale of slaves, &c.   23,259
      Sum L 29,071

CHAP. XIX.

Nicias determines to attack Syracuse.

of the summer, in the inactive quarters of Naxos and Catana.

The impatience of the Athenians murmured against these dilatory and ignoble proceedings, which appeared altogether unworthy the greatness of their armament, the generous spirit with which they felt themselves animated, and the ancient glory of the republic. Nicias, resisting the wary dictates of his own fear or foresight, determined to gratify the inclination of his troops by the vigor of his winter-campaign. The conquest of Syracuse, against which he intended to lead them, might well excite the emulation of the combatants, since that powerful city formed the main obstacle to their ambition, and the principal bulwark not only of Sicily, but of the Italian and African shores.

Description of that city.

Ancient Syracuse, of which the ruined grandeur still forms an object of admiration, was situate on a spacious promontory, washed on three sides by the sea, and defended on the west by abrupt and almost inaccessible mountains. The town was built in a triangular form, whose summit may be conceived at the lofty mountains Epipolé. Adjacent to these natural fortifications, the western or inland division of the city was distinguished by the name of Tycha, or Fortune, being adorned by a magnificent temple of that flattering divinity. The triangle gradually widening towards the base, comprehended the vast extent of Achradina, reaching from the northern shore of the promontory to the southern island Ortygia. This small island, composing the whole of modern Syracuse, formed but the

third

third and the least extensive division of the ancient; which was fortified by walls eighteen miles in circuit, enriched by a triple harbour, and peopled by above two hundred thousand warlike citizens or industrious slaves[10].

When the Syracusans heard the first rumors of the Athenian invasion, they despised, or affected to despise them, as idle lies invented to amuse the ignorance of the populace. The hostile armament had arrived at Rhegium before they could be persuaded, by the wisdom of Hermocrates, to provide against a danger which their presumption painted as imaginary. But when they received undoubted intelligence that the enemy had reached the Italian coast; when they beheld their numerous fleet commanding the sea of Sicily, and ready to make a descent on their defenceless island, they were seized with a degree of just terror and alarm proportional to their false security. They condemned their former incredulity and indifference, which had been nourished by the interested adulation of the demagogue Athenagoras, who vainly assured them that the strength of Syracuse was sufficient not only to defy the assailants, but to deter the attempts, of any Grecian foe. From the heights of presumption they plunged into the depths of despair, and their spirits were, with difficulty, restored by the animating voice of Hermocrates, who was not more prudent in prosperity than intrepid in danger[11].

CHAP. XIX.

Temper of the Syracusans.

[10] Strabo, p. 246, et seqq. et Thucydid. passim. l. vi.
[11] Thucydid. p. 436, et seqq.

By *his* exhortations they were encouraged to make ready their arms, to equip their fleet, to strengthen their garrisons, and to summon the assistance of their allies. These measures were undertaken with ardor, and carried on with unremitting activity; and the dilatory operations of the enemy not only removed the recent terror and trepidation of the Syracusans, but inspired them with unusual firmness. They requested the generals, whom they had appointed to the number of fifteen, to lead them to Catana, that they might attack the hostile camp. Their cavalry harassed the Athenians by frequent incursions, beat up their quarters, intercepted their convoys, destroyed their advanced posts, and even proceeded so near to the main body, that they were distinctly heard demanding, with loud insults, Whether those boasted lords of Greece had left their native country, that they might form a precarious settlement at the foot of Mount Ætna[11].

Provoked by these indignities, and excited by the impatient resentment of his own troops, Nicias was still restrained from an open attempt against Syracuse by the difficulties attending that enterprise. The distance between Catana and the Sicilian capital was more than thirty miles; but, after the most prosperous voyage, the Athenians could not expect, without extreme danger, to make a

[11] Plutarch. The same is differently expressed in Thucydides: "Whether they had not come to gain a settlement for themselves in a foreign country, rather than to replace the Leontines in *their own*." Thucyd. p. 415.

descent on the fortified coast of a powerful and vigilant enemy. If they determined to march by land, they must be harassed by the numerous cavalry of Syracuse, which actually watched their motions, and with whose activity, in a broken and intricate country, the strength of heavy-armed troops was exceedingly ill qualified to contend. To avoid both inconveniences, Nicias employed a stratagem. A citizen of Catana, whose subtile and daring genius, prepared alike to die or to deceive, ought to have preserved his name from oblivion, appeared in Syracuse as a deserter from his native city; the unhappy fate of which, in being subjected to the imperious commands, or licentious disorder of the Athenians, he lamented with perfidious tears, and with the plaintive accents of well-dissembled sorrow. "He was not the only man who bewailed, with filial compassion, the misfortunes and ignominy of his country. A numerous band of Cataneans, whose resentment was repressed by fear, longed to take up arms, that they might deliver themselves from a disgraceful yoke, and repel the tyranny of the invaders. Nor could the design fail of success, if Syracuse should second their generous ardor. The Athenians, so liberally endowed with courage and ambition, were destitute of wisdom and of discipline. They spurned the confinement of the military life; their posts were forsaken, their ships unguarded; they disdained the duties of the camp, and indulged in the pleasures of the city. On an appointed day it would be easy for the Syracusans, assisted by the

CHAP.
XIX.

conspirators of Catana, to attack them unprepared, to mount their undefended ramparts, to demolish their encampment, and to burn their fleet." This daring proposal well corresponded with the keen sentiments of revenge which animated the inhabitants of Syracuse. The day was named, the plan of the enterprise was concerted, and the treacherous Catanean returned home to revive the hopes, and to confirm the resolution, of his pretended associates.

Falls through the activity of the Syracusans.

The success of this intrigue gave the utmost satisfaction to Nicias, whose armament prepared to sail for Syracuse on the day appointed by the inhabitants of that city for assaulting, with their whole force, the Athenian camp. Already had they marched, with this view, to the fertile plain of Leontium, when, after twelve hours sail, the Athenian fleet arrived in the great harbour, disembarked their troops, and fortified a camp without the western wall, near to a celebrated temple of Olympian Jupiter; a situation which had been pointed out by some Syracusan exiles, and which was well adapted to every purpose of accommodation and defence. Meanwhile the cavalry of Syracuse, having proceeded to the walls of Catana, had discovered, to their infinite regret, the departure of the Athenians. The unwelcome intelligence was conveyed, with the utmost expedition, to the infantry, who immediately marched back to protect Syracuse. The rapid return of the warlike youth restored the courage of the aged Syracusans. They were joined by the forces of Gela,

Selinus, and Camarina; and it was determined, without loss of time, to attack the hostile encampment".

Only a few days elapsed before the Athenians gave them a fairer opportunity of revenge. The two armies prepared to engage, respectively inflamed by resentment and ambition; the one formidable in courage and numbers, the other elated by superior discipline and habitual victory. The Syracusan generals drew up their troops, sixteen, and the Athenians only eight, deep: but the latter had, in their camp, a body of reserve, which was kept ready for action on the first signal. Nicias went round the ranks, exhorting his soldiers by a short discourse, in which he observed, "that the strength of their present preparations was better fitted to inspire confidence, than the most eloquent speech with a weak army, especially as they contended against the Syracusans, a promiscuous crowd, whose presumption was founded on inexperience, and whose desultorious ardor, however successful in predatory incursions, would yield to the first shock of regular war. They fought, indeed, in defence of their city; so did the Athenians and their allies, whom nothing but military valor and success would restore in safety to their respective countries". "Having thus spoken, he led his troops to the enemy, who did not decline the engagement. The light-armed archers" skirmished

CHAP. XIX.
Nicias defeats the Syracusans in a battle. Olymp. xci. 2. A. C. 415.

[18] Thucydid. p. 415—417.
[19] Thucydid. p. 418 et 419.
[20] Thucydides mentions, besides the archers (τοξόται), the λιθοβόλοι and σφενδονῆται, "the throwers of stones and slingers." P. 419. They were all ψιλοί, as he says immediately below.

CHAP.
XIX.

Cause of their defeat.

in the van: the priests brought forth the accustomed sacrifices: the trumpets summoned for a general charge.

The attack was begun with fury, and continued with perseverance for several hours. Both sides were animated by every principle that can inspire and urge the utmost vigor of exertion, and victory was still doubtful, when a tempest suddenly arose, accompanied with unusual peals of thunder. This event, which little affected the Athenians, confounded the unexperienced credulity of the enemy, who were broken and put to flight. Nicias restrained the eagerness of his men in the pursuit, lest they should be exposed to danger from a body of twelve hundred Syracusan cavalry, who had not engaged in the battle, but who impatiently watched an opportunity to assault the disordered phalanx. The Syracusans escaped to their city, and the Athenians returned to their camp. In such an obstinate conflict the vanquished lost two hundred and sixty, the victors only fifty men; numbers that might occasion much surprise, if we reflected not that, to oppose the offensive weapons used by antiquity, the warriors of Greece (in every circumstance so unlike the miserable and naked peasants of modern Europe, whose lives are sacrificed without defence, as without remorse, to the ambition of men whom the Greeks would have styled tyrants) being armed with the helmet and cuirass, the ample buckler, the firm corselet, and the manly greaves, they often displayed their skill, their courage, and their love of liberty, at a very small expense of human blood.

CHAP.
XIX.

The voyage, the encampment, and the battle, employed the dangerous activity, and gratified the impetuous ardor of the Athenians, but did not facilitate the conquest of Syracuse. Without more powerful preparations, Nicias defpaired of taking the place, either by affault, or by a regular fiege. Soon after his victory he returned with the whole armament to Naxos and Catana; a meafure which fufficiently proves that the late enterprife had been undertaken, not in confequence of any permanent fyftem of operations formed by the general, but in compliance with the ungovernable" temper of his troops, whofe ideas of military fubordination were confined to the field of battle.

The Athenians return to Catana and Naxos.

" Without attending to this circumftance, the conduct of Grecian generals muft, on many occafions, appear altogether unaccountable. The fame obfervation applies to modern hiftory preceding the peace of Munfter. The famous war of thirty years, which ended in that peace, laid the foundation for the exact military fubordination which diftinguifhes the prefent century. See Pere Bougeant, *Hiftoire de la Guerre de 30 Ans.*

CHAP. XX.

Preparations for the ensuing Campaign. — The Athenians begin the Siege with Vigor. — Distress and Sedition in Syracuse. — Arrival of Gylippus — Who defeats the Athenians. — Transactions in Greece. — A second Armament arrives at Syracuse — Its first Operations successful. — The Athenians defeated. — Prepare to raise the Siege. — Naval Engagement in the Great Harbour. — Despondency of the Athenians. — Stratagem of Hermocrates. — The Athenians raise their camp. — Melancholy Firmness of Nicias. — Demosthenes capitulates. — Nicias surrenders. — Cruel Treatment of the Athenian Captives. — Singular Exception.

CHAP. XX.
Nicias prepares for the ensuing campaign.
Olymp. xcl. 2.
A. C. 414.

NICIAS had reason to expect that his victory over the Syracusans would procure him respect and assistance from the inferior states of Sicily. His emissaries were diffused over that island and the neighbouring coast of Italy. Messengers were sent to Tuscany, where Pisa and other cities had been founded by Greek colonies[1]. An embassy was dispatched to Carthage, the rival and enemy of Syracuse. Nicias gave orders to collect materials for circumvallation, iron, bricks, and all necessary stores. He demanded horses

[1] Strabo, p. 243, et p. 283, et seqq.

from the Egeſtæans; and required from Athens reinforcements and a large pecuniary ſupply; and neglected nothing that might enable him to open the enſuing campaign with vigor and effect[*].

While the Athenians thus prepared for the attack of Syracuſe, the citizens of that capital diſplayed equal activity in providing for their own defence. By the advice of Hermocrates, they appointed *himſelf*, Heraclides, and Sicanus; three, inſtead of fifteen generals. The commanders newly elected, both in civil and military affairs, were inveſted with unlimited power, which was uſefully employed to purchaſe or prepare arms, daily to exerciſe the troops, and to ſtrengthen and extend the fortifications of Syracuſe. They likewiſe diſpatched ambaſſadors to the numerous cities and republics with which they had been connected in peace, or allied in war, to ſolicit the continuance of their friendſhip, and to counteract the dangerous deſigns of the Athenians.

The importance of the city Camerina, ſituate on the ſouthern coaſt of Sicily, demanded the preſence of Hermocrates himſelf. The Camerineans had given a very feeble and reluctant aſſiſtance to their allies of Syracuſe; and the orator Euphemus employed all the reſources of his genius to unite

CHAP. XX.

The Syracuſans prepare for defence.

Both parties court the friendſhip of the Camerineans. Olymp: xcl. 2. A. C. 415.

[*] It is remarkable that though Nicias, after the removal of Alcibiades, enjoyed the principal, or rather ſole, command of the army, he acted quite contrary to the opinion which he had declared at the commencement of the expedition. The plan which he purſued was that of Alcibiades, not his own: the views of the baniſhed general ſtill actuated the army; but the ardent ſpirit was withdrawn, that could alone enſure their ſucceſs.

CHAP.
XX.

Argument of the Syracusans.

them to the Athenian confederacy. An assembly being summoned, Hermocrates informed them, "That a desire to prevent the deception of the Camerineans, not the dread of the Athenian power, had occasioned his present journey. That restless and ambitious nation, which had so often kindled the flames of war on the continent of Greece, had lately sailed to Sicily, under pretence of re-establishing the affairs of the Leontines and Egestæans, but from a motive more selfish, which it was easy to conjecture, and impossible to mistake. Their real and only design was to sow dissension and disagreement among the Sicilian states, which, fighting singly, might be successively subdued. How could effrontery affirm, or simplicity believe, that the Athenians should undertake a voyage to vindicate the freedom of Egesta; they who oppressed, with all the rigors of slavery, the unhappy islanders of Eubœa, by whom Egesta had been built, and from whom its inhabitants were descended! Under pretence of delivering from the tyranny of the great king, the Greeks of Asia, of the Hellespont, of Thrace, and of the Ægean, they had conquered and enslaved those various countries. They actually employed the same perfidious contrivance against the safety of the Sicilians; but he trusted that their present undertaking, though carried on with equal artifice, would be attended with very different success; and that they would learn, by experience, to distinguish between the effeminate Ionians and Hellespontines, whose minds had been enfeebled and debased by the Persian yoke, and the

THE HISTORY OF GREECE. 107

magnanimous Dorians of Sicily, the genuine offspring of Peloponnesus, the source of valor and of liberty¹."

Euphemus, the Athenian, repelled, with force and spirit, these reproachful accusations. "The colonies of Athens were kept in a dependence, not less advantageous to themselves than honorable to the parent state. The general interest of Greece required that the same republic which at first had so bravely established, should still continue to maintain, the national independence. They who yield protection, must assume authority; but this authority the Athenians had exerted in a manner essential to their own and to the public safety. If they had subjected the neighbouring coasts and islands, their *interest* might justify that odious but necessary measure; and the same dictates of sound policy which induced them to conquer and to enslave the Hellespontine and Asiatic Greeks, would engage them to emancipate and to deliver the oppressed Sicilians. To this office they were invited by the Leontines and Egestæans; to this duty they were prompted by the ties of friendship and consanguinity; to this enterprise they were determined by the strongest of all motives, a well-grounded fear lest the inhabitants of Sicily (whose numbers and distance rendered it impossible for Athens to subdue, far less to retain them in subjection) should fall a prey to the watchful encroachments of Syracuse, and thus become an accession to the Peloponnesian confederacy." The Camerineans dreaded

CHAP. XX.

Of the Athenians.

---

¹ Thucydid. l. vi. p. 463, et seqq.

108 THE HISTORY OF GREECE.

CHAP. XX.

The Camerineans determine to observe neutrality.

the distant ambition of Athens, but dreaded still more the neighbouring hostility of Syracuse. Their fears dictated a reply in friendly and respectful terms; but they craved leave to preserve a neutrality between the contending powers, hoping, by this expedient, to irritate the resentment of neither, yet to defeat the designs of both.

The Athenians are reinforced, and begin the siege with vigor.

Olymp. xci. 3.
A. C. 414.

Meanwhile the expected reinforcements arrived from Athens. In addition to his original force, Nicias had likewise collected a body of six hundred cavalry, and the sum of four hundred talents; and, in the eighteenth summer of the war, the activity of the troops and workmen had completed all necessary preparations for undertaking the siege of Syracuse. The Athenian armament enjoyed a prosperous voyage to the northern harbour of Trogilé, and the troops were no sooner disembarked than they seized an opportunity of signalizing their valor against a body of seven hundred men, who marched to reinforce the garrison of Labdalus; an important fortress, situate on the highest of the mountains which overlook and command the city. Three hundred Syracusans were killed in the pursuit; the rest took refuge behind their walls; and the castle of Labdalus was taken, and strongly guarded by the victors. The plan which Nicias adopted for conquering the city, was to draw a wall on either side from the neighbourhood of Labdalus, towards the port of Trogilé on the north, and towards the gulph, extending two leagues in circumference, and justly called the Great Harbour, on the south. When these circumvallations had

surrounded the place by land, he expected, by his
numerous fleet, to block up the wide extent of the
Syracufan harbours. The whole ftrength of the
Athenian armament was employed in the former
operations; and, as all neceffary materials had been
provided with due attention, the works rofe with a
rapidity which furprifed and terrified the befieged.
Their former, as well as their recent defeat, deterred them from oppofing the enemy in a general
engagement; but the advice of Hermocrates perfuaded them to raife walls, which might traverfe
and interrupt thofe of the Athenians*. The im-
minent danger urged the activity of the workmen;
the hoftile bulwarks approached each other; frequent fkirmifhes took place, in one of which the
brave Lamachus unfortunately fell a victim to his
rafh valor'; but the Athenian troops maintained
their ufual fuperiority.

Encouraged by fuccefs, Nicias pufhed the enemy with vigor. The Syracufans loft hopes of
defending their new works, or of preventing the
complete circumvallation of their city; and this
defpair was increafed by the abundant fupplies
which arrived from all quarters to the befiegers,
while the intereft of Syracufe feemed to be univer-
fally abandoned by the indifference or cowardice of
her allies. In the turbulent democracies of Greece,
the moment of public danger commonly gave the
fignal for domeftic fedition. The populace clamored, with their ufual licentioufnefs, againft the
incapacity or perfidy of their leaders, to whom

* Thucydid. L vi. p. 483, et feqq. ¹ Plutarch. in Nicia.

110 THE HISTORY OF GREECE.

CHAP. IX.

alone they ascribed their misfortunes. New generals were named in the room of Hermocrates and his colleagues; and this injudicious alteration increased the calamities of Syracuse, which at length prepared to capitulate^a.

The Syracusans unexpectedly relieved by their Peloponnesian allies.
Olymp. xcl. 1.
A. C. 414.

While the assembly deliberated concerning the execution of a measure, which, however disgraceful, was declared to be necessary, a Corinthian galley, commanded by Gongylus, entered the central harbour of Ortygia, which being strongly fortified, and penetrating into the heart of the city, served as the principal and most secure station for the Syracusan fleet. The news immediately reached the assembly, and all ranks of men eagerly crowded around Gongylus the Corinthian, that they might learn the design of his voyage, and the intentions of their Peloponnesian allies. Gongylus announced a speedy and effectual relief to the besieged city[b]. He acquainted the Syracusans, that the embassy, sent the preceding year, to crave the assistance of Peloponnesus, had been crowned with success. His own countrymen had warmly embraced the cause of their kinsmen, and most respectable colony. They had fitted out a considerable fleet, the arrival of which might be expected every hour. The Lacedæmonians also had sent a small squadron, and the whole armament was conducted by the Spartan Gylippus, an officer of tried valor and ability.

Arrival of the Spartan Gylippus.

While the desponding citizens of Syracuse listened to this intelligence with pleasing astonishment,

[a] Thucydid. p. 457. [b] Id. p. 460.

a messenger arrived by land from Gylippus himself. That experienced commander, instead of pursuing a direct course to Sicily, which might have been intercepted by the Athenian fleet, had landed with four gallies on the western coast of the island. The name of a Spartan general determined the wavering irresolution of the Sicilians. The troops of Himera, Selinus, and Gela, flocked to his standard; and he approached Syracuse on the side of Epipolé, where the line of contravallation was still unfinished, with a body of several thousand men.

The most courageous of the citizens sallied forth to meet this generous and powerful protector. The junction was happily effected; the ardor of the troops kindled into enthusiasm; and they distinguished that memorable day by surprising several important Athenian posts. This first success re-animated the activity of the soldiers and workmen. The traverse wall was extended with the utmost diligence, and a vigorous sally deprived the enemy of the strong castle of Labdalus. Nicias perceiving that the interest of the Athenians in Sicily would be continually weakened by delay, wished to bring the fortune of the war to the decision of a battle. Nor did Gylippus decline the engagement. The first action was unfavorable to the Syracusans, who had been imprudently posted in the defiles between their own and the enemy's walls, which rendered of no avail their superiority in cavalry and archers. The magnanimity of Gylippus acknowledged this error, for which he

CHAP. XX.

who defeats the Athenians.

completely atoned by his judicious conduct in the succeeding engagements. His forces were drawn up in a more spacious ground. The pikemen received the shock of the enemy's front. The horses and light-armed troops assailed and harassed their undefended flanks. The Athenians were thrown into disorder, repulsed, and pursued to their camp with considerable loss, and with irreparable disgrace.

Consequences of the victory.

The important consequences of this victory appeared in the subsequent events of the siege. The Syracusans soon extended their works beyond the line of circumvallation, so that it was impossible to block up their city, without forcing their ramparts. The besiegers, while they maintained the superiority of their arms, had been abundantly supplied with necessaries from the neighbouring territory; but every place was alike hostile to them after their defeat. The soldiers who went out in quest of wood and water, were unexpectedly attaked and cut off by the enemy's cavalry, or by the reinforcements which arrived from every quarter to the assistance of Syracuse; and they were at length reduced to depend, for every necessary supply, on the precarious bounty of the Italian shore.

Nicias demands a reinforcement from Athens.

Nicias, whose sensibility deeply felt the public distress, wrote a most desponding letter to the Athenians. He honestly described, and lamented, the misfortunes and disorders of his army. The slaves deserted in great numbers; the mercenary troops, who fought only for pay and subsistence, preferred

the

the more secure and lucrative service of Syracuse; even the Athenian citizens, disgusted with the unexpected length and intolerable hardships of the war, abandoned the care of the gallies, to unexperienced hands; an abuse too easily permitted by the captains, whose weakness and partiality had corrupted the discipline, and ruined the strength, of the fleet. Nicias frankly acknowledged his inability to check the disorder; observing, that he wrote to those who knew the difficulty of governing the licentious spirit of their domestic troops. He therefore exhorted the assembly, either to call them home without delay, or to send immediately a second armament, not less powerful than the first.

Gylippus and Hermocrates (for the latter had again assumed the authority due to his abilities,) were acquainted with the actual distress, as well as the future hopes of the besiegers, who might derive, in consequence of Nicias's letter, more effectual succours from Attica than the besieged city could expect from Peloponnesus. They were prompted by interest, therefore, as well as by inclination, to press the enemy on every side, and at once to assail them by sea and land. Besides the bad condition of the Athenian fleet, the absence of a considerable number of gallies employed in conducting the convoys of provisions, encouraged this resolution. The Corinthian squadron of twelve sail, long expected with anxiety, had escaped the dangers of a winter's voyage; and at the commencement of the ensuing spring, the harbours of

CHAP. XX.

Syracuse were crowded with the whole naval strength of Sicily. Hermocrates persuaded his countrymen, "That the advantages of skill and experience, which he honestly ascribed to the Athenians, could not compensate their terror and confusion at being suddenly attacked by a superior force, on an element which they affected to command. Athens had assumed this boasted empire of the sea in repelling the invasion of Persia. Syracuse had a similar, yet stronger motive; and as she possessed greater power, was entitled to expect more distinguished success."

Alternate success.

The principal squadrons of Syracuse lay in the harbour of Ortygia, separated, by an island of the same name, from the station of the Athenian fleet. While Hermocrates sailed forth with eighty gallies, to venture a naval engagement, Gylippus attacked the hostile fortifications at Plemmyrium, a promontory opposite to Ortygia, which confined the entrance of the Great Harbour. The defeat of the Syracusans at sea, whereby they lost fourteen vessels, was balanced by their victory at land, in which they took three fortresses, containing a large quantity of military and naval stores, and a considerable sum of money. In some subsequent actions, which scarcely deserve the name of battles, their fleet was still unsuccessful; but as they engaged with great caution, and found every where a secure retreat on a friendly shore, their loss was extremely inconsiderable. The want of success, in their first attempt, did not abate their resolution to gain the command at sea. The hopes of defending their country sharpened their invention, and animated their activity. They could not, indeed, contend with the Athenians in the rapidity of naval evolution, or in the skill of seamanship; but in the destined scene of action, there was little opportunity for displaying those advantages; and by strengthening, with unremitting labor, the prows of their ships, they compensated, by superior weight, the defect of velocity. They provided also a great number of small vessels, which might approach so near the hostile fleet, that the light-armed troops with which they were filled could aim their darts against the Athenian mariners.

By unexampled assiduity in completing these preparations, the Syracusans at length prevailed in a general engagement, which was fought in the Great Harbour. Seven Athenian ships were sunk, many more were disabled, and Nicias saved the remains of his shattered and dishonored armament, by retiring behind a line of merchantmen and transports, from the masts of which had been suspended huge masses of lead, named dolphins from their form, sufficient to crush, by their falling weight, the stoutest gallies of antiquity. This unexpected obstacle arrested the progress of the victors; but the advantages already obtained elevated them with the highest hopes, and reduced the enemy to despair.

The Athenian misfortunes in Sicily were attended by misfortunes at home, still more dreadful. In the eighteenth year of the war, Alcibiades accompanied to Sparta the ambassadors of Corinth and

CHAP.
XX.

Syracuse, who had solicited and obtained assistance to the besieged city. On that occasion, the Athenian exile first acquired the confidence of the Spartans, by condemning, in the strongest terms, the injustice and ambition of his ungrateful countrymen, "whose cruelty towards himself equalled their inveterate hostility to the Lacedæmonian republic; but that republic might, by following his advice, disarm their resentment. The town of Decelia was situated on the Attic frontier, at an equal distance of fifteen miles from Thebes and Athens. This place, which commanded an extensive and fertile plain, might be surprised and fortified by the Spartans [1], who, instead of harassing their foes by annual incursions, might thus infest them by a continual war. The wisdom of Sparta had too long neglected such a salutary and decisive measure, especially as the existence of a similar design had often been suggested by the fears of the enemy, who trembled even at the apprehension of seeing a foreign garrison in their territory."

The Peloponnesians raise a fortress in Attica. Olympiad. 4. A. C. 413.

[1] This advice, first proposed, and often urged, by Alcibiades, was adopted in the commencement of the ensuing spring, when the warlike Agis led a powerful army into Attica. The defenceless inhabitants of the frontier fled before his irresistible arms; but instead of pursuing them, as usual, into the heart of the country, he stopped short at Decelia. As all

---

[1] The Athenians, with their usual imprudence, facilitated the success of Alcibiades's intrigues. At the time they ought, if possible, to have soothed, they exasperated the Spartans to the utmost, by frequent incursions from Pylos, and by openly assisting the Argives. Thucydid. l. vi. sub fin.

THE HISTORY OF GREECE. 117

neceſſary materials had been provided in great abundance, the place was ſpeedily fortified on every ſide, and the walls of Decelia, which might be diſtinctly ſeen acroſs the intermediate plain, bid defiance to thoſe of Athens[l].

The latter city was kept in continual alarm by the watchful hoſtility of a neighbouring garriſon. The open country was entirely laid waſte, and the uſual communication was interrupted with the valuable iſland of Eubœa, from which, in ſeaſons of ſcarcity, or during the ravages of war, the Athenians commonly derived their ſupplies of corn, wine, and oil, and whatever is moſt neceſſary to life. Haraſſed by the fatigues of unremitting ſervice, and deprived of daily bread, the ſlaves murmured, complained, and revolted to the enemy; and their defection robbed the ſtate of twenty thouſand uſeful artiſans. Since the latter years of Pericles, the Athenians had not been involved in ſuch diſtreſs. But their preſent were far more grievous than their paſt ſufferings. Theſe had been chiefly occaſioned by the temporary rage of the peſtilence, the abatement of which there was always reaſon to expect; but thoſe were inflicted by the unextinguiſhable hatred of a cruel and unrelenting foe[m].

The domeſtic calamities of the republic did not, however, prevent the moſt vigorous exertions abroad. Twenty gallies, ſtationed at Naupactus, watched the motions of the Peloponneſian fleet deſtined to the aſſiſtance of Syracuſe: thirty carried on the war in Macedonia, to reduce the rebellion

CHAP. XX.

The miſerable ſtate of that country.

The Athenians exert great vigor in the midſt of their calamities.

[l] Thucydid. p. 100, et ſeqq. [m] Id. ibid.

I 3

CHAP. XX.

of Amphipolis; a confiderable fquadron collected tribute, and levied foldiers, in the colonies of Afia; another, ftill more powerful, ravaged the coaft of Peloponnefus. Never did any kingdom or republic equal the magnanimity of Athens; never, in ancient or modern times, did the courage of any ftate entertain an ambition fo far fuperior to its power, or exert efforts fo difproportionate to its ftrength. Amidft the difficulties and dangers which encompaffed them on every fide, the Athenians perfifted in the fiege of Syracufe, a city little inferior to their own; and, undaunted by the actual devaftation of their country, unterrified by the menaced affault of their walls, they fent, without delay, fuch a reinforcement into Sicily, as afforded the moft promifing hopes of fuccefs in their expedition againft that ifland [11].

The Athenian armament, commanded by Demofthenes, arrives at Syracufe. Olymp. XCI. 4. A. C. 413

The Syracufans had fcarcely time to rejoice at their victory, or Nicias to bewail his defeat, when a numerous and formidable armament appeared on the Sicilian coaft. The foremoft gallies, their prows adorned with gaudy ftreamers, purfued a fecure courfe towards the harbours of Syracufe. The emulation of the rowers was animated by the mingled founds of the trumpet and clarion; and the regular decoration, the elegant fplendor, which diftinguifhed every part of the equipment, exhibited a pompous fpectacle of naval triumph. Their appearance, even at a diftance, announced the country to which they belonged; and both the joy

[11] Thucydid. p. 507, et feqq.

of the besiegers, and the terror of the besieged, acknowledged that Athens was the only city in the world capable of sending to the sea such a beautiful and magnificent contribution. The Syracusans employed not unavailing efforts to check the progress, or to hinder the approach, of the hostile armament; which, besides innumerable foreign vessels and transports, consisted of seventy-three Athenian gallies, commanded by the experienced valor of Demosthenes and Eurymedon. The pikemen on board exceeded five thousand; the light-armed troops were nearly as numerous; and, including the rowers, workmen, and attendants, the whole strength may be reckoned equal to that originally sent with Nicias [11], which amounted to above twenty thousand men.

The misfortunes hitherto attending the operations in Sicily had lowered the character of the general; and this circumstance, as well as the superior abilities of Demosthenes, entitled him to assume the tone of authority in their conjunct deliberations. His advice, which Eurymedon highly approved, and in which the dilatory caution of Nicias finally acquiesced, was clear and simple. " They ought to avail themselves of the alarm which the unexpected arrival of such a powerful reinforcement had spread among the enemy; and instead of submitting to the tedious formalities of a siege; at once assault the walls of Syracuse. He trusted, by the valor of his troops, to obtain, in one day,

[11] Comp. Thucydid. supra citat. Diodor. l. xiii. p. 336. Plut. in Nicia.

120 THE HISTORY OF GREECE.

CHAP.
XX.

the valuable reward of long and severe labors. But if the gods had otherwise determined, it would be time to desist from an enterprise, in which delay was equal to defeat, and to employ the bravery of the Athenian youth in repelling the invaders of their country "".

Their first operations successful.

After ravaging the banks of the Anapus, and making some ineffectual attempts against the fortifications on that side, probably with a view to divert the attention of the enemy, Demosthenes chose the first hour of a moonshine night, to proceed with the flower of the army to seize the fortresses in Epipolé. The march was performed with successful celerity; the out-posts were surprised; the guards put to the sword; and three separate encampments, of the Syracusans, the Sicilians, and allies, formed a feeble opposition to the Athenian ardor. As if their victory had already been complete, the assailants began to pull down the wooden battlements, or to urge the pursuit with a rapidity which disordered their ranks.

A general engagement, in which the Athenians are defeated.

Meanwhile, the vigilant activity of Gylippus had assembled the whole force of Syracuse. At the approach of the enemy his vanguard retired. The Athenians were decoyed within the intricate windings of the walls, and their irregular fury was first checked by the firmness of a Theban phalanx. A resistance so sudden and unexpected might alone have been decisive; but other circumstances were adverse to the Athenians: their ignorance of the

" Thucydid. L. vii. p. 519.

THE HISTORY OF GREECE. 121

ground, the alternate obscurity of night, and the deceitful glare of the moon, which, shining in the front of the Thebans, illumined the splendor of their arms, and multiplied the terror of their numbers. The foremost ranks of the pursuers were repelled; and, as they retreated to the main body, encountered the advancing Argives and Corcyreans, who, singing the Pœan in their Doric dialect and accent, were unfortunately taken for enemies. Fear, and then rage, seized the Athenians, who thinking themselves encompassed on all sides, determined to force their way, and committed much bloodshed among their allies, before the mistake could be discovered. To prevent the repetition of this dreadful error, their scattered bands were obliged at every moment to demand the watch-word, which was at length betrayed to their adversaries. The consequence of this was doubly fatal. At every rencounter the silent Athenians were slaughtered without mercy, while the enemy, who knew their watch-word, might at pleasure join, or decline, the battle, and easily oppress their weakness, or elude their strength. The terror and confusion increased; the rout became general; Gylippus pursued in good order with his victorious troops. The vanquished could not descent in a body with the celerity of fear, by the narrow passages through which they had mounted. Many abandoned their arms, and explored the unknown paths of the rocky Epipolé. Others threw themselves from precipices, rather than await the pursuers. Several thousands were left dead or wounded on the scene

CHAP.
XX.

CHAP.
XX.

The salutary measures proposed by Demosthenes prevented by Nicias.

of action; and in the morning the greater part of the stragglers were intercepted and cut off by the Syracusan cavalry [14].

This dreadful and unexpected disaster suspended the operations of the siege. The Athenian generals spent the time in fruitless deliberations concerning their future measures, while the army lay encamped on the marshy and unhealthy banks of the Anapus. The vicissitudes of an autumnal atmosphere, corrupted by the foul vapors of an unwholesome soil, made a severe impression on the irritable fibres of men, exhausted by fatigue, dejected by disgrace, and deprived of hope. A general sickness broke out in the camp. Demosthenes urged this calamity as a new reason for hastening their departure, while it was yet possible to cross the Ionian sea, without risking the danger of a winter's tempest. But Nicias dissuaded the design of leaving Sicily until they should be warranted to take this important step by the positive authority of the republic. "Those who were actually the most bent on ignominious flight, would, after their return, be the foremost to accuse the weakness or the treachery of their commanders; and for his own part, he would rather die honorably in the field of battle, than perish by the unjust sentence of his country." Demosthenes and Eurymedon knew, by fatal experience, the irascible temper of an Athenian assembly; they only insisted, that the armament should at least remove to

[14] Thucydid. p. 520, et seqq.

a more convenient station, from whence, after the troops had recovered their usual health and spirits, they might harass the enemy by continual descents, until they obtained an opportunity of fighting the Syracusan fleet on the open sea.

But even this resolution was strenuously opposed by Nicias, who knew by the secret correspondence which he maintained with certain traitors in Syracuse, that the treasury of that city had been exhausted by the enormous expense of two thousand talents already incurred in the war, and that the magistrates had stretched their credit to its utmost limits, in borrowing from their allies; and who therefore naturally flattered himself, that the vigor of their resistance would abate with the decay of their faculties. The colleagues of Nicias were confounded with the firmness of an opposition so unlike the flexible timidity of his ordinary character, and so inconsistent with the sentiments which he had often expressed concerning the Sicilian expedition. They imagined that he might rely on some more important ground of confidence, which his caution was unwilling to explain; they submitted therefore to his opinion, an opinion equally fatal to himself and to them, and to the armament which they commanded[85].

Meanwhile the prudence of Gylippus profited of the fame of his victory, to draw a powerful reinforcement from the Sicilian cities; and the transports, so long expected from Peloponnesus, finally

[85] Comp. Thucydid. p. 524. et Plut. in Nicia.

CHAP.
XX.

arrived in the harbour of Ortygia. The Peloponnesian forces had sailed from Greece early in the spring; and it is not explained for what reason they touched on the coast of Cyrenaica. There they continued for some months, that they might defend their Grecian brethren, actually threatened by the barbarous assaults of the Lybians; and having conquered that dangerous enemy, they augmented their fleet with a few Cyrenian gallies [19], and safely reached Syracuse, the place of their first destination. This squadron formed the last assistance sent to either of the contending parties, and nothing farther was required to complete the actors in the following dreadful scene; for by the accession of the Cyrenians, Syracuse was either attacked or defended by all the various divisions of the Grecian name, which formed, in that age, the most civilized portion of the inhabitants of Asia, Africa, and Europe.

The Athenians prepare to raise the siege.

The arrival of such powerful auxiliaries to the besieged, and the increasing force of the malady, totally disconcerted the Athenians. Even Nicias agreed to set sail. Every necessary preparation was made for this purpose, and the cover of night was chosen, as most proper for concealing their own disgrace, and for eluding the vengeance of the enemy. But the night appointed for their departure was distinguished by an inauspicious eclipse of the moon, for so at least it was judged by the superstitious fears of Nicias, and by the ignorance

[19] Thucydid. p. 127.

of his diviners [17], even in the vain art which they professed. The voyage was deferred til the mystical number of thrice nine days. But before the expiration of that time it was no longer practicable; for the design was soon discovered to the Syracusans, and this discovery, added to the encouragement derived from the circumstances of which we have already taken notice, increased their eagerness to attack the enemy by sea and land. Their attempts failed to destroy, by fire-ships, the Athenian fleet. They were more successful in employing superior numbers to divide the strength, and to weaken the resistance, of an enfeebled and dejected foe. During three days there was a perpetual succession of military and naval exploits. On the first day fortune hung in suspense; the second deprived the Athenians of a considerable squadron commanded by Eurymedon; and this misfortune was embittered, on the third, by the loss of eighteen gallies, with their crews [18].

The Syracusans celebrated their victory with triumphant enthusiasm; while their orators "extolled and magnified the glory of a city, which, by its native prowess and single danger, had not only maintained the independence of Sicily, but avenged the injuries of the whole Grecian name, too long dishonored and afflicted by the oppressive tyranny of Athens. That tyranny had been acquired and confirmed by the usurped sovereignty of

[17] The rules of divination, we are told, should have taught them, that the obscuring of an eclipse betokened a successful retreat. Plutarch. in Nicia.
[18] Thucydid. p. 528, et seqq.

CHAP.
XI.

the fea; but even on that element, the courage of Syracufe had defeated the experience of the enemy. Their renown would be immortal, if they accomplifhed the ufeful and meritorious work; and if, by intercepting the retreat, and deftroying the armament of the Athenians, they crufhed at once the power, and for ever humbled the pride, of that afpiring people".

who throw a chain acrofs the Great Harbour.

This defign, fuggefted by the wifdom of Hermocrates, was eagerly adopted by the active zeal of his fellow-citizens, who ftrove, with unremitting ardor, to throw a chain of veffels acrofs the mouth of the Great Harbour, about a mile in breadth. The labor was complete before Nicias, totally occupied by other objects, attempted to interrupt it. After repeated defeats, and although he was fo miferably tormented by the ftone, that he had frequently folicited his recal, that virtuous commander, whofe courage rofe in adverfity, ufed the utmoft diligence to retrieve the affairs of his country. The fhattered gallies were fpeedily refitted; and again prepared, to the number of an hundred and ten, to rifk the event of a battle. As they had fuffered greatly, on former occafions, by the hardnefs and maffive folidity of the Syracufan prows, Nicias provided them with grappling-irons, fitted to prevent the recoil of their opponents, and the repetition of the hoftile ftroke. The decks were crowded with armed men, and the contrivance to which the enemy had hitherto chiefly owed their fuccefs, of introducing the firmnefs and ftability of a military, into a naval engagement, was adopted

THE HISTORY OF GREECE.

in its full extent by the Athenians. When the fleet was ready for sea, Nicias recalled the troops from the various posts and fortresses still occupied by their arms, and formed them into one camp on the shore, where, on the day of battle, their ranks might be extended as widely as the vicinity of the Syracusan ramparts could safely permit; that a spacious retreat might be secured to the Athenian ships, if persecuted by their usual bad fortune; in which fatal alternative nothing remained, but to retire by land with the miserable remnant of the army. But Nicias did not yet despair, that the last efforts of his countrymen would break the enemy's chain at the mouth of the Great Harbour; and that they would return victorious; to transport their encamped companions to the friendly ports of Naxos and Catana.

Elevated by this hope, he forgot his bodily infirmities and suppressed the anguish of his soul. With a cheerful and magnanimous firmness, he removed the dejection of the Athenians, exhorting them, before they embarked, by an affecting and manly speech, " to remember the vicissitudes of war, and the instability of fortune ". Though hitherto unsuccessful, they had every thing to expect from the strength of their actual preparations; nor ought men, who had tried and surmounted so many dangers, to yield to the weak prejudices of unexperienced folly, and cloud the prospect of future victory, by the gloomy remembrance of past

CHAP. XX.

Both sides prepare for battle.

³⁰ Thucydid. p. 135, et seqq.

defeat. They yet enjoyed an opportunity to defend their lives, their liberty, their friends, their country, and the mighty name of Athens; an opportunity which never could return, since the whole fortune of the republic was embarked in the present fleet[20]. When Gylippus and the Syracusan commanders were apprized of the designs of the enemy, they hastened to the defence of the bar which had been thrown across the entrance of the harbour. It is uncertain for what reason they had left open one narrow passage[21], on either side of which they stationed a powerful squadron. Gylippus animated the sailors with such topics as the occasion naturally furnished, and returned to take the conduct of the land-forces, leaving Sicanus, Agatharchus, and Pythen, the two first to command the wings, and the last, a citizen of Corinth, to command the centre, of the Syracusan fleet, which fell short of the Athenian by the number of twenty gallies. But the former was admirably provided with whatever seemed most necessary for attack or for defence; even the Athenian grappling-irons had not been overlooked; to elude the dangerous grasp of these instruments, the prows of the Syracusan vessels were covered with wet and slippery hides.

Naval engagement in the Great Harbour.

Before the Athenians set sail, Nicias, that nothing might be neglected to obtain success, went round the whole armament, addressing, in the most pathetic terms, the several commanders by name,

[20] Και των ναυπηγουντα δεινολων. Thucydid. p. 411.

recalling

recalling to them the objects most dear and most respectable, which they were engaged by every tie of honor and affection to defend, and conjuring them by their families, their friends, and their paternal gods, to exert whatever skill or courage they collectively, or as individuals, possessed, on this ever memorable and most important occasion. He then returned to the camp with an enfeebled body and an anxious mind, committing the last hope of the republic to the active valor of Demosthenes, Eudemus, and Menander. The first impression of the Athenians was irresistible; they burst through the passage of the bar, and repelled the squadrons on either side. As the entrance widened, the Syracusans, in their turn, rushed into the harbour, which was more favorable than the open sea to their mode of fighting. Thither the foremost of the Athenians returned, either compelled by superior force, or that they might assist their companions. The engagement became general in the mouth of the harbour; and in this narrow space two hundred gallies fought, during the greatest part of the day, with an obstinate and persevering valor. It would require the expressive energy of Thucydides, and the imitative, though inimitable, sounds and expressions of the Grecian tongue, to describe the noise, the tumult, and the ardor of the contending squadrons. The battle was not long confined to the shock of adverse prows, and to the distant hostility of darts and arrows. The nearest vessels grappled, and closed with each other, and their decks were soon converted

CHAP.
XX.

130 THE HISTORY OF GREECE.

CHAP. XX.

into a field of blood. While the heavy-armed troops boarded the enemy's ships, they left their own exposed to a similar misfortune; the fleets were divided into massive clusters of adhering gallies; and the confusion of their mingled shouts overpowered the voice of authority; the Athenians exhorting, not to abandon an element on which their republic had ever acquired victory and glory, for the dangerous protection of an hostile shore; and the Syracusans encouraging each other not to fly from an enemy, whose weakness or cowardice had long meditated flight [11].

The Athenians defeated.

The singular and tremendous spectacle of an engagement more fierce and obstinate than any that had ever been beheld in the Grecian seas, restrained the activity, and totally suspended the powers, of the numerous and adverse battalions which encircled the coast. The spectators and the actors were equally interested in the important scene; but the former, the current of whose sensibility was undiverted by any exertion of mind or body, felt more deeply, and expressed more forcibly, the various emotions by which they were agitated [12]. Hope, fear, the shouts of victory, the shrieks of despair, the anxious solicitude of doubtful success, animated the countenances, the voice, and the gesture of the Athenians, whose whole reliance centered in their fleet. When at length their gallies evidently gave way on every side, the contrast of alternate, and the rapid tumult of successive

[11] Thucydid. p. 543, et seqq. [12] Id. p. 544.

THE HISTORY OF GREECE 131

passions, subsided in a melancholy calm. This dreadful pause of astonishment and terror was followed by the disordered trepidation of flight and fear: many escaped to the camp: others ran, uncertain whither to direct their steps; while Nicias, with a small, but undismayed band, remained on the shore, to protect the landing of their unfortunate gallies. But the retreat of the Athenians could not probably have been effected, had it not been favored by the actual circumstances of the enemy, as well as by the peculiar prejudices of ancient superstition. In this well-fought battle, the vanquished had lost fifty, and the victors forty vessels. It was incumbent on the latter to employ their immediate and most strenuous efforts to recover the dead bodies of their friends, that they might be honored with the sacred and indispensable rites of funeral. The day was far spent; the strength of the sailors had been exhausted by a long continuance of unremitting labor; and both they and their companions on shore were more desirous to return to Syracuse to enjoy the fruits of victory, than to irritate the dangerous despair of the vanquished Athenians[a].

CHAP. XX.

It is observed by the Roman orator[b], with no less truth than elegance, that not only the navy of Athens, but the glory and the empire of that republic, suffered shipwreck in the fatal harbour of Syracuse. The despondent degeneracy which immediately followed this ever memorable engagement was

Their extreme despondency.

[a] Thucydid. p. 449. [b] Cic. in Verr. v, 37.

K 2

CHAP.
XX.
testified in the neglect of a duty which the Athenians had never neglected before, and in denying a part of their national character, which it had hitherto been their greatest glory to maintain. They abandoned to insult and indignity the bodies of the slain; and when it was proposed to them by their commanders to prepare next day for a second engagement, since their vessels were still more numerous than those of the enemy, they, who had seldom avoided a superior, and who had never declined the encounter of an equal force, declared, that no motive could induce them to withstand the weaker armament of Syracuse. Their only desire was to escape by land, under cover of the night, from a foe whom they had not courage to oppose, and from a place where every object was offensive to their sight, and most painful to their reflection [21].

The Syracusans celebrate the festival of Hercules with riotous joy.

The behaviour of the Syracusans might have proved extremely favorable to this design. The evening after the battle was the vigil of the feast of Hercules; and the still agitated combatants awakened, after a short and feverish repose, to celebrate the memory of their favorite hero, to whose propitious influence they probably ascribed the merit of the most splendid trophy that ever adorned the fame of Syracuse. From the triumph of victory, and grateful emotions of religious enthusiasm, there was an easy transition, in the creed and in the practice of the Greeks, to the extravagance of licentious joy, and the excesses of sensual indulgence.

[21] Thucyd. p. 465.

Sports, proceffions, mufic, dancing, the pleafures of the table, of the elegant arts, and of unguarded converfation, were incorporated in the texture of their religious worfhip. But the coincidence of a feftival and a victory demanded an accumulated profufion of fuch objects as footh the fenfes and pleafe the fancy. Amidft thefe giddy tranfports, the Syracufans loft all remembrance of an enemy whom they defpifed; even the foldiers on guard joined the diffolute or frivolous amufements of their companions; and, during the greateft part of the night, Syracufe prefented a mixed fcene of fecure gaiety, of thoughtlefs jollity, and of mad and dangerous diforder[24].

The firm and vigilant mind of Hermocrates alone withftood, but was unable to divert, the general current. It was impoffible to roufe to the fatigues of war men buried in wine and pleafure, and intoxicated with victory; and, as he could not intercept by force, he determined to retard by ftratagem, the intended retreat of the Athenians, whofe numbers and refentment would ftill render them formidable to whatever part of Sicily they might remove their camp. A felect band of horfemen, affuming the character of traitors, fearlefsly approached the hoftile ramparts, and warned the Athenians of the danger of departing that night, as many ambufcades lurked in the way, and all the moft important paffes were occupied by the enemy. The frequency of treafon gained credit to the

[24] Thucydid. p. 546.

THE HISTORY OF GREECE.

CHAP. XI.

perfidious advice; and the Athenians, having changed their first resolution, were persuaded by Nicias to wait two days longer, that such measures might be taken as seemed best adapted to promote the safety and celerity of their march [1].

The Athenians raise their camp.

The camp was raised on the third morning after the battle. Forty thousand men, of whom many were afflicted with wounds and disease, and all exhausted by fatigue, and dejected by calamity, exhibited the appearance, not of a flying army, but of a great and populous community, driven from their ancient habitations by the cruel vengeance of a conqueror. They had miserably fallen from the lofty expectations with which they sailed in triumph to the harbour of Syracuse. They had abandoned their fleet, their transports, the hopes of victory, and the glory of the Athenian name; and these collective sufferings were enhanced and exasperated by the painful images which struck the eyes and the fancy of each unfortunate individual. The mangled bodies of their companions and friends, deprived of the sacred rites of funeral, affected them with a sentiment of religious horror, on which the weakness of human nature is happily unable to dwell. They removed their attention from this dreadful sight; but they could not divert their compassion from a spectacle still more melancholy, the numerous crowds of sick and wounded, who followed them with enfeebled and unequal steps, entreating, in the accent and attitude of unutterable

Their dreadful afflictions.

[1] Thucydid. p. 147.

anguish, to be delivered from the horrors of famine, or the rage of an exasperated foe. Amidst such affecting scenes, the heart of a stranger would have melted with tender sympathy; but how much more must it have afflicted the Athenians, to see their parents, brothers, children, and friends, involved in unexampled misery! to hear, without the possibility of relieving, their lamentable complaints! and reluctantly to throw the clinging victims from their wearied necks and arms! Yet the care of personal safety prevailed over every other care; for the soldiers, either destitute of slaves, or distrusting their fidelity, were not only encumbered by their armor, but oppressed by the weight of their provisions[22].

The superior rank of Nicias entitled him to a pre-eminence of toil and of woe; and he deserves the regard of posterity by his character and sufferings, and still more by the melancholy firmness of his conduct. The load of accumulated disasters did not sink him into inactive despondency. He moved with a rapid pace around every part of the army, and the ardor of his mind re-animating the languor of his debilitated frame, he exclaimed, with a loud and distinct voice, "Athenians and allies! there is yet room for hope. Many have escaped from still greater evils; nor ought you rashly to accuse either fortune or yourselves. As to me, who, in bodily strength, excel not the weakest among you (for you see to what a miserable condition my disease has reduced me), and

[22] Thucydid. p. 548.

who, in the happiness of private life, and the deceitful gifts of prosperity, had long been distinguished above the most illustrious of my contemporaries, I am now confounded in affliction with the meanest and most worthless. Yet am I unconscious of deserving such a fatal reverse of fortune. My conduct towards men has been irreproachable; my piety towards the gods conspicuous and sincere. For this reason I am still animated with confidence; calamities, unmerited by guilt, are disarmed of their terrors. If we have incurred the indignation of the gods by our ambitious designs against Sicily, our offence, surely, is sufficiently expiated by past sufferings, which now render us the objects of compassion. Other nations have attacked their neighbours with less provocation, and have yet escaped with a gentler punishment; nor will experience warrant the belief, that for the frailties and errors of passion, providence should impose penalties too heavy to be borne. We have the less reason to adopt an impious prejudice, so dishonorable to the gods, when we consider the means which their goodness has still left us to provide for our defence. Our numbers, our resolution, and even our misfortunes, still render us formidable. There is not any army in Sicily capable to intercept our course; much less to expel us from the first friendly territory in which we may fix our camp. If we can secure, therefore, our present safety, by a prudent, speedy, and courageous retreat, we may afterwards retrieve our lost honor, and restore the fallen glory of Athens;

since the chief ornament of a state consists in brave and virtuous men, not in empty ships and undefended walls".

The actions of Nicias fully corresponded with his words. He neglected none of the duties of a great general. Instead of leading the army towards Naxos and Catana, in which direction there was reason to apprehend many secret ambushes of the enemy, he conducted them by the western route towards Gela and Camerina; expecting, by this measure, to find provisions in greater plenty, as well as to elude the latent snares of the Syracusans. That nothing might be omitted which promised the hope of relief, messengers were immediately dispatched to the neighbouring cities, which might possibly be tempted by their natural jealousy of the growing prosperity of Syracuse, to favor the retreat of the vanquished. The troops were then divided into two squares, as the most secure and capacious arrangement. Nicias led the van; Demosthenes conducted the rear; the baggage, and unarmed multitude, occupied the centre. In this order of march they passed the river Anapus, the ford of which was feebly disputed by an inconsiderable guard; and having proceeded the first day only five miles, they encamped in the evening on a rising ground, after being much harassed during the latter part of their journey by the Syracusan cavalry and archers, who galled them at a distance, intercepted the stragglers, and avoided, by a seasonable retreat, to commit the security of their own

⁹ Thucydid. p. 550.

CHAP. IX.

fortune with the dangerous despair of the Athenians. Next day, having marched only twenty furlongs, they reached a spacious plain, the convenience of which invited them to repose; especially as they needed a supply of water and provisions, which might be easily obtained from the surrounding country[10].

Interrupted by the enemy.

Before this time, the enemy were apprized of their line of march; and, in order to interrupt it, they sent a numerous detachment to fortify the mountain of Acræum. This mountain, which probably gave name to the small town situate in its neighbourhood, intersected the direct road to Gela and Camerina. It was distant a few miles from the Athenian encampment, and a small degree of art might render it impregnable, since it was of a steep and rapid ascent, and encompassed on every side by the rocky channel of a loud and foaming torrent. In vain the Athenians attempted, on three successive days, to force the passage. They were repelled with loss in every new attack, which became more feeble than the preceding. In the first and most desperate, an accidental storm of thunder increased the courage of the Syracusans and the terror of the Athenians. A similar event had, in the first engagement after the invasion of Sicily, produced an opposite effect on the contending nations. But the hopes and the fears of men change with their fortune.

Change their line of march.

In the evening after the last unsuccessful contest, the condition of the Athenians was peculiarly

[10] Thucydid. p. 513, et seqq.

deplorable. The numbers of the wounded had been increased by the fruitless attempts to pass the mountain; the enemy had continually galled and insulted them as they retreated to their camp; the adjacent territory could no longer supply them with the necessaries of life; and they must be compelled, after all their hardships and fatigues, to make a long circuit by the sea-shore, if they expected to reach, in safety, the places of their respective destination. Even this resolution (for there was no alternative), however dreadful to men in their comfortless and exhausted state, was recommended by Nicias, who, to conceal his design from the enemy, caused innumerable fires to be lighted in every part of the camp [11]. The troops then marched out under cover of the night, and in the same order which they had hitherto observed. But they had not proceeded far in this nocturnal expedition, when the obscurity of the skies, the deceitful tracks of an unknown and hostile country, filled the most timid or unfortunate with imaginary terrors. Their panic, as is usual in great bodies of men, was speedily communicated to those around them; and Demosthenes, with above one half of his division, fatally mistook the road, and quitted, never more to rejoin, the rest of the army.

The scouts of Gylippus and the Syracusans immediately brought intelligence of this important event, which furnished an opportunity to attack the divided strength of the Athenians. His superior knowledge of the country enabled Gylippus, by

[11] Thucydid. p. 112, et seqq.

CHAP.
XX.

the celerity of his march, to intercept the smaller division, and to surround them on every side, in the difficult and intricate defiles which led to the ford of the river Erinios. There he assaulted them with impunity, during a whole day, with darts, arrows, and javelins. When the measure of their sufferings was complete, he proclaimed towards the evening, by the sound of the trumpet, and with the loud voice of the herald, freedom, forgiveness, and protection to all who should desert and abandon the bad fortune of their leaders; an offer which was accepted by the troops of several Asiatic islands, and other dependent and tributary countries. At length he entered into treaty with Demosthenes himself, whose soldiers laid down their arms, and delivered their money (which filled the capacious hollow of four broad bucklers), on condition that they should not suffer death, imprisonment, or famine[19]. Notwithstanding the number of the deserters and of the slain, the remainder still amounted to six thousand, who were sent to Syracuse with their captive general, under a powerful and vigilant escort, while the activity of Gylippus followed the flying battalions of the enemy, which had been conducted by Nicias to the distance of twenty miles, towards the fatal banks of the river Assinaros.

The division under Nicias overtaken by the enemy.

The Syracusans overtook the rear before the van could arrive at the lofty and abrupt margin of this rapid stream; and an herald was sent to Nicias,

[19] Thucydid. p. 513.

exhorting him to imitate the example of his colleague, and to surrender, without farther bloodshed, to the irresistible valor of his victorious pursuers. Nicias disbelieved, or affected to disbelieve, the report; but when a confidential messenger, whom he was allowed to dispatch for information, brought certain intelligence of the surrender and disgrace of Demosthenes, he also condescended to propose terms, in the name of the Athenians, engaging, on the immediate cessation of hostilities, to reimburse the magistrates of Syracuse for the expense of the war, and to deliver Athenian hostages (a citizen for a talent) until the debt should be liquidated [51].

These terms were rejected by the Syracusans with disdain; and Gylippus having occupied the most advantageous posts on every side, attacked the army of Nicias with the same mode of warfare which had, two days before, proved so destructive to their unfortunate companions. During the whole day they bore, with extraordinary patience, the hostile assault, still expecting, under cover of the night, to escape the cruel vigilance of the enemy. But that hope was vain: Gylippus perceived their departure; and although three hundred men of determined courage gallantly broke through the guards, and effected their escape, the rest were no sooner discovered than they returned to their former station, and laid down their arms in silent despair. Yet the return of the morning brought back their courage. They again took up their arms, and marched towards

[51] Thucydid. p. 554.

CHAP.
XX.

the river, miserably galled and afflicted by the hostile archers and cavalry. Their distress was most lamentable and incurable: yet hope did not totally forsake them; for like men in the oppression and languor of a consuming disease, they still entertained a confused idea, that their sufferings would end, could they but reach the opposite banks of the neighbouring river [10].

Horrid scene on the banks of the Assinaros.

The desire of assuaging their thirst encouraged this daring design. They rushed with frantic disorder into the rapidity of the stream; the pursuing Syracusans, who had occupied the rocky banks, destroying them with innumerable volleys of missile weapons. In the Assinaros they had a new enemy to contend with. The depth and force of the waters triumphed over their single, and shook their implicated strength. Many were borne down the stream. At length the weight of their numbers resisted the violence of the torrent; but a new form of danger and of horror presented itself to the eyes of Nicias. His soldiers turned their fury against each other, disputing, with the point of the sword, the unwholesome draughts of the agitated and turbid current. This spectacle melted the firmness of his manly soul. He surrendered to Gylippus, and asked quarter for the miserable remnant of his troops, who had not perished in the Assinaros, or been destroyed by the Syracusan archers and cavalry [11]. Before the commands of the Lacedæmonian general could pervade the army, many of the soldiers had, according to the barbarous

[10] Thucydid. p. 114. [11] Ibid. p. 115.

practice of the age, seized their prisoners and slaves; so that the Athenian captives were afterwards distributed among several communities of Sicily, which had sent assistance to Syracuse. The rest, upon laying down their arms, were entitled to the pity and protection of Gylippus; who, after sending proper detachments to intercept and collect the stragglers, returned in triumph to the city with the inestimable trophies of his valor and conduct.

Nicias had little to expect from the *humanity* of a proud and victorious Spartan; but Demosthenes might naturally flatter himself with the hope of *justice*. He urged with energy, but urged in vain, the observance of the capitulation which had been ratified with due forms, on the faith of which he had surrendered himself and the troops intrusted to his command. The public prisoners, conducted successively to Syracuse, and exceeding together the number of seven thousand, were treated with the same inhuman cruelty. They were universally condemned to labor in the mines and quarries of Sicily [10]: their whole sustenance was bread and water: they suffered alternately the ardors of a scorching sun, and the chilling damps of autumn. For seventy days and nights they languished in this dreadful captivity, during which, the diseases incident to their manner of life were rendered infectious by the stench of the dead bodies, which corrupted the purity of the surrounding air. At length an eternal separation was made between

[10] Thucydid. p. 516.

CHAP. XX.

those who should enjoy the happier lot of being sold as slaves into distant lands, and those who should for ever be confined to their terrible dungeons. The Athenians, with such Italians and Sicilians as had unnaturally embraced their cause, were reserved for the latter doom. Their generals, Nicias and Demosthenes, had not lived to behold this melancholy hour. Gylippus would have spared their lives, not from any motives of humanity and esteem, but that his joyous return to Sparta might have been graced by their presence. But the resentment of the Syracusans, the fears of the Corinthians; above all, the suspicious jealousy of those perfidious traitors who had maintained a secret correspondence with Nicias, which they dreaded lest the accidents of his future life might discover, loudly demanded the immediate execution of the captive generals[17]. The Athenians of those times justly regretted the loss of Demosthenes, a gallant and enterprising commander; but posterity will for ever lament the fate of Nicias, the most pious, the most virtuous, and the most unfortunate man of the age in which he lived.

A singular exception to this general cruelty.

Amidst this dark and dreadful scene of cruelty and revenge, we must not omit to mention one singular example of humanity, which broke forth like a meteor in the gloom of a nocturnal tempest. The Syracusans, who could punish their helpless captives with such unrelenting severity, had often melted into tears at the affecting strains of Euripides[18], an Athenian poet, who had learned in the Socratic

[17] Thucydid. l. vii. ad fin. [18] See above, vol. II. p. 274.

school

school to adorn the lessons of philosophy with the
charms of fancy, and who was regarded by the taste
of his contemporaries, as he still is by many enlightened judges, as the most tender and pathetic,
the most philosophical and instructive, of all tra-
gic writers. The pleasure which the Syracusans
had derived from his inimitable poetry, made them
long to hear it rehearsed by the flexible voices and
harmonious pronunciation of the Athenians, so unlike, and so superior, to the rudeness and asperity
of their own Doric dialect. They desired their
captives to repeat the plaintive scenes of their favorite bard. The captives obeyed; and affecting
to represent the woes of ancient kings and heroes,
they too faithfully expressed their own. Their
taste and sensibility endeared them to the Syracusans, who released their bonds, received them with
kindness into their families[19], and, after treating
them with all the honorable distinctions of ancient
hospitality, restored them to their longing and afflicted country, as a small but precious wreck of
the most formidable armament that had ever sailed
from a Grecian harbour. At their return to
Athens, the grateful captives walked in solemn procession to the house of Euripides, whom they hailed
as their deliverer from slavery and death[20]. This
acknowledgment, infinitely more honorable than

[19] Ητοι τεθνηκεν η διδασκει γραμματα, "he is either dead or teaching verses," an expression first introduced at this time, was afterwards applied proverbially, in speaking of travellers in foreign countries, whose fate was uncertain.
[20] Plutarch. in Nicia.

CHAP.
XX.

all the crowns and splendor that ever surrounded the person, and even than all the altars and temples that ever adorned the memory of a poet⁹¹, must have transported Euripides with the *second* triumph which the heart of man can feel. He would have enjoyed the *first*, if his countrymen had owed to his virtues the tribute which they paid to his talents; and if, instead of the beauty and elegance of his verses, they had been saved by his probity, his courage, or his patriotism; qualities which, still more than genius and fancy, constitute the real excellence and dignity of human nature.

[91] See above, chapter VI.

CHAP. XXI.

Confequences of the Athenian Misfortunes in Sicily. — Formidable Confederacy againft Athens. — Peculiar Refources of free Governments. — Naval Operations. — Battle of Miletus. — Intrigues of Alcibiades. — The Athenian Democracy fubverted. — Tyrannical Government of the Four Hundred. — Battle of Eretria. — Democracy re-eftablifhed in Athens. — Naval Succefs of the Athenians. — Triumphant Return of Alcibiades. — The Eleufinian Myfteries — and Plynteria.

IN the populous and extenfive kingdoms of modern Europe, the revolutions of public affairs feldom difturb the humble obfcurity of private life; but the national tranfactions of Greece involved the intereft of every family, and deeply affected the fortune and happinefs of every individual. Had the arms of the Athenians proved fuccefsful in Sicily, each citizen would have derived from that event an immediate acceffion of wealth, as well as of power, and have felt a proportional increafe of honor and fecurity. But their proud hopes perifhed for ever in the harbour of Syracufe. The fucceeding difafters fhook to the foundation the fabric of their empire. In one rafh enterprife they loft their army, their fleet, the prudence of

CHAP. XXI.

Extent of the Athenian misfortunes in Sicily.

CHAP.
XXI.

their experienced generals, and the flourishing vigor of their manly youth'—Irreparable disasters! which totally disabled them to resist the confederacy of Peloponnesus, reinforced by the resentment of a new and powerful enemy. While a Lacedæmonian army invested their city, they had reason to dread that a Syracusan fleet should assault the Piræus; that Athens must finally yield to these combined attacks, and her once prosperous citizens destroyed by the sword, or dragged into captivity, atone by their death or disgrace for the cruelties which they had recently inflicted on the wretched republics of Melos and Scioné,

The news brought to Athens. Olymp. xcl. 4. A. C. 413.

The dreadful alternative of victory and defeat, renders it little surprising that the Athenians should have rejected intelligence, which they must have received with horror. The first messengers of such sad news were treated with contempt: but it was impossible long ² to with-hold belief from the miserable fugitives, whose squalid and dejected countenances too faithfully attested the public cala-

---

¹ Thucydid. l. vii. p. 547. Cicero goes farther. Hic primum opes Attica civitatis victæ, comminutæ, depressæque sunt: in hoc portu Atheniensium nobilitatis, imperii, gloriæ naufragium factum existimatur. Cicer. in Verrem, v. 37.

² The calamity was so great that the boldest imagination had never dared to conceive its existence. Their minds being thus unprepared, the Athenians, says Thucydides, disbelieved και τους πανυ των στρατιωτων αυτη τη εργω διαπεφευγοτας; even those soldiers who escaped from this melancholy business. The Stories of Plutarch in Nicia, of Athenæus, etc. may be safely condemned as fictions, since they are inconsistent with Thucydides's narrative.

mity. Such evidence could not be refused; the arrogance of incredulity was abashed, and the whole republic thrown into consternation, or seized with despair. The venerable members of the Areopagus expressed the majesty of silent sorrow; but the piercing cries of woe extended many a mile along the lofty walls which joined the Piræus to the city; and the licentious populace raged with unbridled fury against the diviners and orators, whose blind predictions, and ambitious harangues, had promoted an expedition eternally fatal to their country [1].

The distress of the Athenians was too great to admit the comfort of sympathy; but had they been capable of receiving, they had little reason to expect, that melancholy consolation. The tidings so afflicting to *them* gave unspeakable joy to their neighbours; many feared, most hated, and all envied a people who had long usurped the dominion of Greece. The Athenian allies, or rather subjects, scattered over so many coasts and islands, prepared to assert their independence; the confederates of Sparta, among whom the Syracusans justly assumed the first rank, were unsatisfied with victory, and longed for revenge: even those communities, which had hitherto declined the danger of a doubtful contest, meanly solicited to become parties in a war, which they expected must finally terminate in the destruction of Athens [2].

---

[1] Thucyd. l. viii. p. 118, et seqq.
[2] Thucyd. l. viii. p. 118, et seqq. Diodor. l. xiii. p. 148.

CHAP.
XXI.
Abetted by the resentment of Persia.

Should all the efforts of such a powerful confederacy still prove insufficient to accomplish the ruin of the devoted city, there was yet another enemy behind, from whose strength and animosity the Athenians had every thing to fear. The long and peaceful reign of Artaxerxes, king of Persia, expired four hundred and twenty-five years before the Christian æra. The two following years were remarkable for a rapid succession of kings, Xerxes, Sogdianus, Ochus; the last of whom assumed the name of Darius, to which historians have added the epithet of Nothus, the bastard, to distinguish this effeminate prince from his illustrious predecessor [1]. The first years of Darius Nothus were employed in confirming his disputed authority, and in watching the dangerous intrigues of his numerous kinsmen who aspired to the throne. When every rival was removed that could either disturb his quiet or offend his suspicion, the monarch sunk into an indolent security, and his voluptuous court was governed by the feeble administration of women and eunuchs [2]. But in the ninth year of his reign Darius was roused from his lethargy by the revolt of Egypt and Lydia. The defection of the latter threatened to tear from his dominion the valuable provinces of Asia Minor; a consequence which he determined to prevent by employing the bravery of Pharnabazus, and the

[1] Diodor. l. xii. p. 322. Ctesias, Persic. c. xlv. et seqq.
[2] Ctesias, c. xvii.

policy of the crafty Tissaphernes, to govern respectively the northern and southern districts of that rich and fertile peninsula. The abilities of these generals not only quelled the rebellion in Lydia, but extended the arms of their master towards the shores of the Ægean, as well as of the Hellespont and Propontis; in direct opposition to the treaty which forty years before had been ratified between the Athenians, then in the height of their prosperity, and the unwarlike Artaxerxes. But the recent misfortunes of that ambitious people flattered the Persian commanders with the hope of restoring the whole Asiatic coast to the great king [7], as well as of inflicting exemplary punishment on the proud city, which had resisted the power, dismembered the empire, and tarnished the glory of Persia.

CHAP. XXI.

The terror of such a formidable combination might have reduced the Athenians to despair; and our surprise that this consequence should not immediately follow, will be increased by the following reflection. Not to mention the immortal trophies of Alexander, or the extensive ravages of Zingis Khan, Tamerlane, and the Tartar princes of their race; the Spaniards, the Portuguese, and other nations of modern Europe, have, with a handful of men, marched victorious over the effeminate or barbarous coasts of the eastern and western world. The hardy discipline of Europe easily prevailed

The Athenian allies prepare to revolt.

[7] Thucydid. l. viii. p. 560. et Ctesias, Persic. c. li.

152 THE HISTORY OF GREECE.

CHAP.
XXI.

over the unwarlike softness of India and the savage ignorance of America. But the rapid success of all these conquerors was owing to their military knowledge * and experience. By the superiority of their arms and of their discipline, the Romans subdued the nations of the earth. But the Athenians afford the only example of a people, who, by the virtues of the mind alone, acquired an extensive dominion over men equally improved with themselves in the arts of war and government. They possessed, or were believed to possess, superior courage and capacity to the nations around them; and this opinion, which should seem not entirely destitute of foundation, enabled them to maintain, by very feeble garrisons, an absolute authority in the islands of the Ægean, as well as in the cities of the Asiatic coast. Their disasters and disgrace in Sicily destroyed at once the real and the ideal supports of their power; the loss of one third of their citizens made it impossible to supply, with fresh recruits, the exhausted strength of their garrisons in foreign parts; the terror of their fleet was no more; and their multiplied defeats, before the walls of Syracuse, had converted into contempt that admiration in which Athens had been long held by Greeks and Barbarians.

Peculiar
resources
of free
governments.

But in free governments there are many latent resources which public calamities alone can bring to

* If that of the Tartars should be doubted, the reader may consult Monf. de Guignes's Hist. des Huns, and Mr. Gibbon's admirable description of the manners of the pastoral nations, iv. 273.

light; and adversity, which, to individuals endowed with inborn vigor of mind, is the great school of virtue and of heroism, furnishes also to the enthusiasm of popular assemblies the noblest field for the display of national honor and magnanimity. Had the measures of the Athenians depended on one man, or even on a few, it is probable that the selfish timidity of a prince, and the cautious prudence of a council, would have sunk under the weight of misfortunes, too heavy for the unsupported strength of ordinary minds. But the first spark of generous ardor, which the love of virtue, of glory, and the republic, or even the meaner motives of ambition and vanity, excited in the assembled multitude, was diffused and increased by the natural contagion of sympathy; the patriotic flame was communicated to every breast; and the social warmth, reflected from such a variety of objects, became too intense to be resisted by the coldness of caution and the damps of despair.

CHAP. XXI.

With one mind and resolution the Athenians determined to brave the severity of fortune, and to withstand the assaults of the enemy. Nor did this noble design evaporate in useless speculation: the wisest measures were adopted for reducing it to practice. The great work began, as national reformation ought always to begin, by regulating the finances, and lopping off every branch of superfluous expense. The clamor of turbulent demagogues was silenced; aged wisdom and

Prudent and vigorous measures of the Athenians.

CHAP.
XXI.

experience were allowed calmly to direct the public councils; new levies were raised; the remainder of their fleet was equipped for sea; the motions of the colonies and tributary states were watched with an anxious solicitude, and every proper expedient was employed that might appease their animosity, or render it impotent[1]. Yet these measures, prudent and vigorous as they were, could not, probably, have suspended the fall of Athens, had not several concurring causes facilitated their operation. The weak, dilatory, and ineffectual proceedings of the Spartan confederacy; the temporizing, equivocal, and capricious conduct of the Persian governors; above all, the intrigues and enterprising genius of Alcibiades, who, after involving his country in inextricable calamities, finally undertook its defence, and retarded, though he could not prevent, its destiny.

The Peloponnesians and Persians prepare to assist the Asiatic dependents of Athens.
Olymp. xcii. 1.
A. C. 412.

In the year following the unfortunate expedition into Sicily, the Spartans prepared a fleet of an hundred sail, of which twenty-five gallies were furnished by their own sea-ports; twenty-five by the Thebans; fifteen by the Corinthians; and the remainder by Locris, Phocis, Megara, and the maritime cities on the coast of Peloponnesus. This armament was destined to encourage and support the revolt of the Asiatic subjects of the Athenians. The islands of Chios and Lesbos, as well as the city Erythræ on the continent, solicited the

[1] Thucydid. l. viii. p. 119. Diodor. l. xiii. p. 349.

Spartans to join them with their naval force. Their request was enforced by Tissaphernes, who promised to pay the sailors, and to victual the ships. At the same time, an ambassador from Cyzicus, a populous town situate on an island of the Propontis, entreated the Lacedæmonian armament to sail to the safe and capacious harbours which had long formed the wealth and the ornament of that city, and to expel the Athenian garrisons, to which the Cyzicenes and their neighbours reluctantly submitted. The Persian Pharnabazus seconded their proposal; offered the same conditions with Tissaphernes; and so little harmony subsisted between the lieutenants of the great king, that each urged his particular demand with a total unconcern about the important interests of their common master[10]. The Lacedæmonians held many consultations among themselves, and with their allies; hesitated, deliberated, resolved, and changed their resolution; and at length were persuaded by Alcibiades to prefer the overture of Tissaphernes and the Ionians to that of the Hellespontines and Pharnabazus.

The delay occasioned by this deliberation was the principal, but not the only cause; which hindered the allies from acting expeditiously, at a time when expedition was of the utmost importance. A variety of private views diverted them from the general aim of the confederacy; and the

[10] Thucydid. p. 561 et 562.

season was far advanced before the Corinthians, who had been distinguished by excess of antipathy to Athens, were prepared to sail. They determined, from pride perhaps, as well as superstition, to celebrate[11], before leaving their harbours, the Isthmian games, consecrated to Neptune, the third of the Grecian festivals in point of dignity and splendor. From this ceremony the Athenians, though enemies, were not excluded by the Corinthian magistrates; nor did they exclude themselves, though oppressed by the weight of past misfortunes, and totally occupied by the thoughts of providing against future evils. While their representatives shared the amusements of this sacred spectacle, they neglected not the commission recommended by their country. They secretly informed themselves of the plan and particular circumstances of the intended revolt, and learned the precise time fixed for the departure of the Corinthian fleet. In consequence of this important intelligence, the Athenians anticipated the designs of the rebels of Chios, and carried off seven ships as pledges of their fidelity. The squadron which returned from this useful enterprise, intercepted the Corinthians as they sailed through the Saronic gulph; and having attacked and conquered them, pursued and blocked them up in their harbours[12].

---

[11] "Πριν τα Ισθμια διαπραχθηι." The Scholiast justly observes, the force of the "δια," "thoroughly, completely," *i. e.* until they had celebrated the games, the complete number of days, appointed by antiquity. Vid. Æ. Part. ad loc. p. 563.

[12] Thucydid. p. 164.

Meanwhile the Spartans and their allies sent to the Ionian coast such squadrons as were successively ready for sea, under the conduct of Alcibiades, Chalcideus, and Astyochus. The first of these commanders sailed to the isle of Chios, which was distracted by contending factions. The Athenian partisans were surprised, and compelled to submit; and the city, which possessed forty gallies, and yielded in wealth and populousness to none of the neighbouring colonies, became an accession to the Peloponnesian confederacy. The strong and rich town of Miletus followed the example: Erythræ and Clazomené surrendered to Chalcideus, several places of less note were conquered by Astyochus.

When the Athenians received the unwelcome intelligence of these events, they voted the expenditure of a thousand talents, which, in more prosperous times, they had deposited in the citadel, under the sanction of a decree of the senate and people, to reserve it for an occasion of the utmost danger. This seasonable supply enabled them to increase the fleet, which sailed, under Phrynichus and other leaders, to the isle of Lesbos. Having secured the fidelity of the Lesbians, who were ripe for rebellion, they endeavoured to recover their authority in Miletus, anciently regarded as the capital of the Ionic coast. A bloody battle was fought before the walls of that place, between the Athenians and Argives on one side, and the Peloponnesians, assisted by the troops of Tissaphernes and the revolted Milesians, on the other. The Athenian bravery defeated, on this occasion, the superior numbers of Greeks and Barbarians to whom they were opposed; but their Argive auxiliaries were repulsed by the gallant citizens of Miletus: so that, in both parts of the engagement, the Ionic race, commonly reckoned the less warlike, prevailed over their Dorian rivals and enemies. Elevated with the joy of victory, the Athenians prepared to assault the town, when they were alarmed by the approach of a fleet of fifty-five sail, which advanced in two divisions, the one commanded by the celebrated Hermocrates, the other by Therameries the Spartan. Phrynichus prudently considered, that his own strength only amounted to forty-eight gallies, and refused to commit the last hope of the republic to the danger of an unequal combat. His firmness despised the clamors of the Athenian sailors, who insulted[11], under the name of cowardice, the caution of their admiral; and he calmly retired with his whole force to the isle of Samos, where the popular faction having lately treated the nobles with shocking injustice and cruelty, too frequent in Grecian democracies, were ready to receive with open arms

The Athenian fleet retired.

---

[11] Like Fabius,

Non ponebat enim rumores ante salutem."

ENNIUS apud Cic.

which Thucydides expresses with more vigor, " γὰρ ἔστι τῷ ἀνάγκῃ παιδὺ ἀφεῖς κλεῆις ἀποδοῦνται, " p. 174.

THE HISTORY OF GREECE.   159

the patrons of that fierce and licentious form of government.

CHAP.
XXI.

The retreat of the Athenian fleet acknowledged the naval superiority of the enemy; a superiority which was alone sufficient either to acquire or to maintain the submission of the neighbouring coasts and islands. In other respects too, the Peloponnesians enjoyed the most decisive advantages. Their gallies were victualled, their soldiers were paid by Tissaphernes, and they daily expected a re-inforcement of an hundred and fifty Phœnician ships, which, it was said, had already reached Aspendus, a sea-port of Pamphylia. But, in this dangerous crisis, fortune seemed to respect, the declining age of Athens, and, by a train of accidents, singular and almost incredible, enabled Alcibiades, so long the misfortune and the scourge, to become the defence and the saviour, of his country.

The Athenian affairs retrieved by Alcibiades.

During his long residence in Sparta, Alcibiades assumed the outward gravity of deportment, and conformed himself to the spare diet, and laborious exercises, which prevailed in that austere republic; but his character and his principles remained as licentious as ever. His intrigue with Timea, the spouse of king Agis, was discovered by an excess of female levity. The queen, vain of the attachment of so celebrated a character, familiarly gave the name of Alcibiades to her son Leotychides; a name which, first confined to the privacy of her female companions, was soon spread abroad in the world. Alcibiades punished her folly by a most

His intrigues.

mortifying, but well-merited declaration, boasting that he had solicited her favors from no other motive but that he might indulge the ambitious desire of giving a king to Sparta. The offence itself, and the shameless avowal, still more provoking than the offence, excited the keenest resentment in the breast of the injured husband[10]. The magistrates and generals of Sparta, jealous of the fame, and envious of the merit of a stranger, readily sympathized with the misfortune, and encouraged the revenge of Agis; and, as the horrid practice of assassination still disgraced the manners of Greece, orders were sent to Astyochus, who commanded in chief the Peloponnesian forces in Asia, secretly to destroy Alcibiades, whose power defied those laws which in every Grecian republic condemned adulterers to death[11]. But the active and subtile Athenian had secured too faithful domestic intelligence in the principal families of Sparta to become the victim of this execrable design. With his usual address he eluded all the snares of Astyochus; his safety, however, required perpetual vigilance and caution, and he determined to escape from a situation, which subjected him to such irksome constraint.

Publicly banished from Athens, secretly persecuted by Sparta, he had recourse to the friendship of Tissaphernes, who admired his accomplishments, and respected his abilities; which, though far superior in degree, were similar in kind to his own.

[10] Plutarch, II. 49. in Alcibiad.
[11] Lysias in defence of Euphiletus, etc. p. 469.

Tissaphernes,

Tissaphernes was of a temper the more readily to serve a friend, in proportion as he less needed his services. Alcibiades, therefore, carefully concealed from him the dangerous resentment of the Spartans. In the selfish breast of the Persian no attachment could be durable unless founded on interest; and Alcibiades, who had deeply studied his character, began to flatter his avarice, that he might ensure his protection. He informed him, that by allowing the Peloponnesian sailors a drachma, or seven-pence sterling, of daily pay, he treated them with an useless and even dangerous liberality; that the pay given by the Athenians, even in the most flourishing times, amounted only to three oboli; which proceeded, not from a disinclination to reward the skill and valor of their seamen, but from an experience, that if they received more than half a drachma each day, the superfluity would be squandered in such profligate pleasures as enfeebled and corrupted their minds and bodies, and rendered them equally incapable of activity and of discipline. Should the sailors prove dissatisfied with this equitable reduction, the Grecian character afforded an easy expedient for silencing their licentious clamors. It would be sufficient to bribe the naval commanders and a few mercenary orators; and the careless and improvident seamen would submit, without suspicion, the rate of their pay, as well as every other concern, to the influence and authority of those who were accustomed to govern them[16].

[16] Thucyd'd. p. 184, et seqq.

CHAP.
XXL.
Persuades
him to di-
minish his
subsidies
to the
Peloponnesians.

Tissaphernes heard this advice with the attention of an avaricious man to every proposal for saving his money, and so true a judgment had Alcibiades formed of the Greeks, that Hermocrates the Syracusan was the only officer who disdained, meanly and perfidiously, to betray the interest of the men under his command: yet through the influence of his colleagues, the plan of œconomy was universally adopted, and on a future occasion, Tissaphernes boasted that Hermocrates, though more coy, was not less corruptible than others, and that the only reason for which he undertook the patronage of the sailors, was to compel his own reluctance to comply with the exorbitance of his demands. This reproach illustrates the opinion entertained by foreign nations of Grecian virtue; but it is probably an aspersion on the fame of the illustrious Syracusan.

Alienates
him from
the interest of
Sparta.

The intrigues of Alcibiades had sown jealousy and distrust in the Peloponnesian fleet: they had alienated the minds of the troops both from Tissaphernes and their commanders: the Persian was ready to forsake those whom he had learned to despise; and Alcibiades profited of this disposition to insinuate that the alliance of the Lacedæmonians was equally expensive and inconvenient for the great king and his lieutenants. " That these haughty republicans were accustomed to take arms to defend the liberties of Greece, a design totally inconsistent with the views of the Persian court. If the Asiatic Greeks and islanders aspired at independence, and hoped to deliver themselves from Athenian governors and garrisons, without submitting to pay tribute to Persia, they ought to carry on the war at their own expense, since they would alone reap the benefit of its success. But if Tissaphernes purposed to recover the ancient possessions of his master, he must beware of giving a decided superiority to either party, especially to the warlike Spartans. By an attention to preserve the balance even, between the hostile republics, he would force them to exhaust each other. Amidst their domestic contests an opportunity would soon arrive, when Darius, without danger or expense, might crush both, and vindicate his just hereditary claim to the dominion of all Asia."

CHAP. XXI.

These artful representations produced almost an open breach between Tissaphernes and his confederates. The advantage which Athens would derive from this rupture might have paved the way for Alcibiades to return to his country: but he dreaded to encounter that popular fury, whose effects he had fatally experienced, and whose mad resentment no degree of merit could appease; he therefore applied secretly to Pisander, Theramenes, and other persons of distinction in the Athenian camp. To them he deplored the desperate state of public affairs, expatiated on his own credit with Tissaphernes, and insinuated that it might be yet possible to prevent the Phœnician fleet at Aspendus from sailing to assist the enemy. Assuming gradually more boldness, as he perceived the success of his

Alcibiades, in order to pave the way for his return to Athens, conspires against the democracy.

CHAP. XXI.

intrigues, he finally declared that the Athenians might obtain not merely the neutrality, but perhaps the assistance of Artaxerxes, should they consent to abolish their turbulent democracy, so odious to the Persians, and intrust the administration of government to men worthy to negociate with so mighty a monarch.

This measure had been already in agitation both in the city and in the camp.

When the illustrious exile proposed this measure, it is uncertain whether he was acquainted with the secret cabals which had been already formed, both in the city and in the camp, for executing the design which he suggested. The misfortunes, occasioned by the giddy insolence of the multitude, had thrown the principal authority into the hands of the noble and wealthy, who, corrupted by the sweets of temporary power, were desirous of rendering it perpetual. Many prompted by ambition, several moved by inconstancy, a few directed by a just sense of the incurable defects of democracy, were prepared to encounter every danger, that they might overturn the established constitution. In the third and most honorable class was Antiphon, a man of an exalted character, and endowed with extraordinary talents. The irresistible energy of his eloquence was suspected by the people. He appeared not in the courts of justice, nor in the assembly; but his artful and elaborate compositions often saved the lives of his friends. *He* was the invisible agent who governed all the motions of the conspiracy; and when compelled, after the ruin of his party to stand trial for his life, he discovered

THE HISTORY OF GREECE. 165

an activity and force of mind that astonished the most discerning of his contemporaries ". Pisander, Theramenes, and the other leaders of the aristocratical party, warmly approved the views of Alcibiades. The Athenian soldiers likewise, though they detested the impiety, admired the valor, of the illustrious exile, and longed to see him restored to the service of his country. All ranks lamented the dangerous situation of Athens; many thought that their affairs must become desperate, should Tissaphernes command the Phœnician fleet to cooperate with that of Peloponnesus; and many rejoiced in the prospect of a Persian alliance, in consequence of which they would enter at once into the pay of that wealthy satrap ".

[17] Thucydid. l. viii. p. 600. A few lines above, Thucydides describes the character of Antiphon with expressive energy: ανηρ Αθηναιων των καθ' ἑαυτον αρετῃ τε ουδενος ὑστερος, και κρατιστος ενθυμηθηναι γενομενος, και ἁ γνοιη ειπειν. "An Athenian, in virtue second to no man then living, endowed with the greatest vigor of thought, and the greatest power of expression." Plutarch in the very inaccurate and imperfect work, entitled, The Lives of the Ten Orators, tells us, that Antiphon was the first who wrote institutions of oratory; and that his pleadings were the most ancient that had come down to posterity. The character given by Plutarch of the writings of Antiphon agrees with the high commendation of Thucydides.

[18] What influence this consideration must have had, may be conjectured from the information of Andocides, Orat. iii. who says, that in the course of this war the Spartans received, from their Persian allies, subsidies to the amount of five thousand talents, about a million sterling. The sum is prodigious, considering the value of money in that age.

CHAP. XXI.
Phrynichus counterplots Alcibiades.

One man, the perfonal enemy of Alcibiades, alone oppofed the general current. But this man was Phrynichus, whofe prudent firmnefs as a commander we have already had occafion to remark. The courage with which he invited dangers many have equalled, but none ever furpaffed the boldnefs with which he extricated himfelf from difficulties. When he perceived that his colleagues were deaf to every objection againft recalling the friend of Tiffaphernes, he fecretly informed the Spartan admiral Aftyochus, of the intrigues which were carrying on to the difadvantage of his country. Daring as this treachery was, Phrynichus addreffed a traitor not lefs perfidious than himfelf. Aftyochus was become the penfioner and creature of Tiffaphernes, to whom he communicated the intelligence. The Perfian again communicated it to his favorite Alcibiades, who complained in ftrong terms to the Athenians of the bafenefs and villany of Phrynichus. The latter exculpated himfelf with confummate addrefs; but as the return of Alcibiades might prove fatal to his fafety, he ventured, a fecond time, to write to Aftyochus, gently reproaching him with his breach of confidence, and explaining by what means he might furprife the whole Athenian fleet at Samos; an exploit that muft for ever eftablifh his fame and fortune. Aftyochus again betrayed the fecret to Tiffaphernes and Alcibiades; but before *their* letters could be conveyed to the Athenian camp, Phrynichus, who, by fome unknown channel, was informed of this second treachery, anticipated the dangerous discovery, by apprizing the Athenians of the enemy's design to surprise their fleet. They had scarcely employed the proper means to counteract that purpose when messengers came from Alcibiades to announce the horrid perfidy of a wretch who had basely sacrificed to private resentment the last hope of his country. But the messengers arrived too late; the prior information of Phrynichus, as well as the bold and singular wickedness of his design, which no common degree of evidence was thought sufficient to prove, were sustained as arguments for his exculpation; and it was believed that Alcibiades had made use of a stratagem most infamous in itself, but not unexampled among the Greeks, for destroying a man whom he detested[19].

The opposition of Phrynichus, though it retarded the designs of Alcibiades, prevented not the measures of Pisander and his associates for abolishing the democracy. The soldiers at Samos were induced, by the reasons above mentioned, to acquiesce in the resolution of their generals. But a more difficult task remained; to deprive the people of Athens of their liberty, which, since the expulsion of the family of Pisistratus, they had enjoyed an hundred years. Pisander headed the deputation which was sent from the camp to the city to effect this important revolution. He acquainted the extraordinary assembly, summoned on that

[19] Thucydid. p. 187—190.

CHAP. XXI.

occasion in the theatre of Bacchus, of the measures which had been adopted by their soldiers and fellow-citizens at Samos. The compact band [18] of conspirators warmly approved the example, but loud murmurs of discontent resounded in different quarters of that spacious theatre. Pisander asked the reason of this disapprobation. "Had his opponents any thing better to propose? If they had, let them come forward and explain the grounds of their dissent: but, above all, let them explain how they could save themselves, their families, and their country, unless they complied with the demand of Tissaphernes. The imperious voice of necessity was superior to law; and when the actual danger had ceased, they might re-establish their ancient constitution." The opponents of Pisander were unable or afraid to reply: and the assembly passed a decree, investing ten ambassadors with full powers to treat with the Persian satrap.

Negociation with Tissaphernes. Olymp. xcii. 1.
A. C. 412.

Soon after the arrival of the Peloponnesian fleet on the coast of Asia, the Spartan commanders had concluded, in the name of their republic, a treaty with Tissaphernes; in which it was stipulated, that the subsidies should be regularly paid by the king of Persia, and that the Peloponnesian forces should employ their utmost endeavours to recover, for

---

[18] Or rather bands, according to Thucydides. Pisander was at pains to gain over to his views τας ξυνωμοσιας, αιπερ ετυγχανον πρστερον εν τη πολει ουσαι επι δικαις και αρχαις. "The factions or juntos already formed in Athens, with a view to thrust themselves into the seats of judicature and the great offices of state." Thucydid. p. 192.

that monarch, the dominions of his ancestors, which had been long unjustly usurped, and cruelly insulted, by the Athenians. This treaty seemed so honorable to the great king, that his lieutenant could not venture openly to infringe it. It is possible, that in the interval between his intrigues with Alcibiades, and the arrival of the Athenian ambassadors at Magnesia, the place of his usual residence, Tissaphernes might receive fresh instructions from his court to make good his agreement with the Spartans. Perhaps the crafty satrap never entertained any serious thoughts of an alliance with the Athenians, although he sufficiently relished the advice given him by Alcibiades to weaken both parties. But whatever motive determined him, it is certain that he showed a disinclination to enter into any negociation with the Athenian ambassadors. Alarmed at the decay of his influence with the Persians, on which he had built the flattering hopes of returning to his country, Alcibiades employed all the resources of his genius to conceal his disgrace. By solicitations, entreaties, and the meanest compliances, he obtained an audience for his fellow-citizens. As the agent of Tissaphernes, he then proposed the conditions on which they might obtain the friendship of the great king. Several demands were made, demands most disgraceful to the name of Athens: to all of which the ambassadors submitted. They even agreed to surrender the whole coast of Ionia to its ancient sovereign. But when the artful Athenian (fearful lest they should, on any terms, admit the treaty which

CHAP. XXI.

Artifices of Alcibiades.

CHAP.
XXI.

Tissaphernes was resolved on no terms to grant) demanded that the Persian fleets should be allowed to sail, undisturbed, in the Grecian seas, the ambassadors, well knowing that should this condition be complied with, no treaty could hinder Greece from becoming a province of Persia, expressed their indignation in very unguarded language, and left the assembly in disgust. This imprudence enabled Alcibiades to affirm, with some appearance of truth, that their own anger and obstinacy, not the reluctance of Tissaphernes, had obstructed the negociation, which was precisely the issue of the affair most favorable to his views[11].

The democracy overturned in Athens.
Olymp. xcii. 2.
A. C. 411.

His artifices succeeded, but were not attended with the consequences expected from them. The Athenians, both in the camp and city, perceived, by this transaction, that his credit with the Persians was less than he represented it; and the aristocratical faction were glad to get rid of a man, whose restless ambition rendered him a dangerous associate. They persisted, however, with great activity, in executing their purpose; of which Phrynichus, who had opposed them only from hatred of Alcibiades, became an active abettor. When persuasion was ineffectual, they had recourse to violence. Androcles, Hyperbolus[12], and other

[11] Thucydid. L. viii. p. 593.
[12] Thucydides paints his character in few words: Τυρβολον τε των Αθηναιων, μοχθηρον ανθρωπον στρατευμενον η δια δυναμιος και αξιωματος φοβον, αλλα δια πονηριαν και αισχυνην της πολεως. "One Hyperbolus, a worthless fellow, and banished by the Ostracism, not from fear of his power and dignity, but on account of his extreme

licentious demagogues, were aſſaſſinated. The people of Athens, ignorant of the ſtrength of the conſpirators, and ſurpriſed to find in the number many whom they leaſt ſuſpected, were reſtrained by inactive timidity, or fluctuated in doubtful ſuſpenſe. The cabal alone acted with union and with vigor; and difficult as it ſeemed to ſubvert the Athenian democracy, which had ſubſiſted an hundred years with unexampled glory, yet this deſign was undertaken and accompliſhed by the enterpriſing activity of Piſander, the artful eloquence of Theramenes, the firm intrepidity of Phrynichus, and the ſuperintending wiſdom of Antiphon [15].

He it was who formed the plan, and regulated the mode of attack, which was carried on by his aſſociates. In a deliberation concerning the means of retrieving the affairs of the public, Piſander propoſed the electing of ten men, who ſhould be charged with the important truſt of preparing and digeſting reſolutions, to be on an appointed day laid before the aſſembly of the people. When the day arrived, the commiſſioners had but one reſolution to propoſe: "That every citizen ſhould be free to offer his opinion, however contrary to law, without fear of impeachment or trial;" a matter eſſential to the intereſts of the cabal, ſince by a ſtrange contradiction in government, the

Government of the four hundred.

profligacy, and his being a diſgrace to the city. " The Oſtraciſm was thought to be for ever diſgraced by being applied to ſuch an unworthy object, and thenceforth laid aſide. See Plut. in Nicia, and Ariſtoph. in Pac. ver. 680.

[15] Thucydid. ibid. et Lyſias adverſ. Agorat.

CHAP.
XXI.

Athenian orators and statesmen were liable to prosecution " before the ordinary courts of justice, for such speeches and decrees as had been approved and confirmed by the assembly. In consequence of this act of indemnity, Pisander and his party boldly declared, that neither the spirit nor the forms of the established constitution (which had recently subjected them to such a weight of misfortunes) suited the present dangerous and alarming crisis. That it was necessary to new-model the whole fabric of government; for which purpose five persons (whose names he read) ought to be appointed by the people, to chuse an hundred others; each of whom should select three associates; and the four hundred thus chosen, men of dignity and opulence, who would serve their country without fee or reward, ought immediately to be invested with the majesty of the republic. They alone should conduct the administration uncontrolled, and assemble, as often as seemed proper, five thousand citizens, whom they judged most worthy of being consulted in the management of public affairs. This extraordinary proposal was accepted without opposition: the partisans of democracy dreaded the strength of the cabal; and the undiscerning multitude, dazzled by the imposing name of five thousand, a number far exceeding the ordinary assemblies of Athens, perceived not that they surrendered their liberties to the artifice of an ambitious faction ".

¹⁴ By the γραϕη παρανομων. See Chap. xlii.
¹⁵ Thucydid. et Lysias, ubi supra.

But the conduct of the four hundred tyrants (for historians have justly adopted the language of Athenian resentment) soon opened the eyes and understanding of the most thoughtless. They abolished every vestige of ancient freedom; employed mercenary troops levied from the small islands of the Ægean, to overawe the multitude, and to intimidate, in some instances to destroy, their real or suspected enemies. Instead of seizing the opportunity of annoying the Peloponnesians, enraged at the treachery of Tissaphernes, and mutinous for want of pay and subsistence, they sent ambassadors to solicit peace from the Spartans on the most dishonorable terms. Their tyranny rendered them odious in the city, and their cowardice made them contemptible in the camp at Samos. Their cruelty and injustice were described, and exaggerated, by the fugitives who continually arrived in that island. The generous youth, employed in the sea and land service, were impatient of the indignities offered to their fellow-citizens. The same indignities might be inflicted on themselves, if they did not vindicate their freedom. These secret murmurs broke out into loud and licentious clamors, which were encouraged by the approbation of the Samians. Thrasybulus and Thrasyllus, two officers of high merit and distinction, though not actually intrusted with a share in the principal command [16], gave activity and boldness

[16] Neither generals nor admirals; for Thrasybulus only commanded a galley; and Thrasyllus served in the heavy-armed infantry;

CHAP.
XXI.

The former conduct of Alcibiades to the Athenian camp.

to the infurgents. The abettors of the new government were attacked by furprife: thirty of the moſt criminal were put to death, feveral others were baniſhed, democracy was re-eſtabliſhed in the camp, and the foldiers were bound by oath to maintain their hereditary government againſt the confpiracy of domeſtic foes, and to act with vigor and unanimity againſt the public enemy.

Thrafybulus, who headed this fuccefsful and meritorious fedition, had a mind to conceive, a tongue to perfuade, and a hand to execute, the moſt daring defigns. He exhorted the foldiers not to defpair of effecting in the capital the fame revolution which they had produced in the camp. But ſhould they fail in that defign they ought no longer to obey a city which had neither wealth nor wifdom, neither fupplies nor good counfel to fend them. They were themfelves more numerous than the fubjects of the four hundred, and better provided in all things neceſſary for war. They poſſeſſed an iſland which had formerly contended with Athens for the command of the fea, and which, it was hoped, they might defend againſt every foe, foreign and domeſtic. But were they compelled to forfake it, they had ſtill reafon to expect that, with an hundred ſhips of war, and with fo many brave men, they might acquire an eſtabliſhment not lefs valuable elfewhere, in which they would enjoy, undiſturbed, the invaluable

whether as an officer, or in the ranks, the expreſſion leaves uncertain. The fcholiaſt, however, confiders ἐπλήσυντες as fynonymous with τε ὁπλίτης ἄρχιστε. Thucydid. p. 606.

THE HISTORY OF GREECE. 175

possession of liberty. Their most immediate concern was to recal Alcibiades, who had been deceived and disgraced by the tyrants, and who not only felt with peculiar sensibility, but could resent with becoming dignity, the wrongs of his country and his own. The advice of Thrasybulus was approved; soon after he sailed to Magnesia, and returned in company with Alcibiades.

Near four years had elapsed since the eloquent son of Clinias had spoken in an Athenian assembly. Being presented by Thrasybulus to his fellow-citizens, he began by accusing his fortune, and lamenting his calamities. "Yet his banishment ought not to affect him with permanent sorrow, since it had furnished him with an opportunity to serve the cause of his country. This event, otherwise unfortunate, had procured him the acquaintance and friendship of Tissaphernes; who, moved by his entreaties, had withheld the stipulated pay from the Peloponnesian forces, and who, he doubted not, would continue his good offices to the Athenians, supply them with every thing requisite for maintaining the war, and even summon the Phœnician fleet to their assistance." These were magnificent but flattering promises. In making them, Alcibiades however did not consult merely the dictates of vanity. They raised his credit with the army, who immediately saluted him general[17]; they widened the breach between

[17] Μιτα τως προτηρων — They associated him with the former commanders. But Thucydides immediately adds, και τα πραγματα παντα επιτρεψαν, and referred every thing to his management. p. 675.

CHAP.
XXI.

He addresses his countrymen.

176 THE HISTORY OF GREECE.

CHAP. XXI.

His message to the tyrants.

Tissaphernes and the Spartans; and they struck terror (when his speech got abroad) into the tyrants of Athens, who had provoked the resentment of a man capable to subvert their usurpation.

Alcibiades left the care of the troops to his colleagues Thrasybulus and Thrasyllus, and withdrew himself from the applauses of his admiring countrymen, on pretence of concerting with Tissaphernes the system of their future operations. But his principal motive was to show himself to the Persian, in the new and illustrious character with which he was invested; for having raised his authority among the Athenians by his influence with the satrap, he expected to strengthen this influence by the support of that authority. Before he returned to the camp, ambassadors had been sent by the tyrants, to attempt a negociation with the partisans of democracy, who, inflamed by continual reports of the indignities and cruelties committed in Athens, prepared to sail thither to protect their friends and take vengeance on their enemies. Alcibiades judiciously opposed this rash resolution, which must have left the Hellespont, Ionia, and the islands, at the mercy of the hostile fleet. But he commanded the ambassadors to deliver to their masters a short but pithy message: "That they must divest themselves of their illegal power, and restore the ancient constitution. If they delayed obedience, he would sail to the Piræus, and deprive them of their authority and their lives [a]."

[a] Thucydid. ibid. et Plut. lib. 54. in Vit. Alcibiad.

When

When this message was reported at Athens, it added to the disorder and confusion in which that unhappy city was involved. The four hundred, who had acted with unanimity in usurping the government, soon disagreed about the administration, and split into factions, which persecuted each other as furiously as both had persecuted the people [20]. Theramenes and Aristocrates condemned and opposed the tyrannical measures of their colleagues. The perfidious Phrynichus was slain: both parties prepared for taking arms; and the horrors of a Corcyrean sedition were ready to be renewed in Athens, when the old men, the children, the women, and strangers, interposed for the safety of a city which had long been the ornament of Greece, the terror of Persia, and the admiration of the world [19].

CHAP. XXI.
Tumults in Athens.

Had the public enemy availed themselves of this opportunity to assault the Piræus, Athens could not have been saved from immediate destruction. But the Peloponnesian forces at Miletus, long clamorous and discontented, had broken out into open mutiny, when they heard of the recal of Alcibiades, and the hostile intentions of Tissaphernes. To the duplicity of the satrap, and the treachery of their own captains, they justly ascribed the want of pay and subsistence, and all the misfortunes which they felt or dreaded. Their resentment was violent and implacable. They destroyed the Persian fortifications in the neighbourhood of

Mutiny in the Peloponnesian camp.

[20] Lysias adv. Agorat. [19] Thucydid. p. 610.

CHAP. XXI.

Miletus; they put the garrisons to the sword; their treacherous commander, Astyochus, saved his life by flying to an altar; nor was the tumult appeased until the guilty were removed from their sight, and Myndarus, an officer of approved valor and fidelity, arrived from Sparta to assume the principal command [11].

Amidst the tumults in Athens, the Peloponnesian fleet appears on the coast.

The dreadful consequences which must have resulted to the Athenians, if, during the fury of their sedition, the enemy had attacked them with a fleet of an hundred and fifty sail, may be conceived by the terror inspired by a much smaller Peloponnesian squadron of only forty-two vessels, commanded by the Spartan Hegesandridas. The friends of the constitution had assembled in the spacious theatre of Bacchus. Messengers passed between them and the partisans of Antiphon and Pisander, who had convened in a distant quarter of the city. The most important matters were in agitation, when the alarm was given that some Peloponnesian ships had been seen on the coast. Both assemblies were immediately dissolved. All ranks of men hastened to the Piræus; manned the vessels in the harbour; launched others; and prepared thirty-six for taking the sea. When Hegesandridas perceived the ardent opposition which he must encounter in attempting to land, he doubled the promontory of Sunium, and sailed towards the fertile island of Eubœa, from which, since the fortification of Decelia, the Athenians had derived

[11] Thucydid. p. 612.

far more plentiful supplies than from the defolated territory of Attica. To defend a country which formed their principal refource, they failed in purfuit of the enemy and obferved them next day near the fhore of Eretria, the moſt confiderable town in the ifland.

The Eubœans, who had long watched an opportunity to revolt, fupplied the Peloponnefian fquadron with all neceffaries in abundance; but inftead of furnifhing a market to the Athenians, they retired from the coaſt on their approach. The commanders were obliged to weaken their ſtrength, by detaching feveral parties into the country to procure provifions; Hegefandridas feized this opportunity to attack them: moſt of the fhips were taken; the crews fwam to land; many were cruelly murdered by the Eretrians, from whom they expected protection; and fuch only furvived as took refuge in the Athenian garrifons fcattered over the ifland[11].

The news of this misfortune were moſt alarming to the Athenians. Neither the invafion of Xerxes, nor even the defeat in Sicily, occafioned fuch terrible confternation. They dreaded the immediate defection of Eubœa; they had no more fhips to launch; no means of refifting their multiplied enemies: the city was divided againſt the camp, and divided againſt itſelf. Yet the magnanimous firmneſs of Theramenes did not allow the friends of liberty to defpair. He encouraged them

CHAP. XXL.

Battle of Eretria.

Democracy reeſtabliſhed in Athens. Olymp. xcii. 2. A. C. 411.

[11] Thucydid. p. 522.

CHAP.
XXI.

to disburden the republic of its domestic foes, who had summoned, or who were at least believed to have summoned, the assistance of the Lacedæmonian fleet, that they might be enabled to enslave their fellow-citizens. Antiphon, Pisander, and others most obnoxious, seasonably escaped; the rest submitted. A decree was passed, recalling Alcibiades, and approving the conduct of the troops at Samos. The sedition ceased. The democracy, which had been interrupted four months, was restored; and such are the resources of a free government, that even this violent fermentation was not unproductive of benefit to the state. The Athenians completed whatever had been left imperfect in former reformations[11]; and determined to defend, to the last extremity, the ancient glory of the republic.

The Athenians victorious at sea. Olymp. xcii. 2. A. C. 411.

By the imprudent or perfidious conduct of their commanders, and the seditious spirit of their troops, the Peloponnesians lost a seasonable opportunity to terminate the war with equal advantage and honor; and having neglected the prosperous current of their fortune, they were compelled long and laboriously to strive against an unfavorable stream.

[11] The government was brought back to its original principles, as established by Solon. Among other salutary regulations, it was enacted, that no one should receive a salary for any public magistracy. "And now," says Thucydides, "for the first time, in the present age at least, the Athenians modelled their government aright; and this enabled Athens again to raise her head." Thucydid. p. 623. It is remarkable, that neither Diodorus, Plutarch, nor any of the orators make the least mention of those salutary regulations, which, however, failed not long after the return of Alcibiades.

The doubtful Tissaphernes hesitated between the part of an open enemy, or a treacherous ally; the Spartans, who had formerly rejected the friendship, now courted the protection, of his rival Pharnabazus; to whose northern province they sailed with the principal strength of their armament, leaving only a small squadron at Miletus, to defend their southern acquisitions. The Athenians, animated by the manly counsels of Thrasybulus and Thrasyllus, the generous defenders of their freedom, proceeded northwards in pursuit of the enemy; and the important straits, which join the Euxine and Ægean seas, became, and long continued, the scene of conflict. In the twenty-first winter of the war, a year already distinguished by the dissolution and revival of their democracy, the Athenians prevailed in three successive engagements, the event of which became continually more decisive. In the first, which was fought in the narrow channel between Sestos and Abydus, the advantages were in some measure balanced, since Thrasybulus took twenty Peloponnesian ships, with the loss of fifteen of his own. But the glory remained entire to the Athenians, who repelled the enemy, and offered to renew the battle[10]. Not long afterwards, they intercepted a squadron of fourteen Rhodian vessels, near Cape Rhegium. The islanders defended themselves with their usual bravery. Myndarus beheld the engagement from the distance of eight miles, while he performed his morning devotions to

[10] Thucydid. l. viii. p. 624.

182 THE HISTORY OF GREECE.

CHAP. XXI.

Minerva in the lofty temple of Ilium. Alarmed for the safety of his friends, he rushed from that sacred edifice, and hastened with great diligence to the shore, that he might launch his ships, and prevent, by speedy assistance, the capture or destruction of the Rhodians[11]. The principal Athenian squadron attacked him near the shore of Abydus. The engagement was fought from morning till night, and still continued doubtful, when the arrival of eighteen gallies, commanded by Alcibiades, turned the scale of victory. The escape of the Peloponnesians was favored by the bravery of Pharnabazus, who, at the head of his Barbarian troops, had been an impatient spectator of the combat. He gallantly rode into the sea, encouraging his men with his voice, his arm, and his example. The Spartan admiral drew up the greatest part of his fleet along the shore and prepared to resist the assailants; but the Athenians, satisfied with the advantages already obtained, sailed to Sestos, carrying with them a valuable prize, thirty Peloponnesian gallies, as well as fifteen of their own, which they had lost in the former engagement. Thrasyllus was sent to Athens, that he might communicate the good news, and raise such supplies of men and money as could be expected from that exhausted city[12].

Alcibiades surprises, and takes the whole

The Spartans yielded possession of the sea, which they hoped soon to recover, and retired to the friendly harbours of Cyzicus, to repair their

[11] Xenoph. Hellen. l. 1. c. 1. Diodor. xiii. p. 314.   [12] Id. Ibid.

shattered fleet; while the Athenians profited of the fame of their victory, and the terror of their arms, to demand contributions from the numerous and wealthy towns in that neighbourhood. The several divisions returned to Sestos, having met with very indifferent success in their design; nor, without obtaining more decisive and important advantages, could they expect to intimidate such strongly fortified places as Byzantium, Selembria, Perinthus, on the European, or Lampsacus, Parium, Chalcedon, on the Asiatic, coast. It was determined therefore, chiefly by the advice of Alcibiades, to attack the enemy at Cyzicus; for which purpose they sailed, with eighty gallies, to the small island of Proconnesus, near the western extremity of the Propontis, and ten miles distant from the station of the Peloponnesian fleet. Alcibiades surprised sixty vessels in a dark and rainy morning as they were manœuvring at a distance from the harbour, and skilfully intercepted their retreat. As the day cleared up, the rest sailed forth to their assistance; the action became general; the Athenians obtained a complete victory, and their valor was rewarded by the capture of the whole Peloponnesian fleet, except the Syracusan ships, which were burned, in the face of a victorious enemy, by the enterprising Hermocrates. The circumstances and consequences of this important action were related in few, but expressive words, to the Spartan senate, in a letter written by Hippocrates, the second in command, and intercepted by the Athenians; "All is lost;

CHAP.
XXI.

The Athenians diligently improve their advantages.
Olymp.
xcII. 3.
A. C. 410.

our ships are taken; Myndarus is slain; the men want bread; we know not what to do"."

The fatal disaster at Cyzicus prevented the Peloponnesians from obstructing, during the following year, the designs of the enemy, who took possession of that wealthy sea-port, as well as of the strong city Perinthus; raised a large contribution on Selembria; and fortified Chrysopolis, a small town of Chalcedonia, only three miles distant from Byzantium. In this new fortress they placed a considerable body of troops; and guarded the neighbouring strait with a squadron of thirty sail, commanded by Theramenes and Eubulus, and destined to exact, as tribute, a tenth from all ships which sailed through the Bosphorus into the Euxine sea¹². The Peloponnesians were assisted by Pharnabazus in equipping a new fleet; but were deprived of the wise counsels of Hermocrates, whose abilities were well fitted both to prepare and to employ the resources of war. The success of the Asiatic expedition had not corresponded to the sanguine hopes of his countrymen; the insolent populace accused the incapacity of their commanders; and a mandate was sent from Syracuse, depriving

¹¹ Xenoph. Hellen. L. L c. i. et Plut. p. 60. in Alcibiad.

¹² It is well known, that Mahomet the Second obtained the same end, by fortifying two castles, one on the Asiatic, and another on the European side. That next to Chrysopolis is called by the modern Greeks Neocastron; but the name of the town itself is now changed to Scutari, a place deemed by the Turks one of the suburbs of Constantinople.

TOURNEFORT, Lettre 11.

THE HISTORY OF GREECE. 185

them of their office, and punishing them with banishment. The conduct of Hermocrates is worthy of admiration. Having called an assembly, he deplored his hard fortune, but recommended the most submissive obedience to the authority of the republic. He then exhorted the sailors to name temporary commanders, till the arrival of those who had been appointed by their country. But the assembly, especially the captains and pilots, tumultuously called out, "That he and his colleagues ought to continue in the command." Hermocrates then conjured them "not to rebel against the government. When they should return home, they would then enjoy a fair opportunity to do justice to their admirals, by recounting the battles which they had won, by enumerating the ships which they had taken, and by relating how their own courage, and the conduct of their commanders, had entitled them to the most honorable place in every engagement by sea and land." At the earnest and unanimous entreaty of the assembly, he consented, however, to retain his authority, till the arrival of his successors. His colleagues imitated the example; and soon after this memorable scene, Demarchus, Myseo, and Potamis, the admirals named by the state, took the command of the Syracusan forces. Yet the soldiers and sailors would not allow their beloved leaders to depart, before taking in their presence a solemn oath to revoke their unjust banishment, whenever they themselves returned to Syracuse. On Hermocrates in particular, the captains and pilots bestowed many

CHAP. XXI.

Admirable behaviour of Hermocrates the Syracusan.

distinguished tokens of their affection and respect, which his behaviour had justly merited; for every morning and evening he had called them together, communicated his designs, asked their opinion and advice, reviewed the past, and concerted the future, operations of the war; while his popular manners and condescending affability secured the love of those who respected his skill, his vigilance, and his courage[19].

Thrasyllus, at first successful, is defeated in the battle of Ephesus. Olymp. xciii. 4. A. C. 409.

Meanwhile Thrasyllus obtained at Athens the supplies which he had gone to solicit; supplies far more powerful than he had reason to expect. They consisted in a thousand heavy-armed men, an hundred horse, and fifty gallies, manned by five thousand experienced seamen. That the sailors might be usefully employed on every emergency at sea or land, they were provided with the small and light bucklers, the darts, swords, and javelins, appropriated to the Grecian targeteers, who, uniting strength and velocity, formed an intermediate and useful order between the archers and pikemen. With these forces, Thrasyllus sailed to Samos, hoping to render the twenty-third campaign not less glorious than the preceding; and ambitious to rival, by his victories in the central and southern parts of the Asiatic coast, the fame acquired by Alcibiades and Thrasybulus in the north. His first operations were successful. He took Colophon, with several places of less note, in Ionia; penetrated into the heart of Lydia, burning the corn

[19] Xenoph. p. 431.

and villages; and returned to the shore, driving before him a numerous body of slaves, and other valuable booty. His courage was increased by the want of resistance on the part of Tissaphernes, whose province he had invaded; of the Peloponnesian forces at Miletus; and of the revolted colonies of Athens. He resolved, therefore, to attack the beautiful and flourishing city of Ephesus, which was then the principal ornament and defence of the Ionic coast. While his soldiers, in separate divisions, were making their approaches to the walls of that place, the enemy assembled from every quarter to defend the majesty of Ephesian Diana. A vigorous sally of the townsmen increased the strength of Tissaphernes and the Peloponnesians, the latter of whom had been seasonably reinforced by a considerable squadron from Sicily. The Athenians were defeated, with the loss of three hundred men; and retiring from the field of battle, they sought refuge in their ships, and prepared to sail towards the Hellespont[10].

During the voyage thither, they fell in with twenty Sicilian gallies, of which they took four, and pursued the rest to Ephesus. Having soon afterwards reached the Hellespont, they found the Athenian armament at Lampsacus, where Alcibiades thought proper to muster the whole military and naval forces: but, on this occasion, the northern army gave a remarkable proof of pride or spirit. They, who had ever been victorious,

[10] Xenoph. Hellen. L. I. p. 436.

refused to rank with the soldiers of Thrasyllus, who had been so shamefully foiled before the walls of Ephesus. They submitted, however, though not without reluctance, to live in the same winter-quarters; from which they made a conjunct expedition against Abydus. Pharnabazus defended the place with a numerous body of Persian cavalry. The disgraced troops of Thrasyllus rejoiced in an opportunity to retrieve their honor. They attacked, repelled, and routed the enemy. Their victory decided the fate of Abydus, and their courage was approved by the army of Alcibiades, who embraced them as fellow-soldiers and friends.

Alcibiades takes Byzantium. His success by sea and land.
Olymp. xciii. 1.
A. C. 409.

For several years the measures of the Athenians had been almost uniformly successful; but the twenty-fourth campaign was distinguished by peculiar favors of fortune. The invasion of Sicily by the Carthaginians prevented that island from sending any effectual assistance to their Peloponnesian allies. The dangerous revolt of the Medes with-held the Persian reinforcements, which were necessary to support the arms of Pharnabazus [11]. Both nations were repeatedly defeated by the Athenians, driven from their encampments and fortresses near the shore, and pursued into the inland country, which was plundered and desolated by the victors. The Athenians returned in triumph to attack the fortified cities, which still declined submission; an undertaking in which Alcibiades displayed the wonderful resources of his extraordinary genius.

[11] Diodorus, l. xiii.

By gradual approaches, by sudden assaults, by surprise, by treason, or by stratagem, he in a few months became master of Chalcedon, Selembria, and at last of Byzantium itself. His naval success was equally conspicuous. The Athenians again commanded the sea. The small squadrons fitted out by the enemy successively fell into their power; and these multiplied captures, which were made with little difficulty, accumulated the trophies of the well-fought battles which we have already described. It was computed by the partisans of Alcibiades, that, since assuming the command, he had taken or destroyed two hundred Syracusan and Peloponnesian gallies; and his superiority of naval strength enabled him to raise such contributions, both in the Euxine and Mediterranean, as abundantly supplied his fleet and army with every necessary article of subsistence and accommodation [1].

CHAP. XXI.

While the Athenian arms were crowned with such glory abroad, the Attic territory was continually harassed by king Agis, and the Lacedæmonian troops posted at Decelia. Their bold and sudden incursions frequently threatened the safety of the city itself; the desolated lands afforded no advantage to the ruined proprietors; nor could the Athenians venture without their walls, to celebrate their accustomed festivals. Alcibiades, animated by his foreign victories, hoped to relieve the domestic sufferings of his country; and after an absence of many years, distinguished by such a

His triumphant return to Athens. Olymp. xciii. 2. A. C. 407.

[1] Xenoph. Hellen. Diodor. l. xiii. Plut. in Alcibiad.

CHAP. XIII.

variety of fortune, eagerly longed to revisit his native city, and to enjoy the rewards and honors usually bestowed by the Greeks on successful valor. This celebrated voyage, which several ancient historians studiously decorated with every circumstance of naval triumph [1], was performed in the twenty-fifth summer of the war. Notwithstanding all his services, the cautious son of Clinias, instructed by adversity, declined to land in the Piræus, until he was informed that the assembly had repealed the decrees against him, formally revoked his banishment, and prolonged the term of his command. Even after this agreeable intelligence he was still unable to conquer his well-founded distrust of the variable and capricious humors of the people; nor would he approach the crowded shore, till he observed, in the midst of the multitude, his principal friends and relations inviting him by their voice and action. He then landed amidst the universal acclamations of the spectators, who, unattentive to the naval pomp, and regardless of the other commanders, fixed their eyes only on Alcibiades. Next day an extraordinary assembly was summoned, by order of the magistrates, that he might explain and justify his apparent misconduct, and receive the rewards due to his acknowledged merit. The public anticipated his apology, by contrasting the melancholy situation of affairs when Alcibiades assumed the command, with the actual condition of the republic. "At the former

[1] Duris apud Plut. in Alcibiad.

period Athens yielded the command of the sea: the enemy were every where victorious; the state was oppressed by foreign war, torn by sedition, without resources, and without hope. The address and dexterity of Alcibiades were alone capable to have disunited the councils, to have weakened and afterwards repelled the efforts, of a powerful confederacy; his activity and courage could alone have animated the dejection of the citizens to pursue the measures of offensive war: his abilities, his virtue, and his fortune could alone have rendered those measures successful."

Before judges so favorably disposed to hear him, Alcibiades found no difficulty to make his defence; but it was difficult both for him and his friends to moderate the excessive transports of the people, who would have loaded their favorite with honors incompatible with the genius of a free republic, and which might, therefore, have proved dangerous to his future safety. He received, with pleasure, the crowns and garlands, with other accustomed pledges of public gratitude and admiration; but he respectfully declined the royal sceptre, expressing a firm resolution to maintain the hereditary freedom of his country". Athens required not a king, but a general with undivided power, capable of restoring the ancient splendor of the commonwealth. To this illustrious rank, which had been filled by Themistocles and Cimon, the son of Clinias might justly aspire. He was

CHAP. XXI.

His reception there.

" Com. Isocrat. Orat. pro Alcibiad. et Plut. in Alcibiad.

CHAP.
XXI.

appointed commander in chief by sea and land ". An hundred gallies were equipped, and transports were prepared for fifteen hundred heavy-armed men, with a proportional body of cavalry.

The Eleusinian mysteries.

Several months " had passed in these preparations, when the Eleusinian festival approached; a time destined to commemorate and to diffuse the temporal and spiritual gifts of the goddess Ceres, originally bestowed on the Athenians, and by them communicated to the rest of Greece ". Corn, wine, and oil, were the principal productions of Attica; each of which had been introduced into that country by the propitious intervention of a divinity, whose festival was distinguished by appropriated honors. Minerva, who had given not only the olive, but what was regarded as far more valuable, her peculiar protection to the city of Athens, was rewarded with innumerable solemnities. Various also were the professions of gratitude expressed, in stated days of the spring and autumn, to the

---

" Ανωρεθη απαντων ηγεμων αυτοκρατωρ. "He was chosen absolute commander of all." Xenoph. p. 320.

" From the festivals Plynteria and Eleusina, mentioned in the text, it appears that he arrived in July, and failed in November.

" Meursius, apud Gronov. Thesaur. has collected all the passages in ancient writers respecting this festival. It is said to have been celebrated in the month Boedromion, which, according to Father Petaut, answers to our November. But as the Attic year was lunar, the months of that year could not exactly correspond to those of ours. In the computation of their months, the Greeks agreed not with other nations, nor even among themselves. Vid. Plut. in Vit. Romul. et Aristid.

generous

generous author of the vine. The worship of Ceres CHAP.
returned, indeed, less frequently; but was partly, XXI.
on that account, the more solemn and awful; and
partly, because distinguished by the Eleusinian
mysteries, those hidden treasures of wisdom and
happiness, which were poured out on the initiated
in the temple of Eleusis. Fourteen " centuries before the Christian æra, the goddess, it is said, communicated these invaluable rites to Eumolpus and
Keryx, two virtuous men, who had received her in
the form of an unknown traveller with pious hofpitality ". Their descendants, the Eumolpidæ and
Kerykes, continued the ministers and guardians of
this memorable institution, which was finally abolished by the great Theodosius, after it had lasted
eighteen hundred years ". The candidates for ini-
tiation were prepared by watching, abstinence, facrifice, and prayer; and before revealing to them
the divine secrets, the most awful silence was enjoined them. Yet enough transpired among the
prophane vulgar to enable us still to collect, from
impartial " and authentic testimony, that the

" Marsh. Arund. Epoch. 14.
" Diodor. l. v. Isocrat. Panegyr. Pollux, L. viii. c. ix.
" Zosim. Hist. l. iv.
" I say *impartial*, because Isocrates, the scholar of Socrates,
cannot be supposed to exaggerate the merit of ceremonies, which his
master is said to have despised. The passage is remarkable: "Though
what I am going to relate may be disfigured by tradition and fable,
the substance of it is not the less deserving of your regard. When
Ceres travelled to Attica in quest of her daughter, she received the
most hospitable treatment, and those particular good offices which are
known to the initiated. The goddess was not ungrateful for such

VOL. III. O

CHAP. XXI.

mysteries of Ceres expressed by external signs the immortality of the human soul, and the rewards prepared in a future life for the virtuous servants of heaven. The secrecy enjoined by her ministers, so unworthy the truths which they taught, might justify the indifference of Socrates [10], whose doctrines, not less divine, were inculcated with unreserved freedom. But the fate of Socrates may justify in its turn, the circumspection of the hierophants of Ceres.

Alcibiades conducts the Eleusinian procession.

Besides the mysterious ceremonies of the temple, the worship of that bountiful goddess was celebrated by vocal and instrumental music, by public shows, and exhibitions, which continued during several days, and above all, by the pompous procession, which marched for ten miles along the sacred road leading from Athens to Eleusis [11]. This important part of the solemnity had formerly been intermitted, because the Athenians, after the loss of Decelia, were no longer masters of the road, and were compelled, contrary to established custom, to proceed by sea to the temple of Ceres. Alcibiades determined to wipe off the stain of impiety

favors, but in return conferred on our ancestors the two most valuable presents which either heaven can bestow, or mankind can receive; the practice of agriculture, which delivered us from the fierce and precarious manner of life, common to us with wild animals; and the knowledge of those sacred mysteries which fortify the initiated against the terrors of death, and inspire them with the pleasing hopes of an happy immortality. See Panegyr. p. 24. et Euseb. Præpar. Evang. l. iii.

[10] Laert. in Diogene.
[11] Herodot. l. viii. c. Liv. et Plut. in Alcibiad.

which had long adhered to his character, by renewing, in all its lustre, this venerable procession. He prepared to defend, by an armed force, the peaceful ministers and votaries of the gods, persuaded that the Spartans would either allow them to pass undisturbed, which must lessen the military fame of that people, or, if they attempted to interrupt the ceremony, must be exposed not only to the dangerous resistance of men animated by enthusiasm, but to the disgraceful charge of irreligion, and the general detestation of Greece. The priests, the heralds, and the whole body of the initiated, were apprized of his intention, and requested to hold themselves in readiness by the appointed day. Early in the morning the cavalry explored the adjoining country; the eminences were occupied by the light infantry and targeteers; and, after sufficient garrisons had been left to defend the Athenian walls and fortresses, the whole body of heavy-armed troops were drawn out to protect the Eleusinian procession, which marched along the usual road to the temple, and afterwards returned to Athens, without suffering any molestation from the Lacedæmonians; having united, on this occasion alone, all the splendor of war with the pomp of superstition [10].

CHAP. XXI.

Soon after this meritorious enterprise, Alcibiades prepared to sail for Lesser Asia, accompanied by the affectionate admiration of his fellow-citizens, who flattered themselves that the

His glory clouded by the inauspicious return of the Plynteria.

[10] Plut. in Alcibiad.

abilities and fortune of their commander would speedily reduce Chios, Ephesus, Miletus, and the other revolted cities and islands. The general alacrity, however, was somewhat abated by the reflection, that the arrival of Alcibiades in Athens coincided with the anniversary of the Plynteria[11], a day condemned to melancholy idleness, from a superstitious belief that nothing undertaken on that day could be brought to a prosperous conclusion. The celebrated Parthenon, whose remains still attest the magnificence of Pericles, was consecrated by the presence of a goddess, who realized the inspirations of Homer, as far as they were capable of being expressed by the genius of Phidias. Minerva, composed of gold and ivory, and twenty-six cubits high, was represented with the casque, the buckler, the lance, and all her usual emblems; and the warm fancy of the Athenians, enlivened and transported by the graceful majesty of her air and aspect, confounded the painful production of the statuary with the instantaneous creation of Jupiter. To confirm this useful illusion the crafty priests of the temple carefully washed and brightened the image, whose extraordinary lustre increased the veneration of the multitude. The Plynteria, during which this ceremony was performed, required uncommon secrecy and circumspection. The eyes and imagination of the vulgar might have become too

[11] Πλυνω, to wash; πλυντηρις; and in the plural neuter, "the ceremony of ablution."

familiar with their revered goddess, had they beheld her stripped of her accustomed ornaments, and observed every part of her form brightening into new beauty under the plastic hands of the priests. To prevent this dangerous consequence, the Plynteria was veiled in mystic obscurity; the doors of the temple were shut; that sacred edifice was surrounded on all sides to intercept the approach of indiscretion or profanity; and the return of Alcibiades, the favorite hope of his country, happening on the inauspicious day when Minerva hid her countenance, was believed by many to announce the dreadful calamities which soon afterwards befel the republic [56].

[56] Xenoph. p. 438. et Plut. in Alcibiad.

CHAP. XXII.

Character of Lysander. — His Conference with Cyrus. — He defeats the Athenian Fleet. — Disgrace of Alcibiades. — Lysander succeeded by Callicratidas. — His Transactions with the Persians — with the Spartan Allies. — Battle of Arginussa. — Trial of the Athenian Admirals. — Eteonicus checks a Mutiny of the Peloponnesian Troops. — Lysander resumes the Command. — Battle of Ægos Potamos. — Spartan Empire in Asia. — Siege and Surrender of Athens. — Humiliation of the Athenians.

CHAP.
XXII.
Lysander
takes the
command
of the Peloponnesian forces
in the East.
Olymp.
xciii. 2.
A. C. 407.

WHILE the superstitious multitude trembled at the imaginary anger of Minerva, men of reflection and experience dreaded the activity and valor of Lysander, who, during the residence of Alcibiades at Athens, had taken the command of the Peloponnesian forces in the East. The forms of the Spartan constitution required a rapid succession of generals; a circumstance, which amidst the numerous inconveniences with which it was attended, enlarged the sphere of military competition, and multiplying the number of actors on the theatre of war, afforded an opportunity for the display of many illustrious characters, which must otherwise have remained in obscurity. In the rotation

THE HISTORY OF GREECE. 199

of annual elections, offices of importance and dignity will often be intrusted to men unworthy to fill them; but in the vast variety of experiments, abilities of the most distinguished order (if any such exist in the community) must some time be called into exertion, honored with confidence, and armed with authority.

Such abilities the Spartans finally discovered in Lysander; a shoot of the Herculean stock, but not descended from either of the royal branches. He had been educated with all the severity of Spartan discipline; and having spent his youth and his manhood in those honorable employments [1] which became the dignity of his birth, he approached the decline of life, when his superior merit recommended him to the chief command in a season of public danger. Years had added experience to his valor, and enlarged the resources, without abating the ardor, of his ambitious mind. In his transactions with the world, he had learned to soften the harsh asperity of his national manners; to gain by fraud what could not be effected by force; and, in his own figurative language, to "eke out the lion's with the fox's skin [2]." This mixed character admirably

CHAP.
XXII.

His character.

---

[1] He had served in the army and navy; had been employed as ambassador in foreign states, etc. Plut. in Lysand.

[2] This was said, in allusion to the lion's skin of Hercules, to one who asked Lysander, "How he, who sprang from that hero, could condescend to conquer his enemies by fraud?" His character is diffusely described by Plutarch, L. III. p. 4—15.

CHAP.
XXII.

suited the part which he was called to act. His enterprising courage was successfully exerted in the hostile operations against the Greeks; his subtile and insinuating address gave him an ascendant in every negociation with the Persians; and the reunion of those various qualities enabled him, in a few years, finally to terminate the war, and to produce an important and permanent revolution in the affairs of Athens, of Sparta, and of Greece.

His conference with Cyrus.
Olymp. xciii. 2.
A. C. 407.

Since the decisive action at Cyzicus, the Peloponnesians, unable to resist the enemy, had been employed in preparing ships on the coast of their own peninsula, as well as in the harbours of their Persian and Grecian allies. The most considerable squadrons had been equipped in Cos, Rhodes, Miletus, and Ephesus; in the last of which the whole armament, amounting to ninety sail, was collected by Lysander. But the assembling of such a force was a matter of little consequence, unless proper measures should be taken for holding it together, and for enabling it to act with vigor. It was necessary, above all, to secure pay for the seamen; for this purpose, Lysander, accompanied by several Lacedæmonian ambassadors, repaired to Sardis, to congratulate the happy arrival of Cyrus, a generous and valiant youth of seventeen, who had been intrusted by his father Darius with the government of the inland parts of Lesser Asia; or, in the language of the Persian court, with the command of the numerous troops, who rendezvoused in the plains of

Kaſtolus[1]. Lyſander complained to the young and magnanimous prince, "of the perfidious duplicity of Tiſſaphernes, by which the Athenians had been enabled to re-aſſume that aſcendant in the Eaſt, which had formerly proved ſo dangerous and diſgraceful to the Perſian name. That ſatrap ſeemed, on one occaſion indeed, to have diſcovered the fatal tendence of his meaſures; and had attempted to check the victorious career of thoſe ambitious republicans, by ſeizing the perſon of Alcibiades[2]. Pharnabazus had more effectually ſerved the cauſe of his maſter, by his active valor in the field; by detaining the Athenian ambaſſadors, who had been ſent to ſurpriſe the unſuſpecting generoſity of Darius[3]; and by ſupplying the Peloponneſians, after the unfortunate engagement at Cyzicus, with the means of

[1] This was the ſtyle of the letter, confirmed by the royal ſeal. Παρασιασα Κυρος αρχων των ες Καςωλον αθροιζομενων. Xenoph. p. 418.

[2] This event, which happened in the twenty-firſt year of the war, is related by Xenophon, p. 429. It was omitted in the text, becauſe Alcibiades ſoon effected his eſcape; and the treachery of Tiſſaphernes only diſplayed his own worthleſſneſs, without hurting his enemies.

[3] This diſhonorable tranſaction was approved even by Cyrus, which ſhows the diſregard of the Perſians to the laws of nations. He begged Pharnabazus to put the Athenians in his hands; at leaſt, not to ſet them at liberty, that their countrymen might be ignorant of the meaſures in agitation againſt them. But a remorſe of conſcience ſeized Pharnabazus, who had ſworn, either to conduct the ambaſſadors to the great king, or to ſend them to the Ionian coaſt; in conſequence of which, the Athenians were releaſed. Xenoph. p. 438.

202 THE HISTORY OF GREECE.

CHAP.
XXII.

preparing a new fleet, and with the necessaries and conveniences of life, while they were employed in this useful undertaking. But Tissaphernes was unwilling, and Pharnabazus was perhaps unable, to discharge the stipulated pay, without which the Grecian seamen and soldiers could not be kept together, or engaged to act with vigor against the common enemy." Cyrus replied, "That he had been commanded by his father to assist the Lacedæmonians, and to pay their troops with the most exact punctuality. That, for this purpose, he had carried with him five hundred talents (near an hundred thousand pounds sterling); and if such a sum should be found insufficient, he would willingly expend his private fortune, and even melt down and coin into money the golden throne on which he sat[e]."

The pay of the Grecian sailors, and complement of their ships.

This discourse gave extraordinary satisfaction to his Grecian auditors; and Lysander endeavoured to avail himself of what, judging by his own character, he imagined might be nothing more than a sudden transport of generosity, by requesting that the seamen's pay might be raised from three oboli to an Attic drachma a day. Cyrus answered, "That, on this subject too, he had received express orders from his father[f]. That the pay should

[e] Καὶ τὸν θρόνον κατατεμεῖν, ἐν ᾧ καθῆστο, ὄντα ἀργυροῦν καὶ χρυσοῦν. Literally, "that he would cut in pieces the throne on which he sat," which was composed of silver and gold.

[f] Xenophon makes Cyrus answer with more art than truth, "ὁ δὲ ....

continue on the ancient footing, and the Peloponnesians regularly receive thirty minæ (above ninety pounds sterling) a month, for every ship which they fitted out." Lysander acquiesced with some reluctance, determining to seize the first favorable opportunity to renew his petition. But this instructive conversation may enable us to discover an important matter of fact omitted by historians. As the military and naval officers of the Greeks were not distinguished above the common men by the excessive inequality of their appointments, we may compute, from the monthly sum of thirty minæ, distributed at the rate of three oboli of daily pay, that the complement of each ship amounted to about two hundred and forty sailors; so that a fleet of ninety sail employed twenty-one thousand and six hundred men.

Before Lysander returned to Ephesus, he was invited by the Persian prince to a magnificent entertainment, at which, according to the custom of the age, the most serious matters were discussed amidst the freedom and intemperance of the table. This was a seasonable occasion for displaying the arts of insinuation and flattery, in which the Spartan was a complete master. He represented, without moderation, and without decency, the injustice and incapacity of Tissaphernes, who, as he was naturally the rival, might be suspected soon to become the

CHAP. XXII.

Lysander is entertained at Sardis by the Persian prince.

επιστολην αυτω αλλα παιτα. " Cyrus answered, " that they (Lysander and the Lacedæmonian ambassadors) spoke very reasonably, but that he could not act otherwise than he was commanded by his father."

CHAP.
XXII.

personal enemy of Cyrus. He magnified the beauty, the strength, and the courage, of the young prince. His address in military exercises, and the extraordinary endowments of his mind (the fame of which had reached the most distant countries), were extolled with the most elaborate praise. It is not improbable that he might find a topic of panegyric in a quality of which Cyrus was not a little vain; the capacity of bearing, without intoxication, a greater quantity of liquor than any of his equals[1]; and he might possibly suggest, that of all the sons of Darius, Cyrus was the best qualified to succeed his father, to fill with dignity the Persian throne, and to emulate the glory of that illustrious hero whose name he bore, the immortal founder of the monarchy. But whatever were the topics of which he made use, it is certain that he excited the warmest emotions of friendship in the youthful breast of Cyrus, who drinking his health, after the Persian fashion, desired him to ask a boon, with full assurance that nothing should be denied him. Lysander replied, with his usual address, "That he should ask what it would be no less useful for the prince to give, than for him to receive: the addition of an obolus a day to the pay of the mariners; an augmentation which, by inducing the Athenian crews to desert, would not only increase their own strength, but enfeeble the common enemy." Struck with the apparent disinterestedness of this specious proposal, Cyrus ordered

His address in procuring an addition to the seamen's pay.

[1] Plut. Sympos.

him immediately ten thousand Daricks (above five
thousand pounds sterling); with which he returned
to Ephesus, discharged the arrears due to his troops,
gave them a month's pay in advance, raised their
daily allowance, and seduced innumerable deserters
from the Athenian fleet[9].

CHAP. XXII.

While Lysander was usefully employed in manning his ships, and preparing them for action, Alcibiades attacked the small island of Andros. The resistance was more vigorous than he had reason to expect; and the immediate necessity of procuring pay and subsistence for the fleet, obliged him to leave his work imperfect. With a small squadron he sailed to raise contributions on the Ionian or Carian coast[10], committing the principal armament to Antiochus, a man totally unworthy of such an important trust[11]. Even the affectionate partiality of Alcibiades seems to have discerned the unworthiness of his favorite, since he gave him strict orders to continue, during his own absence, in the harbour of Samos, and by no means to risk an engagement. This injunction, as it could not prevent the rashness, might perhaps provoke the vain levity of the vice-admiral; who, after the departure

Defeats the Athenian fleet in the absence of Alcibiades. Olymp. xciii. 2. A. C. 407.

---

[9] Plut. tom. III. p. 7. Xenoph. Hellen. l. I. p. 441. Diodor. l. xiii. p. 300.

[10] Xenophon says, "Alcibiades failed to Phocæa," which is in Ionia; Plutarch says, "to the coast of Caria."

[11] Diodorus gives his character in few words: "Ὁ δὲ Ἀντιοχος ὢν τῇ φύσει προπετης, και ποθουμενος δια ἑαυτε τι πραξαι λαμπρον. Antiochus, naturally precipitate, and desirous, by himself, to perform some splendid exploit."

CHAP.
XXII.

of his friend, failed towards Ephesus, approached the sterns of Lysander's ships, and with the most licentious insults challenged him to battle. The prudent Spartan delayed the moment of attack, until the presumption of his enemies had thrown them into scattered disorder[13]. He then commanded the Peloponnesian squadrons to advance. His manœuvres were judicious, and executed with a prompt obedience. The battle was not obstinate, as the Athenians, who scarcely expected any resistance, much less assault, sunk at once from the insolence of temerity into the despondency of fear. They lost fifteen vessels, with a considerable part of their crews. The remainder retired disgracefully to Samos; while the Lacedæmonians profited of their victory by the taking of Eion and Delphinium. Though fortune thus favored the prudence of Lysander, he declined to venture a second engagement with the superior strength of Alcibiades, who, having resumed the command, employed every artifice and insult that might procure him an opportunity to restore the tarnished lustre of the Athenian fleet.

Alcibiades accused and disgraced.

But such an opportunity he could never again find. The people of Athens, who expected to hear of nothing but victories and triumphs, were mortified to the last degree, when they received intelligence of such a shameful defeat. As they could not suspect the abilities, they distrusted the fidelity, of their commander. Their suspicions

[13] " Διεσπαρμενας τας ναυς. " Xenoph. p. 441.

were increased and confirmed by the arrival of Thrasybulus[11], who, whether actuated by a laudable zeal for the interest of the public service, or animated by a selfish jealousy of the fame and honors that had been so liberally heaped on a rival, formally impeached Alcibiades in the Athenian assembly. "His misconduct had totally ruined the affairs of his country. A talent for low buffoonery was a sure recommendation to his favor. His friends were, partially, selected from the meanest and most abandoned of men, who possessed no other merit than that of being subservient to his passions. To such unworthy instruments the fleet of Athens was intrusted; while the commander in chief revelled in debauchery with the harlots of Abydus and Ionia, or raised exorbitant contributions on the dependent cities, that he might defray the expense of a fortress on the coast of Thrace, in the neighbourhood of Byzantium, which he had erected to shelter himself against the just vengeance of the republic."

[11] Thrasybulus, we have seen, had a principal share in bringing about the recal of Alcibiades. Nor was the latter ungrateful to his benefactor. When the Athenians committed to him their whole military and naval force, "ἁπασας τας δυναμεις," and allowed him to name his own colleagues, or rather substitutes, he named Thrasybulus and Adimantus. Diod. l. xiii. p. 368. Considering this interchange of good offices between Alcibiades and Thrasybulus, it is remarkable that no Greek writer alleges any reason for the animosity that soon afterwards broke out between them. Plutarch says, that Thrasybulus was the bitterest of Alcibiades's enemies, and imputes his accusation of him to enmity, not to patriotism.

CHAP. XXII.
Ten commanders appointed in his stead.

Were it necessary to prove by examples the deceitful emptiness of popular favor, this subject might be copiously illustrated from the history of the Athenians. The same man, whom a few months before they found it impossible sufficiently to reward, was actually exposed to the rage of disappointment and the fury of revenge. They regretted the loss of every moment which intervened between the rapid progress of their resentment, and the execution of their vengeance. In the same assembly, and on the same day, Alcibiades was accused, and almost unanimously condemned; and, that the affairs of the republic might not again suffer by the abuse of undivided power, ten commanders were substituted in his room; among whom were Thrasyllus, Leon, Diomedon, whose approved valor, and love of liberty, justly recommended them to public honors; Conon, a character as yet but little known, but destined, in a future period, to eclipse the fame of his contemporaries; and Pericles, who inherited the name, the merit, and the bad fortune, of his illustrious father. The new generals immediately sailed to Samos; and Alcibiades sought refuge in his Thracian fortress [11].

Callicratidas sent to command the Peloponnesian fleet.
Olymp. xciii. 3.
A. C. 406.

They had scarcely assumed the command, when an important alteration took place in the Peloponnesian fleet. Lysander's year had expired, and Callicratidas, a Spartan of a very opposite character, was sent to succeed him. The active, ambitious,

[11] Xenoph. Hellen. l. 1r. sub fin. Diodor. xiii. 67—74.

and

and intriguing temper of the former had employed as much assiduous and systematic policy during the short term of his precarious power, as if his authority had never been to end. Though endowed with uncommon vigor of mind, and with consummate prudence (if prudence can belong to a character deficient in justice and humanity), he possessed not those amiable and useful qualities which alone deserve, and can alone obtain, public confidence and respect. Lysander, sensible of this imperfection, had recourse to the ordinary expedient by which crafty ambition supplies the want of virtue. He determined to govern by parties[11]. The boldest of the sailors were attached to his person by liberal rewards and more liberal promises. The soldiers were indulged in the most licentious disorders. In every city and in every island, Lysander had his partisans, whom he flattered with the hopes of obtaining the same authority over their fellow-citizens, which the Spartans enjoyed over the inferior ranks of men in Laconia[12].

It was the general expectation at Ephesus, that the Spartans would, for once, depart from established practice, in order to prolong the command of such an able and successful officer. An universal clamor arose, when Callicratidas displayed his

---

[11] His maxims breathed the odious party-spirit. "That it is impossible to do too much good to friends, or too much evil to enemies. That children are to be deceived by trinkets, men by oaths; and others equally flagitious." Plut. in Lysand.

[12] Idem, ibid. et Xenoph. Hellen.

commission in the council of the confederates. The friends of Lysander affirmed, "That it was equally imprudent and ungenerous to check the victorious career of a deserving and fortunate commander; that the important charge of the fleet ought not to be intrusted to men, who were destitute of experience, and perhaps of abilities; nor would it be just to sacrifice the interest of such a numerous and powerful confederacy to a punctilious observance of the Lacedæmonian laws." Lysander maintained a decent silence concerning the character of his successor, only observing that he resigned to him a fleet which commanded the sea. The noisy acclamations of the assembly confirmed his assertion.

His honesty and firmness confounds the partisans of Lysander.

But Callicratidas had a heart untainted with reproach, and incapable of fear. Unabashed by the seditious turbulence of his opponents, he replied, That he must with-hold his assent to the magnified superiority of the Peloponnesian fleet, unless Lysander should set sail from Ephesus, coast along the isle of Samos (where the Athenians then lay), and surrender his victorious squadrons in the harbour of Miletus. The pride of Lysander might have been confounded by this judicious and solid observation; but his ingenuity suggested a plausible or rather an elusive reply, "That he was no longer admiral."

Callicratidas then addressed the assembly, with the manly simplicity of an honest heart, which disdains the artifice of words, defies the insolence of power, and defeats the intrigues of policy.

"Lacedæmonians and allies, I should have been contented to stay at home; nor does it greatly affect me that Lysander, or any other, should be held a better seaman than myself. Hither I have been sent by my countrymen to command the fleet, and my chief concern is to execute their orders, and to perform my duty. It is my earnest desire to promote the public interest; but you can best inform me whether I ought to continue here, or to return to Sparta." Wonderful is the power of honest intentions and unaffected firmness. The assembly listened with admiration; the partisans of Lysander were abashed; none ventured to object; and, after a considerable pause, all unanimously acknowledged that it became both Callicratidas and themselves to obey the orders of the Spartan government[17].

Lysander, not a little mortified by the language of the assembly, reluctantly resigned his employment; but determined to render it painful, and, if possible, too weighty for the abilities of his successor. For this purpose he returned to the court of Cyrus, to whom he restored a considerable sum of money still unexpended in the service of the Grecian fleet, and to whom he misrepresented, under the names of obstinacy, ignorance, and rusticity, the unaffected plainness, the downright sincerity, and the other manly, but uncomplying, virtues of the generous Callicratidas. When that commander repaired to Sardis to demand the

[17] Xenoph. Hellen. L. i. c. 1. et seqq. et Plut. in Lysand.

CHAP.
XXII.

stipulated pay, he could not obtain admission to the royal presence. The first time that he visited the palace he was told that Cyrus was at table. It is well, said the unceremonious Spartan, I will wait till he has dined. The simplicity of this proceeding, confirmed the opinion which Lysander had given the Persians of his character; and his honest frankness, which was construed into low breeding, seemed a proper object of ridicule to the proud retainers of the court. He returned on another occasion, but without being admitted to see the young prince. The injustice of this treatment might have deserved his resentment, but it chiefly excited his contempt. He left the royal city, despising the pride and perfidy of his Persian allies, whose accidental importance depended on the precarious advantage of riches, and lamenting the domestic dissensions of the Greeks, which obliged them to court the favor of insolent Barbarians.

Obtains voluntary contributions from the Ionians.

But Callicratidas could not, with honor or safety, return to the fleet at Ephesus, without having collected money to supply the immediate wants of the sailors. He proceeded, therefore, to Miletus and other friendly towns of Ionia; and having met the principal citizens, in their respective assemblies, he explained openly and fully the mean jealousy of Lysander, and the disdainful arrogance of Cyrus[14]. "The unjust behaviour of

[14] It will appear, in the sequel, that Callicratidas had formed a very false opinion of the Persian prince, whose neglect of a worthy man was occasioned by the perfidious suggestions of his retainers, the friends or creatures of Lysander.

THE HISTORY OF GREECE. 215

both compelled him, much against his inclination, to have recourse to the confederate cities (already too much burdened) for the money requisite to support the war. But he assured them, that, should his arms prove successful, he would repay their favors with gratitude. Their own interest required a cheerful compliance with his demands, since the expedition had been principally undertaken to vindicate their freedom. He had, however, sent messengers to require effectual supplies from Sparta; but until these should arrive, it became the Greeks in general, but especially the Ionians, who had suffered peculiar injuries from the usurping tyranny of the great king, to prove to the world that, 'without the sordid assistance of *his* boasted treasures, they could prosecute their just designs, and take vengeance on their enemies." By those judicious and honorable expedients, Callicratidas, without fraud or violence, obtained such considerable, yet voluntary contributions, as enabled him to gratify the importunate demands of the sailors, and to return with honor to Ephesus, in order to prepare for action".

His first operations were directed against the isle of Lesbos, or rather against the strong and populous towns of Methymna and Mitylené, which respectively commanded the northern and southern divisions of that island. Besides the numerous citizens of an age to bear arms, Methymna was defended by an Athenian garrison. The place

CHAP. XXII.

He takes Methymna.

[11] Xenoph. Hellen. p. 446.

CHAP. XXII.

made a brave resistance; but the persevering efforts of Callicratidas exhausted its strength: Methymna was taken by storm, and subjected to the depredations of the Peloponnesian troops. The garrison and the slaves were treated as part of the booty. The confederates advised, that the Methymneans also should be sold into servitude; but Callicratidas assured them, that, while he enjoyed the command, there should not any Grecian citizen be reduced to the condition of a slave, unless he had taken arms to subvert the public freedom[10].

Takes thirty ships, and blocks up the rest of the fleet in the harbour of Mitylene.

Meanwhile Conon, the most active and enterprising of the Athenian commanders, had put to sea with a squadron of seventy sail, in order to protect the coast of Lesbos. But this design was attempted too late; nor, had it been more early undertaken, was the force of Conon sufficient to accomplish it. Callicratidas observed his motions, discovered his strength, and, with a far superior fleet, intercepted his retreat to the armament of Samos. The Athenians fled towards the coast of Mitylene, but were prevented from entering the harbour of that place by the resentment of the inhabitants, who rejoiced in an opportunity to punish those who had so often conquered, and so long oppressed, their city. In consequence of this unexpected opposition, the Athenian squadron was overtaken by the enemy. The engagement was more sharp and obstinate than might have been expected in such an inequality of strength. Thirty

[10] Xenoph. ubi supra. Diodor. l. xiii. p. 573.

THE HISTORY OF GREECE. 215

empty ships (for most of the men swam to land) were taken by the Peloponnesians. The remaining forty were haled up under the walls of Mitylene; Callicratidas recalled his troops from Methymna, received a reinforcement from Chios, and blocked up the Athenians by sea and land[1].

The condition of Conon was most distressful. He was surrounded on all sides by a superior force; the town of Mitylené was hostile; his men were destitute of provisions, incapable of resistance, yet unwilling to surrender. In this melancholy situation he attempted the only enterprise which could promise a hope of relief. The bravest and most experienced seamen were embarked in two swift-sailing vessels, one of which eluding the vigilance of the enemy, escaped in safety to the Hellespont, and informed the Athenians of the misfortunes and blockade at Lesbos. The intelligence was immediately communicated to Samos and to Athens; and the importance of the object, which was no less than the safety of forty ships, and above eight thousand brave men, excited uncommon exertions of activity. The Athenians reinforced their domestic strength with the assistance of their allies; all able-bodied men were pressed into the service; and, in a few weeks, they had assembled at Samos an hundred and fifty sail, which immediately took the sea, with a resolution to encounter the enemy.

Callicratidas did not decline the engagement. Having left fifty ships to guard the harbour of

CHAP. XXII.

The Athenians fit out a new fleet.

Battle of Arginusæ, in which Callicratidas

[1] Xenoph. ubi supra. Diodor. L. xiii. p. 373.

CHAP. XXII.
Is defeated and slain.
Olymp. xciii. 3.
A.C. 406.

Mitylené, he proceeded with an hundred and twenty to Cape Malea, the most southern point of Lesbos. The Athenians had advanced, the same evening, to the islands, or rather rocks, of Arginussæ, four miles distant from that promontory. The night passed in bold stratagems for mutual surprise, which were rendered ineffectual by a violent tempest of rain and thunder. At the dawn both armaments were eager to engage; but Hermon and Megareus, two experienced seamen, and the chief counsellors of Callicratidas, exhorted him not to commit the weakness of the Peloponnesians with the superior strength and numbers of the enemy. The generous and intrepid Spartan despised danger and death in comparison of glory; but either his magnanimity had not overcome the last imperfection of virtuous minds, and was averse to sacrifice personal glory to public utility, or he imagined that this utility could not be separated from an inflexible adherence to the martial laws of Lycurgus. He answered the prudent admonitions of his friends in these memorable words, which, according to the construction that is put on them [15],

---

[15] Cicero de Offic. l. i. c. xxiv. takes the unfavorable side. "Itaque ipsi multi sunt, qui non modo pecuniam, sed vitam etiam profundere pro patriâ parati essent: iidem gloriæ jacturam ne minimam quidem facere vellent, ne republicâ quidem postulante; ut Callicratidas, qui cum Lacedæmoniorum dux fuisset Peloponnesiaco bello, multaque fecisset egregie; vertit ad extremum omnia, cum consilio non paruit eorum, qui classem ab Arginusis removendam, nec cum Atheniensibus dimicandum putabant. Quibus ille respondit, Lacedæmonios, classe illâ amissâ, aliam parare posse; se fugere sine suo dedecore non posse."

THE HISTORY OF GREECE. 217

deserve our admiration or our pity. "My death cannot be destructive to Sparta, but my flight would be dishonorable both to Sparta and myself." So saying, he gave the signal for his ships to advance. The fight was long and bloody; passing, successively, through all the different gradations, from disciplined order and regularity to the most tumultuous confusion. The Spartan commander was slain charging in the centre of the bravest enemies. The hostile squadrons fought with various fortune in different parts of the battle, and promiscuously conquered, pursued, surrendered, or fled. Thirteen Athenian vessels were taken by the Peloponnesians; but, at length, the latter gave way on all sides: seventy of their ships were captured, the rest escaped to Chios and Phocæa".

CHAP. XXII.

The Athenian admirals, though justly elated with their good fortune, cautiously deliberated concerning the best means of improving their victory. Several advised that the fleet should steer its course to Mitylené, to surprise the Peloponnesian squadron which blocked up the harbour of that city. Diomedon recommended it as a more immediate and essential object of their care to recover the bodies of the slain, and to save the wreck of twelve vessels which had been disabled in the engagement.

Stratagem of Eteonicus.

Notwithstanding the respectable authority of Cicero, whoever attentively considers the laws of Lycurgus and the character of Callicratidas, will be disposed to believe, that an undeviating principle of duty, not the fear of losing his glory, formed the sublime motive of that accomplished Spartan.

" Xenoph. p. 446. et Diodor. p 374.

CHAP. XXII.

Thrasybulus observed, that by dividing their strength, both purposes might be effected. His opinion was approved. The charge of preserving the dying, and collecting the bodies of the dead, was committed to Theramenes and Thrasybulus. Fifty vessels were destined to that important service, doubly recommended by humanity and superstition. The remainder sailed to the isle of Lesbos, in quest of the Peloponnesians on that coast, who narrowly escaped destruction through the well-conducted stratagem of Eteonicus, the Spartan vice-admiral. Soon after the engagement a brigantine arrived at Mitylene, acquainting him with the death of Callicratidas, as well as with the defeat and flight of the Peloponnesian fleet. The sagacity of Eteonicus immediately foresaw the probable consequences of those events. The Athenians would naturally sail from Arginussae to pursue their good fortune, and Conon, who was shut up at Mitylene, would be encouraged to break through the harbour, that he might join his victorious countrymen.

which saves the Peloponnesian squadron at Mitylene.

In order to anticipate those measures, and to facilitate his own retreat, the Spartan commander ordered the brigantine privately to leave the harbour, and to return, at the distance of a short time, with joyous acclamations and music, the rowers crowned with garlands, and calling out that Callicratidas had destroyed the last hope of Athens, and obtained a glorious and decisive victory. The contrivance succeeded; the Spartans thanked heaven for the good news by hymns and sacrifices; the

THE HISTORY OF GREECE. 219

sailors were enjoined to refresh themselves by a copious repast, and to profit of a favorable gale to sail to the isle of Chios; while the soldiers burned their camp, and marched northward to Methymna, to reinforce the garrison there, which was threatened by a speedy visit of the enemy [14].

CHAP. XXII.

While the prudent foresight of Eteonicus saved the Peloponnesian squadron at Mitylené, the violence of a storm prevented Theramenes and Thrasybulus from saving their unfortunate companions, all of whom, excepting one of the admirals and a few others who escaped by their extraordinary dexterity in swimming, were overwhelmed by the waves of a tempestuous sea; nor could their dead bodies ever be recovered. The Athenians were likewise disappointed of the immediate advantages which ought to have resulted from the engagement. Methymna was too strongly fortified to be taken by a sudden assault; they could not spare time for a regular siege; and when they proceeded to Chios in quest of the Peloponnesian fleet, they found it carefully secured in the principal harbour of that island, which had been put in a vigorous posture of defence. These unforeseen circumstances were the more disagreeable and mortifying to the commanders, because, immediately after the battle, they had sent an advice-boat to Athens, acquainting the magistrates with the capture of seventy vessels [15]; mentioning their intended expeditions to

Disappointment of the Athenian admirals.

[14] Xenoph. Hellen. et Diodor. p. 334.
[15] Xenoph. says sixty-nine; Diodorus, seventy-seven.

CHAP.
XXII.

Mitylené, Methymna, and Chios, from which they had reason to hope the most distinguished success; and particularly taking notice that the important charge of recovering the bodies of the drowned or slain had been committed to Theramenes and Thrasybulus, two captains of approved conduct and fidelity.

Discontents in Athens.

The joy which the Athenians received from this flattering intelligence was converted into disappointment and sorrow, when they understood that their fleet had returned to Samos, without reaping the expected fruits of victory. They were afflicted beyond measure with the total loss of the wreck, by which their brave and victorious countrymen had been deprived of the sacred rites of funeral; a circumstance viewed with peculiar horror, because it was supposed, according to a superstition consecrated by the belief of ages, to subject their melancholy shades to wander an hundred years on the gloomy banks of the Styx, before they could be transported to the regions of light and felicity. The relations of the dead lamented their private misfortunes; the enemies of the admirals exaggerated the public calamity; both demanded an immediate and serious examination into the cause of this distressful event, that the guilty might be discovered and punished.

Amidst the ferment of popular discontents, Theramenes sailed to Athens, with a view to exculpate himself and his colleague Thrasybulus. The letter sent thither before them had excited their fear and their resentment; since it rendered them responsible for a duty which they found it impossible to perform. Theramenes accused the admirals of having neglected the favorable moment to save the perishing, and to recover the bodies of the dead; and, after the opportunity of this important service was irrecoverably lost, of having devolved the charge on others, in order to skreen their own misconduct. The Athenians greedily listened to the accusation, and cashiered the absent commanders. Conon, who during the action remained blocked up at Mitylené, was intrusted with the fleet. Protomachus and Aristogenes chose a voluntary banishment. The rest returned home to justify measures which appeared so criminal ⁵⁶.

Among the inestimable rules of jurisprudence, invented by the wisdom of Athens, we may remark that beneficial institution which subjects the life, the character, and the fortune of individuals, not to the capricious will of an arbitrary judge, but to the equitable decision of the public. In every case, civil and criminal, the rights of an Athenian citizen were intrusted to the judgment of his peers; who, according as the question was more or less important, consisted of a committee, more or less numerous, of the popular assembly. But, in order to unite the double advantages of law and liberty, the nine archons, or chief magistrates, men of approved wisdom and fidelity, respectively presided in the several courts of justice, received

Trials of the admirals.

⁵⁶ Xenoph. Hellen. l. l. c. vii. et seqq. Diodor. xiii. 76—97.

complaints, examined the parties, directed process, and regularly conducted the suit through its various steps and stages. In matters of general concernment, such as the treason, perfidy, or malversation of men in power, the senate of the five hundred, or rather the Prytanes, who presided in the senate, performed the functions of the magistrate, and the whole body of the people, convened in full assembly, executed the office of judge and jury. It belonged to the Prytanes to prescribe the form of action or trial, and to admit the accuser to implead or impeach his antagonist. The cause was then referred to the people, who, as judges of the fact, gave their verdict, and, as judges of the law, passed their sentence or decree. Such were the regulations which reason had established, but which passion and interest commonly rendered ineffectual.

Artifices of their accusers.

Archedemus, an opulent and powerful citizen, and Calixenus, a seditious demagogue, partly moved by the entreaties of Theramenes, and partly excited by personal envy and resentment, denounced the admirals to the senate. The accusation was supported by the relations of the deceased, who appeared in mourning robes, their heads shaved, their arms folded, their eyes bathed in tears, piteously lamenting the loss and disgrace of their families, deprived of their protectors, who had been themselves deprived of those last and solemn duties to which all mankind are entitled. A false witness swore in court, that he had been saved, almost by miracle, from the wreck, and that his companions, as they were ready to be drowned, charged him to acquaint his country how they had fallen victims to the cruel neglect of their commanders. During these proceedings it happened that the people had met to celebrate the Apatouria, or festival in January, so named because the Athenians then presented their sons, who had reached their seventh year, to be inscribed in the register of their respective tribes. Callixenus presuming on the evidence given in the senate, and on the actual disposition of the assembly, proposed the following resolution: "That the cause of the admirals should be immediately referred to the people; that the suffrages should be given by tribes, in each of which the criers should make proclamation, having prepared two urns to receive the white and black beans; if the latter were more numerous, the admirals should be delivered to the eleven men, the executioners of public justice, their estates confiscated, and the tenth part consecrated to Minerva."

CHAP. XXII.

This unjust decree, which deprived the commanders of the benefits of a separate trial, of an impartial hearing, and of the time as well as the means necessary to prepare a legal defence, was approved by a majority of the senate, and received with loud acclamations by the people, whose levity, insolence, pride, and cruelty, all eagerly demanded the destruction of the admirals. In such a numerous assembly, two men alone, Euryptolemus and Axiochus, defended the cause of law and justice. The former impeached Callixenus for proposing a

Informality of the trial.

CHAP. XXII.

resolution inconsistent with all the forms of legal procedure. But the rabble made a violent uproar, calling out that none should attempt, with impunity, to abridge their sovereign power. The Prytanes, who attended, as usual, to direct and control the proceedings of the multitude, endeavoured to moderate the ferment: but they were licentiously told, that if they did not concur with the opinion of the majority, they should be involved in the same accusation with the admirals. This absurd menace (such was the popular frenzy) might be carried into immediate execution. The senators were intimidated into a reluctant compliance with measures which they disapproved, and by which they were for ever to be disgraced. Yet the philosophic firmness of Socrates disdained to submit. He protested against the tameness of his colleagues, and declared that neither threats, nor danger, nor violence, could compel him to conspire with injustice for the destruction of the innocent.

They are condemned and executed.

But what could avail the voice of one virtuous man amidst the licentious madness of thousands? The commanders were accused, tried, condemned; and, with the most irregular precipitancy, delivered to the executioner. Before they were led to death, Diomedon addressed the assembly in a short but ever-memorable speech. "I am afraid, Athenians! lest the sentence which you have passed on us, prove hurtful to the republic. Yet I would exhort you to employ the most proper means to avert the vengeance of heaven. You must carefully

perform

perform the sacrifices which, before giving battle at Arginussæ, we promised to the gods in behalf of ourselves and of you. Our misfortunes deprive us of an opportunity to acquit this just debt, and to pay the sincere tribute of our gratitude. But we are deeply sensible that the assistance of the gods enabled us to obtain that glorious and signal victory." The disinterestedness, the patriotism, and the magnanimity of this discourse, must have appeased (if any thing had been able to appease) the tumultuous passions of the vulgar. But their headstrong fury defied every restraint of reason or of sentiment. They persisted in their bloody purpose, which was executed without pity: yet their cruelty was followed by a speedy repentance, and punished by the sharp pangs of remorse, the intolerable pain of which they vainly attempted to mitigate by inflicting a well-merited vengeance on the worthless and detestable Callixenus[17].

The removal of the Athenian admirals, and the defeat and death of the Spartan Callicratidas, suspended for several months the military and naval operations on both sides. The behaviour of Philocles and Adimanthus, who had been joined in authority with Conon, were better fitted to obstruct than promote the measures of that brave and prudent commander. The former was a man of a violent and impetuous temper, unaccustomed to reflection, destitute of experience, and incapable of governing others, or himself. The latter

[17] Xenoph. et Diodor. ibid.

possessed perhaps the virtue of humanity, but was destitute of spirit and activity, qualities so usual in his age and country. Though ready with his tongue, he was slow with his hand, careless of discipline, negligent of duty, and suspected of a treasonable correspondence with the public enemy.

Eteonicus checks a mutiny among the Peloponnesian troops.

Eteonicus, who commanded the Spartans and their confederates, was a man of a very different character. But the distressful situation of affairs prevented him from displaying his abilities in any important enterprise. His armament was inferior in strength; his sailors were disheartened by defeat; he had not money to pay them; even their subsistence at Chios was very sparing and precarious. These vexatious circumstances increased the mutinous spirit by which the confederates were too naturally animated. They reproached the ungenerous parsimony of the Chians, whom they had taken arms to defend; they spurned the authority of their commander; and in order to obtain those advantages which their services deserved, and which had been unjustly denied them, they determined to become rich at once by seizing and plundering the large and wealthy capital of that flourishing island. The design, though secretly formed, was avowed with open boldness. The conspirators, whose numbers seemed to promise success, or at least to secure impunity, assumed a badge of distinction, that they might encourage each other, and intimidate their opponents. Eteonicus was justly alarmed with the progress of sedition. It was dangerous to attack the insurgents by force: if he destroyed them by fraud, he might be exposed to the reproach and obloquy of Greece. The conduct which he pursued was conceived with an enterprising courage, and executed with a resolute firmness. With only fifteen faithful and intrepid followers, armed with concealed daggers, he patrolled the streets of Chios. The first man whom they met distinguished by a reed (for that was the badge of conspiracy) was put to death, and a crowd collecting to know why the man had been slain, they were told it was for wearing a reed on his casque. The report was immediately spread through every quarter of the city. The reed-men (as they were called) were confounded at discovering a conspiracy more secret and more formidable than their own. They dreaded that every man whom they met might know and kill them; and, as they had not time to assemble for their mutual defence, they hastily threw away the reeds, which exposed them to the dangerous assault of their unknown enemies.

The character of Eteonicus, as far as we can judge from his actions, justly entitled him to the command; but the partiality both of Cyrus and of the confederates eagerly solicited the return of Lysander. The Spartans, though inclined to gratify them, were perplexed by an ancient law enacted in the jealousy of freedom to prohibit the same person from being twice intrusted with the fleet. That they might not violate the respect due to the laws, while at the same time they complied with the request of their powerful allies, they invested

Lysander resumes the command, and takes Lampsacus. Olymp. xciii. 3. A. C. 406.

CHAP.
XXII.

Aracus, a weak and obscure man, with the name of admiral, and sent out Lysander as second in command. The latter was received at Sardis by the Persian prince, with the warmest demonstrations of joy. He was supplied with money to satisfy the immediate wants of the troops; and, as Cyrus at that time happened to make a journey into Upper Asia, the revenues of his wealthy province were consigned, in his absence, to the management of his Spartan friend. Such powerful resources could not long remain unemployed in the active hands of Lysander. His emissaries assiduously engaged or pressed the Ionian and Carian seamen. The harbours of Asia Minor, particularly the port of Ephesus, glowed with the ardor of naval preparation, and in a few months Lysander sailed to the Hellespont with a hundred and fifty gallies, and attacked the important town of Lampsacus. The place, though vigorously defended by the natives as well as by the Athenian garrison, was at length taken by storm; and according to the barbarous practice of the age, abandoned to the licentious rapacity, the avarice, the lust, and the fury, of the conquerors [19].

The Athenian commanders prepare to give him battle.

The languid and imprudent measures of the Athenians at Samos accuse the abilities of Tydeus, Menander, and Cephisodotus, who had been lately joined in command with Conon and his unworthy colleagues. They sailed too late to save Lampsacus, but as they possessed an hundred and eighty

[19] Plut. in Lysand.

gallies, a force superior to Lysander's, they anchored on the opposite, or European side of the Hellespont, at the distance of fifteen furlongs, in order to provoke the enemy to an engagement. Their unfortunate station was the mouth of the Ægos Potamos, or river of the goat, distinguished by that name on account of some small islands, which rising high above the surface of the waters, exhibit to a lively imagination the appearance of that animal. This place was injudiciously chosen, since it afforded very insecure riding; and was distant two miles from Sestos, the nearest town from which the fleet could be provided with necessaries. Alcibiades, who in his Thracian retirement was unable to withdraw his attention from the war in which he had long acted such a distinguished part, modestly admonished his countrymen of their imprudence; but he was arrogantly reproached for presuming, while an exile and an outlaw, to give advice to the admirals of Athens. Their subsequent conduct too faithfully corresponded with this insolence and folly. Despising the inferiority of the Peloponnesian fleet, they advanced in order of battle to the harbour of Lampsacus; and when the enemy moved not from their station, they returned in triumph as acknowledged masters of the sea. The prudence of Lysander perceived and indulged their presumption. During four days he bore, with extraordinary patience, their repeated insults, affecting the utmost disinclination to an engagement, carefully retaining his fleet in a place of security, and regularly dispatching a few swift-sailing

CHAP.
XXII.

Derisive battle of Ægos Potamos, in which the Athenians lose their fleet.
Olymp. xciii. 4.
A. C. 405. December.

vessels to observe the motions and behaviour of the Athenians when they returned from their daily cruise to the road of Ægos Potamos.

The fifth day they again bore up with the Peloponnesians, and provoked them to battle by more daring menaces than on any former occasion. As they flattered themselves with an undoubted prospect of success, they yielded without reserve to all the petulance of prosperity, and debated in what manner they should treat the Lacedæmonian prisoners who had the misfortune to fall into their power. The cruel Philocles proposed to cut off their right hands, that those enemies of Athens might be equally incapable to manage the oar and to brandish the spear; and this bloody resolution, though opposed by Adimantus, was approved by the majority of his colleagues. After insulting the enemy in a manner the most mortifying and disgraceful, they retired with an air of exultation mingled with contempt. The Peloponnesian spy-boats followed them as usual at a convenient distance, and observed that they had no sooner reached their stations than the seamen landed, straggled about the shore, advanced into the inland country in quest of provisions or amusement, indulged in indolence, or revelled in disorder. The advice-boats returned with uncommon celerity to convey the welcome intelligence to Lysander, who had embarked the troops, cleared his ships, and made every necessary preparation to avail himself of the favorable opportunity to effect by stratagem what it might have been dangerous to attempt by force. When his scouts approached the middle of the channel, they hoisted their shields (for that was the appointed signal), and at the same moment the Peloponnesian squadrons were commanded to set sail that they might surprise the hostile fleet, and indulge that resentment and animosity which had been rendered more violent and furious by the long and prudent restraint of their commander. The victory was complete, if that can be called a victory where there was scarcely any resistance. The vigilant activity of Conon endeavoured seasonably to assemble the strength of the Athenians; but his advice was disdained by officers incapable and unworthy of command, and his orders were despised by seamen unaccustomed and unwilling to obey. At length they became sensible of the danger when it was too late to avoid it. Their ships were taken, either altogether empty, or manned with such feeble crews as were unable to work, much less to defend them. The troops and sailors who flocked to the shore from indifferent quarters, and with disordered precipitation, were attacked by the regular onset and disciplined valor of the Peloponnesians. Those who fought were slain; the remainder fled into the inmost recesses of the Chersonesus, or took refuge in the Athenian fortresses which were scattered over that peninsula. When Lysander reviewed the extent of his well-merited success, he found that of a fleet of an hundred and eighty sail, only nine vessels had escaped, eight of which were conducted by Conon to the friendly island of

232 THE HISTORY OF GREECE.

CHAP. XXII.

Cyprus, while the ninth carried to Athens the melancholy news of a disaster equally unexpected and fatal. A hundred and seventy-one gallies, and three thousand prisoners (among whom were Philocles and Adimantus), rewarded the patience and fortitude of Lysander, who returned with his invaluable spoil to Lampsacus, amidst the joyous acclamations of naval triumph ".

The Athenian prisoners executed.

Before pursuing the natural consequences of an event the most important that had hitherto happened in all the Grecian wars, it was necessary for Lysander to decide the fate of the Athenian prisoners, against whom the confederates were animated by all that unrelenting hatred which is congenial to the stern character of republicans exasperated by continual provocation and recent insult. The injustice and cruelty of that ambitious people

" Xenoph. p. 416, et seqq. et Plut. in Lysand. By the battle of Ægos Potamos the Athenians lost the empire of the sea, which they had acquired by the conduct of their maritime allies in the fourth year of the seventy-fifth Olympiad. They enjoyed, therefore, that sovereignty, or empire as they styled it, from the year 477 till the year 405 before Christ; that is, a period of seventy-two years. This important computation is not to be found in any ancient writer; and no two authors agree in calculating the duration of the Athenian empire. Lysias in his Funeral Oration, p. 93. says, " During seventy years in which the Athenians commanded the sea." Diodorus Siculus (ad Olymp. 91. 1.) says, the Athenians commanded the Sea Sixty-five years. Isocrates in one place (l. p. 174.) agrees with Lysias; in another (ii. p 209 ; with Diodorus. Andocides (Orat. III. p. 286.) states it at eighty-five years. Lycurgus (adv. Leoc. p. 141.) at ninety. Dionysius Halicarnassus (Ant. Rom. sub init.) at sixty eight. Demosthenes, as we shall see below, states it variously at forty-five, sixty-five, and seventy-three years.

were carefully described and maliciously exaggerated in the dreadful tribunal of their enemies. "It would be tedious to enumerate, though it was impossible ever to forget, their multiplied and abominable crimes, of which so many individuals, and so many communities, had been the innocent and unhappy victims. Even of late they had destroyed without remorse, and without the shadow of necessity, the helpless crews of a Corinthian and an Andrian vessel. The gods had averted the atrocious resolution proposed by the bloody Philocles, of which the author and the approvers were equally criminal; nor could those deserve pardon who were incapable of pity". Such discourse, which resounded from every quarter of the assembly, declared, without the necessity of the formal vote, the unanimous decree of the confederates. As the prisoners had been stripped of their arms, there was nothing to be feared from their numbers and despair. They were conducted into the presence of their armed judges; and, as a prelude to the inhuman massacre, Lysander sternly demanded of Philocles what he deserved to suffer for his intended cruelty. The Athenian replied with firmness, "Accuse not those whom you are entitled to judge, but inflict on us the same punishment which we, in a different fortune, would have inflicted on our enemies". The words were scarcely ended when Lysander hacked him in pieces. The Peloponnesian soldiers followed the bloody example of their commander. Of three thousand Athenians, Adimantus alone was spared either because he had opposed the detestable resolution of Philocles, or because he had engaged in a treacherous correspondence with the Spartans [o].

Views of Lysander.

It might be expected, that immediately after an event which gave him the command of the sea, Lysander should sail to the Piræus, and assault the unfortunate city, which was already grievously oppressed by the Lacedæmonian army at Decelia. But the sagacious Spartan foresaw the numerous obstacles that opposed his conquest of Athens, and prudently restrained the eagerness of the troops and his own. The strongly fortified harbours of that capital, the long and lofty walls which surrounded the city on every side, the ancient renown and actual despair of the Athenians, must render the siege, if not altogether fruitless, at least difficult and tedious; and the precious moments wasted in this doubtful enterprise might be employed in attaining certain, immediate, and most important advantages.

He establishes the Spartan empire over the coasts and islands of Asia and Europe. Olymp. xciii. 4. A. C. 405.

On the coast neither of Greece nor of Asia, nor of any of the intermediate islands, was there a naval force capable of contending with the fleet of Lysander, nor any fortified place in all those countries (except the city of Athens alone) sufficient to resist the impression of his army. It was a design, therefore, which might well deserve his ambition, and which was not condemned by his prudence, to establish or confirm the Lacedæmonian empire over those valuable and extensive coasts. The populous cities of Byzantium and Chalcedon were

[o] Xenoph. Hellen. Plutarch in Lysand.

THE HISTORY OF GREECE. 235

attacked and taken during the astonishment and terror occasioned by the dreadful and irreparable misfortune of their Athenian allies. After these important acquisitions, Lysander sailed to the island of Lesbos, reduced Mitylené, and confirmed the allegiance of Methymna. While he extended his arms over the neighbouring islands, as well as the maritime towns of Lydia and Caria, a powerful squadron, commanded by the enterprising valor of Eteonicus, ravaged the shores of Macedon, subdued the sea-ports of Thrace, and rode victorious in the Hellespont and Propontis, the Ægean and Euxine seas. In six or eight months after the Athenian disaster at Ægos Potamos, the fairest portion of the ancient world, the most favored by nature, and the most adorned by art, reluctantly submitted to the power, or voluntarily accepted the alliance of Sparta.

CHAP. XXII.

During this long series of triumphs, Lysander never lost sight of the reduction of Athens; an object important in itself, and necessary to the completion of his extensive plan. The vigilance of the Peloponnesian squadrons prevented the usual supplies of foreign grain from reaching the distressed city. In all the towns which surrendered, or which were taken by storm, the Athenian garrisons were saved from immediate death, only on condition that they returned to their native country. By such contrivances the crafty Spartan expected that the scarcity of provisions would soon compel the growing multitude of inhabitants to submit to the Lacedæmonian army at Decelia. But

His measures for the reduction of Athens.

the Athenians, who despised the assaults of the enemy, braved the hardships of famine. Even after Lysander had blocked up their harbours with an hundred and fifty sail, they still defended, with vigor, their walls and ramparts; patiently endured fatigue and hunger; and beheld with obstinate unconcern, the affliction of their wives and children. Amidst the ravages of death and disease, which advanced with increasing horror, they punished, with the utmost severity, the ignoble cowardice of Archestratus, who first mentioned capitulation, and declared that the same moment should put an end to their independence and their lives.

But notwithstanding the melancholy firmness of the popular assembly, a numerous and powerful party in the state was governed rather by interest than by honor; and the greatest enemies of Athenian liberty flourished in the bosom of the republic. The aristocratical leven of the Four Hundred had infected the whole body of the senate; and not only the inconstant Theramenes, but several other men of abilities and influence, who had been most active in subverting that cruel tyranny, regretted the restoration of democracy to a people, who (as they had recently proved in many parts of their conduct) were unable to enjoy, without abusing, the invaluable gift of freedom. In republican governments, the misfortunes, which ought to bind all ranks of men in the firmest and most indissoluble union, have often little other tendence than to exasperate the political factions which tear and distract the community. Amidst every form of public distress, the Athenians caballed, clamored, accused, and persecuted each other; and the faction of the nobles, who acted with superior concert, vigor, and address, destroyed, by dark insinuations, false witnesses, perjury, and every other species of legal fraud and cruelty, the seditious Cleophon; and other turbulent demagogues, who might most effectually have opposed their measures [15].

When these obstacles were removed, Theramenes (whose recent merit prevented the suspicion of the assembly) proposed an embassy to Lacedæmon, which should request a suspension of hostilities, and obtain, if possible, some moderate terms of accommodation. He named himself, with nine colleagues, as the persons best qualified to undertake this important commission; flattering the people in the clearest and least ambiguous terms, with an undoubted prospect of success. A decree was immediately passed, investing the ambassadors with full powers. They assumed the sacred badge of their inviolable character, reached in safety the Spartan camp, held a conference with king Agis, and afterwards repaired to the Lacedæmonian capital. During four months they carried on their pretended negociation with the senate, the kings, the ephori, and especially with Lysander, whose authority, being unknown to the ancient constitution of Sparta, was far more extensive than that of

[15] Lysias, p. 272.

all the other magistrates together. With him, principally, the plan was concerted for compelling the Athenians to submit to terms of peace, which they must have regarded as worse, not only than war, but death [15]. The fortifications of their harbours were to be demolished, as well as the long walls which joined them with the city: they were to surrender all their ships, but twelve; to resign every pretension to their ancient possessions in foreign parts; to recal from banishment the surviving members of the late tyrannical aristocracy; to follow the standard of Sparta in war; and, in peace, to mould their political constitution after the model which that victorious republic might think fit to prescribe.

which is confirmed by the Athenians.

When Theramenes produced these unexpected fruits of his boasted negociation, the Athenians had no longer either strength or spirit to resist, or even courage to die. During the long absence of their ambassadors, the siege had been carried on with redoubled vigor. The Lacedæmonians, reinforced by the Thebans as well as by their numerous allies of Peloponnesus, had invested the city on every side, the harbours were closely blocked up by Lysander, who had become master of Melos, Ceos, Ægina, and Salamis; islands so near to Athens that they were almost regarded as a part of the Attic territory. The greatest misery prevailed within the walls; the famine was intolerable, and the diseases more intolerable than the

[15] Lysias against Eratosthenes, p. 273.

famine. The full period of thrice nine years had elapsed, which, if we may credit a most accurate and faithful historian [11], had been assigned by repeated oracles and predictions, as the destined term of the Peloponnesian war and of the Athenian greatness. The principal leaders of the democracy had been cut off by the perfidious snares of their opponents, who were prepared to bear a foreign yoke, provided they might usurp domestic tyranny. That odious faction was ready to approve the measures of Theramenes, who might intimidate the dejected assembly by declaring (a most melancholy truth) that the severity of the Lacedæmonians, excessive as it seemed, was yet moderation and lenity when compared with the furious and unextinguishable rage of the Thebans and Corinthians, who maintained that the Athenians deserved not any terms of accommodation; that their crimes ought to be persecuted with unrelenting vengeance; their proud city demolished with such perfect destruction, that not even its vestige should remain; and the insolent inhabitants utterly extirpated from Greece, which they had so long disturbed by their ambition, and provoked by their tyranny and cruelty. Such an argument Theramenes might have

[11] The words of Thucydides, l. v. p. 362. are very remarkable. "He remembers, that from the first commencement of hostilities, it had been constantly prophesied that the war would last thrice nine years, which, of all predictions, was alone firm and stable;" or as the idiom of the Greek language will bear, "the most firm and stable."

CHAP. XXII.

Athens surrenders —its humiliation excites the compassion of its enemies. Olymp. xciv. 1. A. C. 404.

employed, if it had been necessary to employ any argument, to justify his negociation with the Spartans, which was confirmed and ratified by the voice of the aristocratical cabal, and submitted to, rather than accepted, by the majority of the assembly, with the gloomy silence of despair.

On the sixteenth of May, the day on which the Athenians had been accustomed to celebrate the anniversary of the immortal victory of Salamis, the hostile armament took possession of their harbours; the combined army entered their gates. The walls and fortresses of the city of Minerva, which the generous magnanimity of its inhabitants, preferring the public safety to their own, had abandoned in defence of Greece to the fury of a barbarian invader, were ungratefully levelled to the ground by the implacable resentment of the Greeks; who executed their destructive purpose with all the eagerness of emulation, boasting, amidst the triumphs of martial music, that the demolition of Athens would be regarded, in succeeding ages, as the true æra of Grecian freedom. Yet after they had satisfied their vengeance, they seemed to regret its effects. The day was concluded with a magnificent festival, in which the recitation of the poets formed, as usual, the principal ornament of the entertainment. Among other pieces was rehearsed the Electra of Euripides, and particularly that affecting chorus, "We come, O daughter of Agamemnon! to thy rustic and humble roof". The words were scarcely uttered, when the whole assembly melted into tears, the

forlorn

forlorn condition of that young and virtuous princess, expelled the royal palace of her father, and inhabiting a miserable cottage, in want and wretchedness, recalling the dreadful vicissitude of fortune which had befallen Athens, once mistress of the sea, and sovereign of Greece, but deprived, in one fatal hour, of her ships, her walls, and her strength, and reduced from the pride of power and prosperity, to misery, dependence, and servitude, without exerting one memorable effort to brighten the last moment of her destiny, and to render her fall illustrious [14].

[14] Xenoph. Hellen. l. II. c. 1. et seqq. Diodor. l. xIII. 104—107. Plut. in Lysand. p. 438. Lysias in Eratosth. et Agorat.

CHAP. XXIII.

Rapacity and Cruelty of the Spartan Government. — The Thirty Tyrants in Athens. — Persecution of Lysias and his Family. — Theramenes opposes the Tyrants. — Sanguinary Speech of Critias. — Death of Theramenes. — Persecution and Death of Alcibiades. — Thrasybulus seizes Phylé — Defeats the Tyrants. —. Memorable Speech of Thrasybulus. — Oath of Amnesty — not faithfully observed.

THE conquest of Athens, and the acknowledged dominion of Sparta, terminated the memorable war of twenty-seven years. It still remained for Lysander to reduce the island of Samos [1], which enjoys the honorable distinction of being the last settlement in the East that defied the ambition of Pericles, and the last which submitted to the arms of Lysander. The conquered islands and cities suffered still greater vexations under the Spartan, than they had done under the Athenian, empire. Among the hostile factions [2]

---

[1] Comp. Xenoph. Hellen. L. ii. p. 461. et Plut. lib. p. 31. in Lysand. Lysias adv. Eratosth. p. 274. et Diodor. p. 396. It is remarkable, that Xenophon and Lysias, both contemporaries, should differ in a matter of chronology; the one placing the conquest of Samos before, and the other after, Lysander's voyage to Athens.

[2] These were the συνωμοσιαι επι δικαις και αρχαις, mentioned by Thucydides and Xenophon; — associations, or rather conspiracies, for mutual defence in courts of justice, and for mutual assistance in obtaining offices of power."

which ambition or danger had formed in those
turbulent republics, Lysander always preferred that
party which possessed most craft, and least patriotism. At the head of this cabal, he placed a
Spartan Harmostes, or governor, on whose obsequious cruelty he could depend. The citadels were
garrisoned by mercenaries; a tyrannical faction insulted as subjects, those whom they had envied as
rivals, or dreaded as enemies; and every species of
licence and disorder was exercised, with a presumption that could be equalled only by the tameness
with which it was endured.[1]. The Asiatic Greeks
regretted the dishonorable yoke of Persia; they
regretted the stern dominion of Athens; both which
seemed tolerable evils, compared to the oppressive
cruelty of Sparta and Lysander. The contributions, of which they had formerly so much complained, no longer appeared exorbitant. Lysander
was the first and the last conqueror who imposed on
those feeble communities the enormous tribute of
a thousand talents[2].

---

[1] Instead of the sweet draught of Liberty, Sparta, according to Theopompus, gave Greece the bitter cup of Slavery. In the city of Miletus, he sacrificed at once eight hundred men, of the democratical faction, to the implacable rage of their adversaries. Plut. in Lysand.

[2] Diodorus, p. 606. says, πλειω των χιλιων ταλαντων κατ' ενιαυτον, "more than a thousand talents yearly;" that is, above two hundred thousand pounds. It may be computed from Plut. in Lysand. et Xenoph. p. 462. that Lysander first borne a still larger sum after the surrender of Samos. The law of Lycurgus respecting gold and silver, which had been long virtually, was now formally, abolished. The use of the precious metals was allowed to the state, but forbidden to

CHAP.
XXIII.
Causes
to which
ascribed.

The unrelenting severity of Sparta has usually been ascribed to the personal character of her general, whose natural arrogance and cruelty were heightened and confirmed by the sudden exaltation of his fortune. From the simple citizen of a small, and then unfortunate republic, he became, in a few years, the arbiter of Greece. Athens acknowledged his authority; the smaller cities courted his protection; venal poets and orators extolled him with odes and panegyrics; he was honored with crowns and statues, and worshipped by hymns and sacrifices [f]. Yet it is obvious to remark, that whatever might be the temper and manners of Lysander, his country is justly accountable for the wrongs which he was allowed to commit with impunity; and it is uncertain whether another general, placed in the same situation, would have acted on different principles; since the nature of the Spartan institutions, and the ambitious views of the republic, seemed to demand and justify uncommon exertions of severity. In the administration of their domestic government, five or six thousand Spartans tyrannized over thirty thousand Lacedæmonians; these tyrannized, with still greater rigor, over thrice that number of slaves; and it was natural to expect, that when the slaves were associated

individuals, under pain of death. The prohibition, however, was universally disregarded; many Spartans possessed abundance of gold and silver; none incurred the penalty of the law. Compar. Plut. et Xenoph. loc. citat. et Isocrat. in Archidam.

[f] Plut. in Lysand.

THE HISTORY OF GREECE. 245

with the troops[f], all these descriptions of men, Spartans, Lacedæmonians, and Helots, would tyrannize, with the emulation of cruelty, over their conquered subjects.

The scanty materials of ancient history cannot enable us minutely to explain the humiliation and distress of the Asiatic Greeks, oppressed by the double tyranny of the Spartans, and of their fellow-citizens. Contemporary writers, who beheld this scene of misery and desolation, seem at a loss for words to impress its horror. Isocrates endeavours to grasp the amplitude of the subject in the vague language of general description; by strokes of exaggeration and hyperbole, he supplies the place of clear and positive information; but all the copiousness and energy of the Greek tongue sink beneath the heavy afflictions of that unfortunate people, and the mind of the orator seems to labor with a thought which he is unable to express[g]. It

---

[f] The Helots then took the title of νεοδαμώδεις, Libertini, ἥντινα δὲ τὸ νεοδαμώδεις ἐλευθέρων τῶν εἱλώτων. Thucydid. l. v. p. 532. From some passages in Isocrates (Panegyr. et de Pace.), it should seem that Lysander often appointed these freed men to offices of great trust and authority.

[g] See the oration of Isocrates on the peace, p. 172, etc. In the panegyric of Athens, speaking of the aristocratical factions supported by Lysander and the Lacedæmonians, Isocrates says, they consisted of wretches, "whose cruelty and injustice are unexampled in the history of mankind. From what indignity did they abstain? Into what excesses were they not transported? They, who regarded the most factious as the most faithful; the most treacherous as the most deserving. Their crimes proved infectious, and changed the mildness of human nature into savage ferocity," etc. See p. 53, etc.

R 3

is not, however, from such rhetorical descriptions that we can attain an adequate and satisfactory knowledge of the Spartan administration: history delights in plain and authentic facts; and the rigorous treatment of the Athenians themselves, will best represent the hardships inflicted on their Asiatic colonies and dependences.

The thirty tyrants in Athens. Olymp. xciv. 1. A. C. 404.

The Athenians had surrendered their fleet; their walls and harbours were demolished; their citadel was occupied by a Lacedæmonian garrison, commanded by Callibius, the friend of Lysander; and their government was usurped by thirty men, the dependants and creatures of Sparta. The furious and profligate Critias formed a proper head for this aristocratical council, whose members have been justly branded in history under the name of the Thirty Tyrants. On pretence of delivering the state from the malice of informers, and the turbulence of seditious demagogues, they destroyed the most valuable portion of the community. Niceratus, the son of Nicias, and a son who inherited not only the opulence, but the virtues of his illustrious father, was condemned to death;

---

* Their names are preserved in Xenophon, Hellen. li. 3.

* Xenoph. p. 462. which Cufas, ap. Sallust. de Bello Catil. c. 11. evidently had in view. "Lacedæmonii devictis Atheniensibus, triginta viros imposuere.... Hi primo cœpere pessimum quemque, et omnibus invisum, indemnatum necare. Eo populus lætari, et merito dicere feri. Post ubi paulatim licentia crevit juxta bonos et malos libidinose interficere.... Ita civitas, servitute oppressa, stultæ lætitiæ graves pœnas dedit."

Leon, the moſt public-ſpirited, and Antiphon, the moſt eloquent of his contemporaries, ſhared the ſame fate; Thraſybulus and Anytus were baniſhed. Whoever was known to be powerful, was regarded as dangerous; whoever was ſuppoſed to be rich, was accuſed as criminal. Strangers and citizens were involved in one promiſcuous ruin [10].

CHAP. XXIII.

Amidſt this general wreck of whatever was moſt worthy and reſpectable, 'I ſhall ſelect the perſecution of Lyſias and his family, the only tranſaction of that kind, recorded with ſuch circumſtances as anſwer the ends of hiſtory. Cephalus, the father of that ingenious orator, was by birth a Syracuſan. The friendſhip of Pericles perſuaded him to ſettle in Athens, where, under the protection of that powerful ſtateſman, he obtained wealth and honors. His inoffenſive and generous character eſcaped the enmity and perſecution to which the opulent Athenians were commonly expoſed; and he enjoyed the rare felicity of living thirty years in the midſt of continual trials and impeachments, without being obliged to appear as plaintiff or defendant in any litigation. His ſons, Lyſias and Polemarchus, inherited his innocence, his generoſity, and his good fortune. Though poſſeſſed of the moſt valuable accompliſhments, natural and acquired, the brothers prudently kept aloof from the dangerous paths of public life; contented

Illuſtrated by the perſecution of Lyſias and his family.

[10] Xenoph. l. II. p. 443, et ſeqq.

CHAP.
XXIII.

with their domestic felicity, they aspired not to the rank of Athenian citizens; but liberally contributed to supply the exigences of the state, from the profits of a flourishing manufacture of shields, which they carried on by the labor of an hundred and twenty slaves. The cruelty of the thirty tyrants, from whose rapacious eye neither obscurity could conceal, nor merit defend, occasioned the death of Polemarchus, and the immediate misfortunes, as well as the future glory of Lysias, who acted a distinguished part in overturning that detestable tyranny, and in bringing its authors and abettors to condign punishment[11].

The orator's account of this matter.

The history is related by himself with perspicuous precision and graceful simplicity: "The tyrants Theognis and Piso acquainted their associates, that many strangers established at Athens were disaffected to the government. This was a plausible pretence for rifling the effects of these unhappy men; a measure to which the thirty were not only excited by avarice, but prompted by fear. Money was become necessary for the preservation of their power, which, being founded on usurpation, and tyrannically administered, could only be maintained by the influence of corruption, and the mercenary aid of foreign troops. The life of man, therefore, they regarded as a matter of little moment; the amassing of wealth was the principal object of their desire; to gratify which, ten strangers were at once devoted to destruction. In this number,

[11] See the Life of Lysias, and the Orations there referred to, p. 110, et seqq.

indeed, were two poor men; a base and cruel artifice to perfuade you, Athenians! that the remaining eight had been condemned, not for the fake of their riches, but in order to preferve the public tranquillity; as if the intereft of the public had ever been the concern of that tyrannical cabal! Their infamous defign was executed with inhuman cruelty. Their victims were taken in their beds, at fupper, in the privacy of domeftic retirement. Me they feized exercifing the rites of hofpitality; my guefts were rudely difmiffed; I was delivered into the cuftody of the worthlefs Pifo. While his accomplices continued in the workfhop, taking a lift of our flaves and effects, I afked him, "Whether money could fave my life?" "Yes, a confiderable fum." "I will give you a talent of filver." This he confented to accept, as the price of my fafety; and to fuch a melancholy fituation was I reduced, that it afforded me a momentary confolation to depend on the precarious faith of a man, who (as I well knew) defpifed every law, human and divine. But my comfort was of fhort duration; for I had no fooner opened my coffer to pay him the talent, than he ordered his attendant to feize the contents, confifting of three talents of filver, an hundred Daricks, three hundred Cyzicenes, and three filver cups. I entreated Pifo to allow me a fmall fum to defray the expenfe of my journey. But he defired me to be thankful to efcape with my life. Going out together, we met the tyrants Melobius and Mnefitheides, returning from the workfhop. They

CHAP. XXIII. inquired, where we were going? Pifo anfwered, to examine the houfe of my brother Polemarchus. They defired him to proceed; but commanded me to follow them to the houfe of Damafippus. Pifo whifpered me to be filent, and to fear nothing, becaufe he would immediately come there. Upon our arrival, we found Theognis guarding feveral of my companions in calamity. I increafed the number of his prifoners; but obtained an opportunity to reprefent my innocence and misfortunes to Damafippus, entreating him, by our paft friendfhip, to employ his influence in my behalf. He affured me of his intention to intercede with Theognis, whofe avarice would eafily perfuade him to betray his truft. While they converfed on this fubject, I took advantage of my knowledge of the houfe to efcape through three fecret paffages, which all happened to be open and unguarded; and fortunately reaching the country-houfe of my friend Archimaus, a fhip-mafter, fent him to the city, that he might bring me intelligence of my brother. He difcovered, that the tyrant Eratofthenes had dragged him from the road, and conducted him to prifon, where he was ordered to drink hemlock. At this melancholy news, I failed to Megara, under cover of the night. Our effects became the property of the tyrants, whofe mean avarice fpared not the fmalleft trifle belonging to us. Even the gold ear-rings of Polemarchus's wife were forcibly torn away by the brutal Melobius [13]."

[13] See the difcourfes of Lyfias againft Agoratus and Eratofthenes, p. 218, et feqq.

The Thirty justified these abominable acts of cruelty by the authority of a servile senate, which they still allowed to subsist as the instrument and accomplice of their tyranny. It could not be expected, however, that in a city accustomed to the utmost liberty of opinion and freedom of debate, a body of five hundred, or even of thirty men, should continue to agree in the same odious and oppressive measures. The first seeds of discord, or rather the first symptoms of repentance, appeared in the speeches and behaviour of the bold and active Theramenes; who, though the principal author of the usurpation, was already disposed by the humanity of his nature, or by the singular inconstancy of his temper[11], to destroy the work of his own hands. His strenuous endeavours were used to save the innocent and unhappy victims whom his furious colleagues daily devoted to destruction; under his protection the citizens assembled, and expressed their resentment or despair; and it was justly apprehended that the government of the Thirty might be dissolved by the same means, and by the same man, who had set on foot and subverted the short-lived tyranny of the four hundred. The present usurpation, indeed, was defended by a Lacedæmonian garrison; but the Thirty dreaded the influence of Theramenes over

CHAP. XXIII.
Theramenes opposes the tyrants.

[11] Thucydid. viii. 68. et seqq. Lysias adverf. Eratosth. Xenophon paints him more favorably; and Aristot. apud Plut. lib. 337. et Diodor. p. 350. et seqq. still more favorably than Xenophon.

CHAP.
XXIII.

the foreign troops; they dreaded still more his influence over the Athenian citizens. When they considered the precarious tenure of their authority, and the unjust violence of their administration, they reflected on the past with pain, and viewed the future with terror. But they had gone too far to retreat, and nothing remained but to prop the tottering fabric of their power by enlarging its base. Three thousand citizens were invited to participate in the advantages and dangers of their government. The rest were disarmed and treated with an increase of severity.

He is accused by Critias.

Theramenes vainly opposed the criminal designs of his colleagues, who implicitly submitted their opinions to the implacable fury of Critias. He it was who chiefly encouraged them boldly to persevere, and to remove every obstacle to the unlimited gratification of their passions. The safety of Theramenes, he assured them, was no longer compatible with their own. His delicacy, real or affected, was totally inconsistent with the spirit of the present administration; nor could the government of Thirty, any more than that of *one* tyrant, admit of being curiously canvassed, or fastidiously opposed. These sentiments being received with approbation, we might expect that Theramenes should have been destroyed by that sudden and open violence which had proved fatal to so many others. But as the most daring violators of the laws of society are obliged to establish and observe some rules of justice, in their conduct towards each other, it had been resolved by the Thirty, that, amidst the violent and capricious outrages which they committed against their subjects, none of their own number should be put to death without the benefit of a trial before the senate; a privilege extending to the three thousand intrusted with the use of arms, and sufficiently denoting the miserable condition of the other citizens. The senate was assembled to try Theramenes; but this tribunal was surrounded by armed men. When the pretended criminal appeared, Critias addressed the court in a speech too remarkable ever to be forgotten.

"Should you imagine, O senators! considering the great numbers who have suffered death, that we have been guilty of unnecessary cruelty, you will alter that opinion on reflecting that revolutions of government must always be attended with bloodshed; but particularly when a populous city like Athens, which has been long pampered with liberty, is reduced under the dominion of a few. The actual form of administration was imposed by the Lacedæmonians as the condition of the public safety. In order to maintain its authority we have removed those seditious demagogues, whose democratical madness hath occasioned all our past calamities. It is our duty to proceed in this useful work, and to destroy, without fear or compassion, all who would disturb the public tranquillity. Should a man of this dangerous disposition be found in our own order, he ought to be punished with double rigor, and treated not only as an enemy but as a traitor. That Theramenes is liable

CHAP. XXIII.

Theramenes's defence.

to this accusation appears from the whole tenor of his conduct. He concluded the treaty with the Lacedæmonians; he dissolved the popular government; he directed and approved the first and boldest measures of our administration: but no sooner did difficulties arise than he deserted his associates, declared his opposition to their designs, and undertook the protection of the populace. When the weather was fair and favorable, he pursued the same course with his companions, but, on the first change of wind, he thought proper to alter his navigation. With such an irresolute steersman it is impossible to govern the helm of the republic, and to guide the vessel to her destined harbour. This dangerous inconsistency ought, indeed, to have been expected from a man to whose character perfidy is congenial. He began his political career under the direction of his father Hagnon, a violent partisan of democracy. He afterwards changed his system, in order to obtain the favor of the nobles. He both established and dissolved the government of the four hundred; and the whole strain of his behaviour proves him unfit to govern, and unworthy to live[10]."

Theramenes made a copious and persuasive defence; acknowledging, "That he had often changed his conduct, but denying that he had ever varied his principles. When the democracy flourished, he had maintained the just rights, but repressed the insolence, of the people. When it

[10] Xenoph. p. 464—466.

THE HISTORY OF GREECE. 255

became neceſſary to alter the form of the republic, in compliance with the command of the Spartans, he had ſupported the legal power, but oppoſed the tyranny, of the magiſtrates. Under every adminiſtration of government he had approved himſelf the friend of moderation and juſtice, which he ſtill continued, and ever would continue, to recommend and enforce, convinced that thoſe virtues alone could give ſtability and permanence to any ſyſtem of government, whether ariſtocratical or popular."

The ſenators murmured applauſe, unawed by the preſence of Critias and his aſſociates. But this furious tyrant made a ſignal to the armed men, who ſurrounded the ſenate-houſe, to ſhow the points of their daggers; and then ſtepping forward, ſaid, "It is the duty, O ſenators! of a prudent magiſtrate, to prevent the deception and danger of his friends. The countenance of thoſe brave youths (pointing to his armed partiſans) ſufficiently diſcovers that they will not permit you to ſave a man who is manifeſtly ſubverting the government: I, therefore, with the general conſent, ſtrike the name of Theramenes from the liſt of thoſe who have a right to be tried before the ſenate; and, with the approbation of my colleagues, I condemn him to immediate death." Rouſed by this unexpected and bloody ſentence, Theramenes ſtarted from his ſeat, and ſprang to the altar of the ſenate-houſe, at once imploring the compaſſion, and urging the intereſt of the ſpectators, whoſe names, he obſerved, might be ſtruck out,

CHAP. XXIII.

His death.

and whose lives might be sacrificed, as unjustly and cruelly as his own. But the terror of armed violence prevented any assistance or intercession; and the eleven men (for thus the Athenian delicacy styled the executioners of public justice) dragged him from the altar, and hurried him to execution.

In proceeding through the market-place the unhappy victim of tyranny invoked the favor and gratitude of his fellow-citizens, who had often been protected by his eloquence, and defended by his valor. But the impudent Satyrus, the chief minister of vengeance both in authority and cruelty, sternly told him, that if he continued his lamentations and uproar he should soon cry in good earnest[13]: "And shall I not," said Theramenes, "though I remain silent?" When he drank the fatal hemlock, he poured a libation on the ground with a health to the honest Critias; circumstances unworthy to relate, if they proved not, that even in his last moments, he was forsaken neither by his factiousness nor by his fortitude[14].

[13] Ὅτι οἰμώξοιτο, εἰ μὴ σιωπήσειεν. Literally, that he would cry out unless he were silent. The inaccurate language of the executioner furnished occasion to the smart reply of Theramenes.

[14] Xenoph. p. 470. The glorious death of Theramenes cancelled the imperfections of his life. That his character was inconstant, most writers allow. Lysias adversus Eratosthen. accuses him of many deliberate crimes; but he died in a virtuous cause, and, however he acted, left the scene gracefully. "Quam me delectat Theramenes! quam elato animo est! Etsi enim flemus, cum legimus, tamen non miserabiliter vir clarus moritur." Cic. Tusc. Quæst.

THE HISTORY OF GREECE. 257

The death of Theramenes delivered the tyrants from the only restraint which tended to control their insolence, and to moderate their cruelty. They might now indulge in all the licentiousness of outrage, without the fear of reproach or the danger of resistance. Their miserable subjects were driven from the city, from the Pyræus, from their houses, their farms, and their villages, which were divided among the detestable instruments of an odious usurpation. Nor did the tyrants stop here. A mandate was published, enforced by the authority of the Spartan senate, prohibiting any Grecian city to receive the unfortunate fugitives. But this inhuman order was almost universally disobeyed; the sacred laws of hospitality prevailed over the terror of an unjust decree; Thebes, Argos, and Megara, were crowded with Athenian exiles[17].

In exercising those abominable acts of cruelty, the Thirty probably consulted the immediate safety of their persons, but they precipitated the downfal of their power. The oppressed Athenians, whose sufferings seemed no longer tolerable, required only a leader to rouse them to arms, and to conduct them to victory and to vengeance. This danger the tyrants had greater reason to apprehend, since they could not expect a reinforcement to the garrison, while the efforts of Lysander and the Spartans were principally directed towards the extension of their Asiatic conquests. The abilities

[17] Diodor. l. xiv. p. 236.

CHAP. XXIII.

and resentment of Alcibiades pointed him out as the person best qualified to undertake the arduous and honorable design of reassembling the fugitives, and of animating them with courage to recover their lost country. That illustrious exile had been driven from his Thracian fortress by the terror of the Lacedæmonians, then masters of the Hellespont, and had acquired a settlement under the protection of Pharnabazus, in the little village of Grynium in Phrygia, where, undisturbed by the dangerous contentions of war and politics, he enjoyed an obscure happiness in the bosom of love and friendship. But the cruel fears of the tyrants pursued him to this last retreat.

His death.

Lysander told Pharnabazus that the sacrifice of Alcibiades was necessary for the safety of that form of government which had been recently established in Athens, and which it was the interest both of Sparta and of Persia to maintain. A private reason (which will afterwards appear) prevailed with the satrap to pay immediate attention to this bloody advice. A band of armed Phrygians was sent to surprise and destroy Alcibiades. Such was the fame of his prowess, that these timid assassins durst not attack him in broad day, or by open force. They chose the obscurity of night to surround and set fire to his house, which, according to the fashion of the country, was chiefly composed of light and combustible materials. The crackling noise of the flames alarmed Alcibiades, whose own treacherous character rendered him always suspicious of treachery. He snatched his sword, and, twisting his mantle round his left arm, rushed through the flaming edifice, followed by his faithful Arcadian friend, and by his affectionate mistress Timandra[18]. The cowardice of the Phrygians, declining to meet the fury of his assault, covered him with a shower of javelins. But even these Barbarians spared the weakness and the sex of Timandra, whose tears and entreaties obtained the melancholy consolation of burying her unfortunate lover; a man whose various character can only be represented in the wonderful vicissitudes of his life and fortune; and who, though eminently adorned with the advantages of birth, wealth, valor, and eloquence, and endowed with uncommon gifts of nature and acquirements of art, yet deficient in discretion and probity, involved his country and himself in inextricable calamities.

Although the life of Alcibiades had been highly pernicious to his country, his death, at this particular juncture, might be regarded as a misfortune, if the Athenian exiles at Thebes had not been headed by a man who possessed his excellences, unmingled with his defects and vices. The enterprising courage of Thrasybulus was animated by the love of liberty; and while he generally followed[19] the rules of justice and humanity, he had magnanimity to conceive, abilities to conduct, and perseverance to accomplish, the boldest and most

[18] Corn. Nepos, et Plut. in Alcibiad.
[19] His conduct, as will appear hereafter, was not uniform.

arduous designs. Having communicated his intentions to the unhappy fugitives in Thebes and Megara, he encouraged a body of seventy intrepid followers to seize the important fortress of Phylé, situate on the Bœotian and Athenian frontier. This daring enterprise alarmed the tyrants, who marched forth with the flower of their troops to dislodge the new garrison. But the natural strength of the place baffled their assault; and, when they determined to invest it, the unexpected violence of a tempest, accompanied with an extraordinary fall of snow [10], obliged them to desist from their undertaking. They returned with precipitation to Athens, leaving behind part of their attendants and baggage, which fell a prey to the garrison of Phylé; the strength of which continually augmented by the confluence of Athenian exiles, and soon increased from seventy, to seven hundred, men.

The tyrants had just reason to apprehend that these daring invaders might ravage the surrounding country, and even attack the capital. Alarmed by this danger they dispatched several troops of horse, with the greater part of their Lacedæmonian mercenaries, who encamped in a woody country, at the distance of fifteen furlongs from Phylé, in order to watch the motions and repress the incursions of the enemy. But these forces, which had been sent to guard the territory and city from surprise,

---

[10] Ἐπιγενέσθαι τῆς νυκτὸς χιὼν παμπληθής. Xenoph. p. 471.

were themselves surprised by Thrasybulus, who silently marched forth in the night, posted his men amidst the concealed intricacies of the forest, and suddenly attacked the Lacedæmonians before they had time to recollect themselves, or even to stand to their arms. The dread of an ambush probably prevented the wary general from following them to any great distance from the garrison. An hundred and twenty men were slain in the pursuit; a trophy was erected; the baggage and arms were conveyed in triumph to Phylé[81].

The news of this disaster inspired the Thirty with such terror that they no longer regarded a demolished city like Athens as proper for their residence. They determined to remove to the neighbouring town of Eleusis, which, in case of extremity, seemed more capable of defence. The three thousand, who were intrusted with the use of arms, accompanied them thither, and assisted them in treacherously putting to death all such of the Eleusinians as were thought disaffected to the usurpation. Under pretence of mustering the inhabitants, those unhappy men were singly conducted through a narrow gate leading to the shore, where they were successively disarmed, bound, and executed, by the cruel instruments of tyranny[82].

Meanwhile the garrison of Phylé continually received new reinforcements. The orator Lysias, whose domestic sufferings have been recently

[81] Xenoph. p. 171. [82] Id. ibid.

CHAP.
XXIII.
described, collected three hundred men to take vengeance on the murderers of his brother, and the authors of his own banishment[1]. These useful supplies encouraged Thrasybulus to attempt surprising the Piræus, the inhabitants of which, consisting chiefly of tradesmen, merchants, and mariners, bore with great impatience and indignation the injuries of a subordinate council of Ten, the obsequious imitators of the Thirty. This enterprise was crowned with success, although the tyrants brought forth their whole force to oppose it. Having intercepted their march to the place, Thrasybulus occupied a rising ground, which gave him a decisive advantage in the engagement.

Addresses his followers in sight of the enemy.

Before leading his men to action, he animated their valor and resentment, by reminding them, that the enemy on the right consisted of those Lacedæmonians whom only five days before they had shamefully routed and put to flight; that the troops on the left were commanded by the Thirty tyrants, who had unjustly driven them into banishment, confiscated their property, and murdered their dearest friends. "But the gods have finally given us the opportunity (long ardently desired) to face our oppressors with arms in our hands, and to take vengeance on their multiplied wickedness and cruelty. When they invested us at Phylé, the gods, consulting our safety, ruffled the serenity

[1] Justin. l. v. c. ix. The compiler, with his usual inaccuracy, says, Lysias Syracusanus orator.

THE HISTORY OF GREECE. 263

of the sky with an unexpected tempest. The assistance of Heaven enabled us, with a handful of men, to raise a trophy over our numerous foes; and the same divine Providence still favors us with the most manifest marks of partiality. The enemy are drawn up in a deep and close array; they must be obliged to ascend the eminence; the javelins of their rear cannot reach beyond their van; while, from the reverse of these circumstances, no weapon of ours needs be discharged in vain. Let us avail ourselves, therefore, of an arrangement evidently produced by the favor of Heaven; each soldier remembering, that he never can atchieve a more honorable victory, or obtain a more glorious tomb ".

The revered authority of the priest enforced the exhortation of the general. He promised them complete success, provided they forbore to charge till one of their men were killed or wounded: "Then," added he, "I will conduct you on to victory, though I myself shall fall." He had scarcely ended, when the enemy threw their javelins; upon which, as if guided by a divine impulse, he rushed forward to the attack. Both parts of his prediction were accomplished. The battle was neither long nor bloody; but Critias and Hippomachus, the two most violent of the tyrants, were left among the slain. Thrasybulus judiciously avoided to pursue the scattered fugitives, who

" Xenoph. p. 473. et Diodor. l. xiv. p. 414.

CHAP.
XXIII.

His proclamation to the vanquished.

being superior in number, might still rally and renew the battle, if he quitted the advantage of the ground. But having proceeded to the foot of the hill, he stopped the ardor of his troops, and commanded the herald Cleocritus to proclaim with a loud voice, "Wherefore, Athenians! would you fly from your countrymen? Wherefore have you driven them from the city? Why do you thirst for their blood? We are all united by religious, civil, and domestic ties. Often, with combined arms, have we fought, by sea and land, to defend our common country and common freedom. Even in this unnatural civil war, excited and fomented by the ambition of impious and abominable tyrants, who have shed more blood in eight months, than the Peloponnesians, our public enemies, in ten years. We have lamented your misfortunes as much as our own; nor is there a man whom you have left on the field of battle, whose death does not excite our sympathy, and increase our affliction." The tyrants, dreading the effect of a proclamation well calculated to sow the seeds of disaffection, led off their troops with great precipitation; and Thrasybulus, without stripping the dead, marched to the Piræus[91].

Government of the Decemviri,

Next day the Thirty, shamefully discomfited in the engagement, and deprived of Critias, their furious but intrepid leader, took their melancholy seats in council with strong indications of expected ruin. Their unfortunate subjects accused their

[91] Xenoph. p. 474.

commanders, and each other; a new sedition arose; nor was the ferment allayed, until the tyrants had been deprived of their dignity, and ten magistrates (one elected from each tribe) appointed in their room [16]. The surviving tyrants, with those who were too closely united with them in guilt, not to be united in interest, fled to Eleusis.

{as violent as that of the Thirty.}

It might be expected that the Decemvirs, who now assumed the government, should have been deterred from injustice by the fatal example of their predecessors. But in the turbulent republics of Greece, however free in theory, men were little acquainted with the benefits of practical liberty. Whether the nobles, or people, or a prevailing faction of either; whatever party in the state obtained the chief administration, their authority was almost alike oppressive and tyrannical. Alternately masters and slaves, those fierce republicans were either unable or unwilling to draw that decisive and impervious line between the power of government, and the liberty of the subject; a line which forms the only solid barrier of a uniform, consistent, and rational freedom.

{Lysander marches to the Piræus.}

The Ten had no sooner been invested with the ensigns of command, than they showed an equal inclination with the Thirty to obey the Lacedæmonians, and to tyrannize over their fellow-citizens [17]. After various skirmishes, which happened in the

[16] Xenoph. p. 471. et Iberat. II. p. 426.
[17] Lysias advers. Eratosth. p. 212, et seqq.

CHAP. XXIII.

course of two weeks, and generally proved honorable to the bravery and conduct of Thrasybulus, the tyrants both in Eleusis and in Athens dispatched messengers to solicit farther assistance from Sparta and Lysander. That active and enterprising leader employed his usual diligence to protect the government which he had established. At the head of a powerful body of mercenaries, he marched to the Piræus, which he invested by land; while his brother Libys, who commanded a considerable squadron, blocked up the harbour [11].

His measures thwarted by Pausanias.

These vigorous exertions restored the hopes and courage of the tyrants; nor can it be doubted that Thrasybulus and his followers must have speedily been compelled to surrender, had the Spartan commanders been allowed to act without control. But the proud arrogance of Lysander, and the rapacious avarice of his dependants, provoked the indignation and resentment of whatever was most respectable in his country. The kings, magistrates, and senate, conspired to humble his ambition; and, lest he should enjoy the glory of conquering Athens a second time, Pausanias, the most popular and beloved of the Spartan princes, hastily levied the domestic troops, and a considerable body of Peloponnesian allies, and marching through the Isthmus of Corinth encamped in the neighbourhood of Athens; little solicitous to increase

[11] Xenoph. p. 476. et Diodor. ubi supra.

the diffensions in that city, provided he could anticipate and thwart the measures of Lysander.

While the two Lacedæmonian armies discovered, in the distance of their encampments, a disunion of their views and interests, an incident happened which determined Pausanias to undertake the protection of Thrasybulus and his adherents; a resolution to which he was naturally inclined from opposition to an envied and odious rival. Diognotus, an Athenian of an amiable and respectable character, brought him the children of Niceratus and Eucrates; the former the son, the latter the brother, of the great Nicias, with whom the Spartan king was connected by the hereditary ties of hospitality and friendship. Having placed the helpless infants on his knees, he conjured him, by his religious regard for the memory of their much-respected ancestor, to pity their innocence and weakness, and to defend them against the cruel tyranny of a worthless faction, ambitious to cut off and destroy whatever was distinguished by birth, wealth, or virtue ". This affecting scene, had it failed to touch the heart of Pausanias, must at least have afforded him a plausible pretence for embracing the party of Thrasybulus, which numbered among its adherents the friends and family of Nicias, who had long been suspected of an undue attachment to the Spartan interest.

CHAP. XXIII.

Pausanias espouses the interest of Thrasybulus and his adherents. Olympiad 2. A. C. 408.

" Lysias adv. Pollochum, p. 323. and the translation of Lysias, p. 232.

CHAP.
XXIII.
Commissioners appointed to settle the affairs of Athens.

Before he could fully persuade the enemy of his favorable intentions, several bloody skirmishes were fought, in which the partisans of democracy defended the Piræus with unequal force, but with uncommon resolution [1]. At length Pausanias made them understand, that, instead of destroying their persons, he wished to protect their liberties. In Athens his emissaries made known this unexpected revolution, which excited a numerous party to throw off the yoke of the tyrants, and to desire a reconciliation with their fellow-citizens in the Piræus. The deputies were favorably received by the Spartan king, and sent, under his protection, to propose overtures of accommodation to the ephori and senate. The messengers of Lysander and the tyrants endeavoured to traverse this negociation; but notwithstanding *their* opposition, the Spartans appointed fifteen commissioners, who, in conjunction with Pausanias, were empowered to settle the affairs of Athens [2].

This happily effected.

With the approbation, or rather by the command, of those ministers, the Athenian factions ceased from hostility; the tyrants were divested of their power; the foreign garrison was withdrawn; and the popular government re-established. This important revolution was remarkable for its singular mildness. The authors and instruments of the most oppressive usurpation recorded in the annals of any people were allowed to retire in safety to

[1] Xenoph. Diodor. Lysias, ubi supra.
[2] Xenoph. p. 478.

Eleusis. Thrasybulus conducted a military procession to the temple of Minerva in the citadel, where the acknowledgments of thanks and sacrifice were offered to that protecting divinity, who had restored the virtuous exiles to their country, and healed the divisions of the state. The citizens who had been banished, and those who had driven them into banishment, joined in this solemn exercise of religious duty; after which, convening in full assembly, they were addressed by Thrasybulus in these memorable words:

"The experience of your past transactions may enable you, men of Athens! to know each other, and to know yourselves. On what pretence could you, who drove us from the city, abet a tyrannical faction? Why would you have enslaved your fellow-citizens? On what superiority of merit could you found your claim of dominion? Is it that you are more honest and virtuous? Yet the people whom you insulted never relieved their poverty by unjust gain; whereas the tyrants, whom you served, increased their wealth by the most oppressive rapacity. Is it that you are more brave and warlike? Yet this injured people, alone and unassisted, and almost unarmed, have overcome your superior numbers, reinforced by the Lacedæmonian garrison, the powerful succours of Pausanias, and the experienced mercenaries of Lysander. As you must yield the prize both of probity and of prowess, so neither can you claim the honor of superior prudence and sagacity. You

CHAP. XXIII.

Memorable speech of Thrasybulus.

270 THE HISTORY OF GREECE.

CHAP. XXIII.

have been not only conquered in war, but overcome in negociation, by the people whom you despised; to whom your Lacedæmonian masters have delivered you, like biting curs [11], bound and muzzled, to be justly punished for your unprovoked insolence and audacity. But as to you, my fellow-sufferers and fellow-exiles! you, who shared the hardships of my banishment, and who now share the triumph of my victorious return, I exhort you to forgive and forget our common injuries. Let the dignity of your sentiments adorn the splendor of your actions. Prove yourselves superior to your enemies, not only in valor but in clemency, that moderation may produce concord, and concord strength."

The assembly.

The effect of this generous enthusiasm, excited and diffused by Thrasybulus, appeared in a very extraordinary resolution of the assembly. During the usurpation of the Thirty, a hundred talents had been borrowed from the Lacedæmonians, to support the rigorous cruelty of a government which had banished five thousand [12], and put to death, untried, fifteen hundred citizens. The repayment of this sum was not to be expected from the people at large, against whose interest and safety it had been so notoriously employed. Yet the Athe-

[11] Ὥσπερ τις δάκνοντας κύνας ἱμάντες παραδιδόασι. Xenoph. Hellen. lib. sub fin. In their comparisons the ancients, it is well known, regarded justness more than dignity.

[12] Isocrat. in Areopag. p. 345. says upwards of five hundred. Diodorus says the one-half of the citizens.

nians unanimously resolved, on this occasion, that
the money should be charged indiscriminately on
them all [14]. This unexampled generosity might
have encouraged even the enfeebled party of the
tyrants to return from Eleusis. But they were too
sensible of their guilt to expect forgiveness or impunity. Having fortified their insecure residence,
in the best manner that their circumstances could
permit, they began to prepare arms; to collect
mercenaries; and to try, anew, the fortune of war.
But their unequal hostility, the effect of rage and
despair, was easily defeated by the vigor of the
new republic. The most obnoxious leaders sealed,
with their blood, the safety of their adherents, who
submitted to the clemency of Thrasybulus. That
fortunate and magnanimous commander generously
undertook their cause, and obtained a decree of the
people for restoring them to the city, for reinstat-
ing them in their fortunes and privileges, and for
burying in oblivion the memory of their past offences [15]. The assembly even ratified, by oath, this

[14] Isocrates, ibid. et p. 495 of the translation.
[15] Among these offences were reckoned the arbitrary laws enacted during their usurpation. All these laws were annulled, and those of Solon, Clisthenes, Pericles, etc. re-established. It appears that the Athenians embraced the same opportunity of examining their ancient laws, abolishing such as no longer suited the condition of the times, and enacting some new ones. Andocid. Orat. I. de Myster. p. 212. et Demosth. adv. Timocrat. p. 469. The year in which the democracy was restored, or, in other words, the archonship of Euclides, was regarded, therefore, as an important era in Athenian Jurisprudence. The only material alterations on record consist, 1 In the law confining the right of voting in the assembly to those born of Athenian mothers. Formerly it sufficed that the father was a citizen, the condition of the

CHAP.
XXIII.

not ob-
served.

act of amnesty, of which both the idea and the name have been adopted by most civilized nations, and extolled by all historians, ancient and modern; who, dazzled by the splendor of a transaction so honorable to Thrasybulus and to Athens, have universally forgot to mention, that the conditions of the amnesty were not faithfully observed. Yet there is the fullest evidence to prove[15], that, when the tyrants were no more, the abettors of their usurpation were accused, convicted, and punished, for crimes of which they had been promised indemnity by a solemn oath. So true is it, that the Athenians had wisdom to discern, but wanted constancy to practise, the lessons of sound policy, or even the rules of justice.

mother not being regarded. Athenæus, xiii. p. 189. et Marc. in Vit. Lysiæ, p. 15. 2. In the law of Demophantus, requiring the citizens to take an oath that no personal danger should prevent them from doing their utmost to deliver their country from tyrants. Vid. Licurg. adv. Leocr. p. 180. et Andoc. de Myst. p. 230.

[15] See Lysias's Orations against Agoratus and Eratosthenes, from p. 133. to p. 230.

CHAP. XXIV.

Accusation of Socrates. — Artifices of his Accusers. — His Defence. — Condemnation. — Address to the Judges. — His Conversation in Prison — and Death. — Transient Persecution of his Disciples. — Writings of Cebes — Æschines. — State of Philosophy. — Of the Fine Arts. — Of Literature. — Herodotus — Thucydides — Xenophon. — Transition to the public Transactions of Greece. — The Spartans invade Elis. — The Messenians driven from Greece. — History of Cyrene — Of Sicily. — War with Carthage. — Siege of Agrigentum. — Reign of Dionysius. — Sicily the first Province of Rome.

IT were well for the honor of Athens, if none but the cruel abettors of an aristocratical faction had experienced the unjust rigor of its tribunals. But among the first memorable transactions, after the re-establishment of democracy, happened the trial and condemnation of Socrates; a man guiltless of every offence but that of disgracing, by his illustrious merit, the vices and follies of his contemporaries. His death sealed the inimitable virtues of his useful and honorable life; it seemed to be bestowed as a favor, not inflicted as a punishment; since, had Socrates,

CHAP. XXIV.

who had already passed his seventieth year, yielded to the decays of nature, his fame would have descended less splendid, certainly more doubtful, to posterity.

Principal causes of that measure.

The remote cause of his prosecution was the ludicrous farce of Aristophanes, entitled the Clouds; to which we had occasion formerly to allude. In this infamous performance, Socrates is introduced denying the religion of his country, corrupting the morals of his disciples, and professing the odious arts of sophistry and chicane. The envy of a licentious populace, which ever attends virtue too independent to court, and too sincere to flatter them, gradually envenomed the shafts of the poet, and malignantly insinuated that the pretended sage was really such a person as the petulance of Aristophanes had described him. The calumny was greedily received, and its virulence embittered by the craft of designing priests and ambitious demagogues, as well as by the resentment of bad poets and vain sophists, whose pretended excellences the discernment of Socrates had unmasked, and whose irritable temper his sincerity had grievously offended[1]. From such a powerful combination it seems extraordinary that Socrates should have lived so long, especially since, during

[1] The causes of his persecution, which are hinted at in Xenophon's Apology for Socrates, are more fully explained in that written by Plato. Vid. Plat. Apolog. Socrat. sect. vi. From these two admirable treatises of practical morality, together with the first chapter of Xenophon's Memorabilia, and Plato's Phædo, the narrative in the text is principally extracted.

THE HISTORY OF GREECE. 275

the democracy, he never disguised his contempt for the capricious levity, injustice, and cruelty of the multitude, and during the usurpation of the Thirty openly arraigned the vices, and defied the authority of those odious tyrants. His long escape he himself ascribed to his total want of ambition. Had he intermeddled in public affairs, and endeavoured, by arming himself with authority, to withstand the corruptions of the times, his more formidable opposition would have exposed him to an earlier fate [a]. Notwithstanding his private station, it seems still to have appeared remarkable to his disciples, that amidst the litigious turbulence of democracy, his invidious fame and merit should have escaped persecution during a long life of seventy years.

When his enemies finally determined to raise an accusation against him, it required uncommon

CHAP. XXIV.

Artifices of his accusers.

[a] The memorable words of Socrates will for ever brand the fierce unfeeling spirit of democracy. Ευ γαρ ιστε ω ανδρες Αθηναιοι, ει εγω παλαι επιχειρησα τα πολιτικα πραγματα, παλαι αν απολωλη, και ετι αν υμας ωδεληκα ηδεν ετι αν εμαυτον, και τω με αχθεσθε λεγοντι τ'αληθη. ου γαρ εςιν οςις σωθησεται, ουτε υμιν ουτε αλλῳ ουδενι πληθει γνησιως αντιτιθεμενος, και κωλυων πολλα αδικα και παρανομα εν τη πολει γινεσθαι. αλλα αναγκαιον εςι τῳ οντι μαχουμενῳ υπερ τε δικαιȣ, και ει μελλει ολιγον χρονον σωθησεσθαι, ιδιωτευειν, αλλα μη δημοσιευειν. Plut. Apolog. Socrat. t. xiii. "You well know, Athenians! that had I formerly intermeddled in public affairs, I should formerly have perished, without benefiting either you or myself. Be not offended; but it is impossible that he should live long who arraigns and manfully opposes the injustice and licentiousness of you, Athenians! or of any other multitude. A champion for virtue, if he would survive but a few years, must lead a private life, and not interfere in politics."

T 2

CHAP.
XXIV.

address to give their malignant calumnies the appearance of probability. Socrates conversed in public with every description of men, in all places, and on all occasions. His opinions were as well known as his person, and ever uniform and consistent; he taught no secret doctrines; admitted no private auditors; his lessons were open to all; and that they were gratuitous, his poverty, compared with the exorbitant wealth of the sophists who accused him, furnished abundant proof. To balance these stubborn circumstances, his enemies confided in the hatred of the jury and judges, composed of the meanest populace, and the perjury of false witnesses, which might be purchased at Athens for the small sum of a few drachmas. They trusted, however, not less in the artifices and eloquence of Miletus, Anytus[1], and Lycon; the first of whom appeared on the part of the priests and poets; the second, on that of the politicians and artists; the third, on that of the rhetoricians and sophists[2].

Informality of the trial.

From the nature of an accusation, which principally respected religion, the cause ought to have been regularly tried in the less numerous but more enlightened tribunal of the Areopagus; yet it was immediately carried before the tumultuary assembly,

---

[1] Some personal reasons are glanced at why Miletus and Anytus stepped forth as accusers. Vid. Andocid. Orat. I. et Xenoph. Apol. Socrat. Libanius has swelled to a long story, and strangely disfigured the hint of Xenophon. Apol. Soc. p. 612, et seqq.

[2] Plato Apol. Soc. &. c.

or rather mob of the Heliæa¹, a court, for so it was called, confisting of five hundred persons, most of whom were liable, by their education and way of life, to be seduced by eloquence, intimidated by authority, and corrupted by every species of undue influence.

In a degenerate age and nation, few virtuous or able men ever acquired popularity merely by their virtues or abilities. In such a nation, should a person, otherwise estimable, be unfortunately cursed with ambition, he must endeavour to gratify it at the expense of his feelings and his principles, and can attain general favor only in proportion as he ceases to deserve it. Uncomplying integrity will meet with derision; and wisdom, disdaining artifice, will grovel in obscurity, while those alone will reach fame, or fortune, or honor, who, though endowed with talents just beyond mediocrity, condescend to flatter the prejudices, imitate the manners, gratify the pride, or adopt the resentments, of an insolent populace.

The superior mind of Socrates was incapable of such mean compliances. When called to make his

---

¹ This appears from innumerable circumstances, some of which are mentioned below, though Meursius, in his treatise on the Areopagus (vid. Gronov. Thesaur. vol. v.), maintains that Socrates was tried in that court; an opinion which has been generally followed, but which the slightest attention to the works of the Athenian orators is sufficient to disprove. Vid. Æsch. Orat. Areopag. Lysias adv. Andocid. p. 108. et Andocid. Orat. l. p. 215. The oath to which Socrates alludes in Xenophon's Apology, c. iv. can only apply to the Heliæa. It is recited at length by Demosthenes, Orat. cont. Timocrat.

CHAP. XXIV.

defence, he honestly acknowledged that he himself was much affected by the persuasive eloquence of his adversaries; though, in truth, if he might use the expression, they had said nothing to the purpose [a]. He then observed, that the fond partiality of his friend Chærephon, having asked the Delphic oracle, whether any man was wiser than Socrates?—the oracle replied, that Socrates was the wisest of men. In order to justify the answer of that god, whose veracity they all acknowledged, he had conversed with every distinction of persons, most eminent in the republic; and finding that they universally pretended to know many things of which they were ignorant, he began to suspect, that in this circumstance he excelled them, since he pretended to no sort of knowledge of which he was not really master. What he did know, he freely communicated, striving, to the utmost, to render his fellow-citizens more virtuous and more happy; an employment to which he believed himself called by the god, "whose authority I respect, Athenians! still more than yours [b].

Provokes the anger of his judges.

The judges were seized with indignation at this firm language from a man capitally accused, from whom they expected that, according to the usual practice, he would have brought his wife and children to intercede for him by their tears [c], or

---

[a] The simplicity of the original is inimitable — Και του ακούειν
 ὑτ᾽, ως εποσ ειπειν, οὐδεν ειρηκασι. Plat. Apol.

[b] These circumstances, which are mentioned both by Xenophon and Plato, prove that Socrates was tried before a popular tribunal.

even have employed the elaborate discourse which his friend Lysias, the orator, had composed for his defence; a discourse alike fitted to detect calumny, and to excite compassion. But Socrates, who considered it as a far greater misfortune to commit, than to suffer an injustice, declared, that he thought it unbecoming his fame, and unworthy his character, to employ any other defence than that of an innocent and useful life. Whether to incur the penalties of the delinquency with which he was falsely charged ought to be regarded as an evil, the gods alone knew. For his part he imagined that he should have no reason for sorrow at being delivered from the inconveniences of old age, which were ready to overtake him, and at being commanded to quit life [*] while his mind, still active and vigorous, was likely to leave behind him the most agreeable impression in the remembrance of his friends.

The firm magnanimity of Socrates could not alter the resolution of his judges; yet such is the ascendency of virtue over the worst of minds, that he was found guilty by a majority of only

---

It is well known that the Areopagus rigorously proscribed all such undue methods of biassing the judgment and seducing the passions. Vid. Demosth. In Near. et Aristocrat. Æschin. In Timarch. Lucian. Hermotim. et Isocrat. Areopag.

[*] Xenophon says, that he writes Socrates's Defence, after so many others, who had already executed that task with sufficient skill and fidelity, in order to illustrate one point much insisted on by Socrates, "That it was better for him to die than to live." Xenoph. Apol. sub init.

CHAP. XXIV.

three voices[9]. The court then commanded him, agreeably to a principle which betrays the true spirit of democratical tyranny, to pass sentence of condemnation on himself, and to name the punishment which ought to be inflicted on him. The punishment, said Socrates, which I deserve for having spent my whole life in endeavouring to render my fellow-citizens wiser and better, and particularly in striving to inspire the Athenian youth with the love of justice and temperance, is, "To be maintained, during the remainder of my life, in the Prytanæum; an honor due to *me*, rather than to the victors in the Olympic games, since, as far as depended on me, I have made my countrymen more happy *in reality*; they only in *appearance*". Provoked by this observation, by which they ought to have been confounded, the judges proceeded to pass sentence, and condemned Socrates to drink hemlock[10].

His address to the judges who voted in his favour.

This atrocious injustice excited the indignation of his numerous friends and disciples, most of whom had accompanied him to the court; but it awakened no other passion in the illustrious sage than that of pity for the blind prejudices of the Athenians. He then addressed that part of the court who had been favorable to him, or rather to themselves, since they had avoided the misfortune of passing an unjust sentence, which would have disgraced and embittered the latest moment

[9] Plato Apol. [10] Idem, ibid.

of their lives. "He considered them as friends with whom he would willingly converse for a moment, upon the event which had happened to him, before he was summoned to death. From the commencement of the prosecution, an unusual circumstance, he observed, had attended all his words and actions, and every step which he had taken in the whole course of his trial. The dæmon, who on ordinary occasions had ever been so watchful to restrain him, when he prepared to say or do any thing improper or hurtful, had never once withheld him, during the whole progress of this affair, from following the bent of his own inclination. For this reason he was apt to suspect that the fate which the court had decreed him, although they meant it for an evil, was to him a real good. If to die was only to change the scene, must it not be an advantage to remove from these pretended judges to Minos, Rhadamantus, and other real judges, who, through their love of justice, had been exalted by the divinity to this important function of government? What delight to live and converse with the immortal heroes and poets of antiquity! It becomes you also, my friends! to be of good comfort with regard to death, since no evil, in life or death, can befal virtuous men, whose true interest is ever the concern of heaven. For my part, I am persuaded that it is better for me to die than to live, and therefore am not offended with my judges. I entreat you all to behave towards my sons, when they attain the years of reason, as I have done to you, not ceasing to

CHAP.
XXIV.

blame and accuse them, when they prefer wealth or pleasure, or any other frivolous object, to the inestimable worth of virtue. If they think highly of their own merit, while in fact it is of little value, reproach them severely, Athenians! as I have done you. By so doing you will behave justly to me and to my sons. It is now time for us to part. I go to die, you to live; but which is best, none but the Divinity knows"."

The execution of the sentence deferred on account of the Delian festival.

It is not wonderful that the disciples of Socrates should have believed the events of his extraordinary life, and especially its concluding scene, to be regulated by the interposition of a particular providence". Every circumstance conspired to evince his unalterable firmness, and display his inimitable virtue. It happened, before the day of his trial, that the high-priest had crowned the stern of the vessel, which was annually sent to Delos, to commemorate, by grateful acknowledgments to Apollo, the triumphant return of Theseus from Crete, and the happy deliverance of Athens from a disgraceful tribute". This ceremony announced the commencement of the festival, which ended with the return

" Plato Apol. sub fin.

" According to Plato nothing happened in this transaction ἄνευ θείας μοίρας. Plat. Apol. Yet in the Phædo. sub. init. he says, τύχη τις αυτω, ω Ἐχέκρατες! συνέβη. But τυχη here refers not to the cause, but to the effect; not to blind chance, but to an unaccountable disposition of events produced by a particular interposition of the divinity. In this sense the word is used not only by philosophers but orators, particularly Demosthenes, as we shall see below.

" See vol. I, p. 32.

of the veſſel; and, during the intervening time, which was conſecrated to the honor of Apollo, it was not lawful to inflict any capital puniſhment. Contrary winds protracted the ceremony thirty days, during which Socrates lay in priſon, and in fetters. His friends daily viſited him, repairing, at the dawn, to the priſon-gate, and impatiently waiting till it opened. Their converſation turned on the ſame ſubjects which had formerly occupied them; but afforded not that pure unmixed pleaſure which they uſually derived from the company of Socrates. It occaſioned, however, nothing of that gloom which is naturally excited by the preſence of a friend under ſentence of death. They felt a certain pleaſing melancholy, a mixed ſenſation of ſorrow and delight, for which no language has aſſigned a name [10].

When the fatal veſſel arrived in the harbour of Sunium, and was hourly expected in the Piræus, Crito, the moſt confidential of the diſciples of Socrates [11], firſt brought the melancholy intelligence;

He refuſes to eſcape from priſon.

---

[10] This is admirably deſcribed by Plato: Αλλα ατοπος συνταν τι μοι παθος παρην, και τις αηλης κραςις — απο τε της ηδονης συγκεκραμενη ομου και της λυπης. The following circumſtances are inimitable: Και παντες οι παροντες σχεδον τι ουτω διεκειμεθα, οντε μεν γελωντες, ενιοτε δε δακρυοντες, εις δε ημων διαφεροντως Απολλοδωρος. οισθα γαρ τον ανδρα και τον τροπον αυτου. Phædo, vill. c. ii. Socrates alone felt none of theſe ſenſations; but as Montaigne, who had ſeized his true character, ſays, Et qui ne recommoiſſe en luy, non ſeulement de la fermeté et de la conſtance (c'étoit ſon aſſiette ordinaire que celle là) mais je ne ſçay quel contentement nouveau et une allegreſſe rajouée en ſes propos et façons dernieres.

[11] Finding Socrates in a profound ſleep, he repoſed himſelf by his ſide till he awoke. Plat. ibid.

CHAP.
XXIV.
and, moved by the near danger of his admired friend, ventured to propose a clandestine escape, showing him at the same time that he had collected a sufficient sum of money to corrupt the fidelity of his keepers. This unmanly proposal, which nothing but the undistinguishing ardor of friendship could excuse, Socrates answered in a vein of pleasantry, which showed the perfect freedom of his mind, "In what country, O Crito! can I escape death? where shall I fly to elude this irrevocable doom, passed on all human kind?" To Apollodorus, a man of no great depth of understanding, but his affectionate and zealous admirer, who said, "That what grieved him beyond measure was, that such a man should perish unjustly," he replied, stroking the head of his friend, "And would you be less grieved, O Apollodorus! were I deserving of death"?" When his friends, and Crito especially, insisted, "That it would be no less ungenerous than imprudent, in compliance with the hasty resolution of a malignant or misguided multitude, to render his wife a widow, his children orphans, his disciples for ever miserable and forlorn, and conjured him, by every thing sacred, to save a life so inestimably precious;" Socrates assumed a tone more serious, recalled the maxims which he professed, and the doctrines which he had ever inculcated, "That how unjustly soever we were treated, it could never be our interest to practise injustice, much less to retort

[14] Xenoph. et Plat. Ibid.

THE HISTORY OF GREECE. 285

the injuries of our parents or our country; and to teach, by our example, disobedience to the laws." The strength of his arguments, and still more, the unalterable firmness and cheerful serenity that appeared in his looks, words, and actions [17], silenced the struggling emotions of his disciples. The dignity of virtue elevated their souls; they parted with tears of inexpressible admiration, and with a firm purpose to see their master earlier than usual on the fatal morning.

Having arrived at the prison-gate, they were desired to wait without, because the Eleven (so the delicacy of Athens styled the executioners of public justice) unloosed the fetters of Socrates, and announced to him his death before the setting of the sun. They had not waited long, when they were desired to enter. They found Socrates just relieved from the weight of his bonds, attended by his wife Xantippé, who bore in her arms his infant son. At their appearance, she exclaimed, "Alas! Socrates, here come your friends, whom you for the last time behold, and who for the last time behold you!" Socrates, looking at Crito, desired some one to conduct her home. She departed, beating her breast, and lamenting with that clamorous sorrow natural to her sex [18] and her character.

CHAP. XXIV.

His behaviour during the last day of his confinement.

---

[17] Καὶ ἐμαυτοῦ καὶ σχημασι καὶ βλέμμασι ἀείφρων, Xenoph. Apol.

[18] Βοῶσα τε καὶ κοπτομένη, and a little above, " ἵνα δὴ ποιοῦσι αἱ γυναῖκες." Phædo, sec. III.

CHAP. XXIV.
His conversation with his disciples.

Socrates, meanwhile, reclining on the couch with his usual composure, drew his leg towards him, and gently rubbing the part which had been galled by the fetters, remarked the wonderful connexion between what men call pleasure, and its opposite, pain. The one sensation, he observed (as just happened to his leg after being delivered from the smart of the irons), was generally followed by the other. Neither of them could long exist apart; they are seldom pure and unmixed; and whoever feels the one, may be sure that he will soon feel the other. " I think, that had Æsop the fabulist made this reflection, he would have said, that the Divinity, desirous to reconcile these opposite natures, but finding the design impracticable, had at least joined their summits; for which reason pleasure has ever since dragged pain after it, and pain pleasure."

Why he composed verses in prison, having never done it before.

The mention of Æsop recalled to Cebes, the Theban, a conversation which he had recently had with Euenus of Paros, a celebrated elegiac poet, then resident in Athens[19]. The poet asked Cebes, " Why his master, who had never before addicted himself to poetry, should, since his confinement, have written a hymn to Apollo, and turned into verse several of Æsop's fables?" The Theban seized the present opportunity to satisfy himself in this particular, and to acquire such information as

[19] The following narrative, to the death of Socrates, is entirely borrowed from the Phædo, to which it is therefore unnecessary at every moment to refer.

might satisfy Euenus, who, he assured Socrates, would certainly repeat his question. The illustrious sage, whose inimitable virtues were all tinged, or rather brightened, by enthusiasm, desired Cebes to tell Euenus, "That it was not with a view to rival him, or with a hope to excel his poetry (for *that*, he knew, would not be easy), that he had begun late in life this new pursuit. He had attempted it in compliance with a divine mandate, which frequently commanded him in dreams to cultivate music. He had, therefore, first applied to philosophy, thinking *that* the greatest music; but since he was under sentence of death, he judged it safest to try likewise the popular music, lest any thing should on his part be omitted, which the gods had enjoined him. For this reason, he had composed a hymn to Apollo, whose festival was now celebrating; and not being himself a mythologist, had versified such fables of Æsop as happened most readily to occur to his memory. Tell this to Euenus — bid him farewel; and farther, that if he is wise, he will follow me; for I depart, as it is likely, to day; so the Athenians have ordered it."

The last words introduced an important conversation concerning suicide, and the immortality of the soul. Socrates maintained, that though it was better for a wise man to die than to live, because there was reason to believe that he would be happier in a future than in the present state of existence, yet it could never be allowable for him to perish by his own hand, or even to lay down life

CHAP. XXIV.

without a sufficient motive, such as that which influenced himself, a respectful submission to the laws of his country. This interesting discussion consumed the greatest part of the day. Socrates encouraged his disciples not to spare his opinions from delicacy to his present situation. Those who were of his mind he exhorted to persevere. Intwining his hand in the long hair of Phædo, "These beautiful locks, my dear Phædo, you will this day cut off[*]; but were I in your place, I would not again allow them to grow, but make a vow (as the Argives did in a matter of infinitely less moment) never to resume the wonted ornament of my beauty, until I had confirmed the doctrine of the soul's immortality."

Concerning death, burial, and the duties of friends to the deceased.

The arguments of Socrates convinced and consoled his disciples, as they have often done the learned and virtuous in succeeding times. "Those who had adorned their minds with temperance, justice, and fortitude, and had despised the vain ornaments and vain pleasures of the body, could never regret their separation from this terrestrial companion. And now," continued he, in the language of tragedy, "the destined hour summons me to death; it is almost time to bathe, and surely it will be better that I myself, before I drink the poison, should perform this ceremony, than occasion unnecessary trouble to the women after I am dead." "So let it be," said Crito; "but first

[*] The ceremony of cutting off the hair at funerals was mentioned above, vol. I. c. vii. p. 325. where the transaction of the Argives, alluded to in the text, is related.

inform

inform us, Socrates, in what we can do you pleasure, respecting your children, or any other concern." "Nothing new, O Crito! but what I have always told you. By consulting your own happiness, you will act the best part with regard to my children, to me, and to all mankind; although you bind not yourselves by any new promise. But if you forsake the rules of virtue, which we have just endeavoured to explain, you will benefit neither my children, nor any with whom you live, although you should now swear to the contrary." Crito then asked him, "How he chose to be buried?" "As you please, provided I don't escape you." Saying this, he smiled, adding, that as to his *body*, they might bury it as seemed most decent, and most suitable to the laws of his country.

He then retired into the adjoining chamber, accompanied only by Crito; the rest remained behind, like children mourning a father. When he had bathed and dressed, his sons (one grown up, and two children), together with his female relations[11], were admitted to him. He conversed with them in the presence of Crito, and then returned to his disciples near sun-set, for he tarried long within. Before he had time to begin any new

---

[11] The ριυιαι γυναικες of Plato. This expression seems to have given rise to the absurd fable, that Socrates had two wives, mentioned by Diogenes Laertius, and others; and the absurd explication of that irregularity, "that the Athenians, after the pestilence, had allowed polygamy, at least bigamy, to repair the ravages of that dreadful malady."

CHAP. XXIV.
Is addressed by the messenger of death.

subject, the keeper of the prison entered, and standing near Socrates, "I cannot," said he, "accuse you, O Socrates! of the rage and execrations too often vented against me by those here confined, to whom, by command of the magistrates, I announce that it is time to drink the poison. Your fortitude, mildness, and generosity exceed all that I have ever witnessed; even now I know you pardon me, since I act by compulsion; and as you are acquainted with the purport of my message, farewel and bear your fate with as much patience as possible." At these words the executioner, hardened as he was in scenes of death, dissolved in tears, and, turning from Socrates, went out. The latter following him with his eye, replied, "And you also farewel; as to me, I shall obey your instructions." Then looking at his disciples, "How truly polite," said he, "Is *the man*"! During my confinement, he often visited and conversed with me; and now, how generously does he lament my death! But let the poison be brought, that we may obey his orders."

His conversation before drinking the poison.

Crito then said, "Still, O Socrates! there is time; the sun still brightens the tops of the mountains. Many have I known, who have drank the poison late in the night, after a luxurious supper and generous wines, and lastly, after enjoying the embraces of those with whom they were enamoured".

" 'Ο ἀνϑρωπος, the term for the executioner.

" Συγγενωμην γ᾽ ἐχει ὁτι με τυχον ἀνϑρωποτις. Phæd. c. xlvhh. What an extraordinary picture of Athenian manners!

But haften not; it is yet time." "With good reafon," faid Socrates, "thefe perfons did what you fay, becaufe they believed thereby to be gainers; and with good reafon I fhall act otherwife, becaufe I am convinced that I fhould gain nothing but ridicule by an over-anxious folicitude for life, when it is juft ready to leave me." Crito then made a fign to the boy who waited; he went, ground the hemlock, and returned with him who was to adminifter it. Socrates perceiving his arrival, "Tell me," faid he, "for you are experienced in fuch matters, what have I to do?" "Nothing farther than to walk in the apartment till your limbs feel heavy; then repofe yourfelf on the couch." Socrates then taking the cup in his hand, and looking at him with ineffable ferenity, "Say, as to this beverage, is it lawful to employ any part of it in libation?" The other replied, "There is no more than what is proper to drink." "But it is *proper*," rejoined Socrates," and neceffary, if we would perform our duty, to pray the gods, that our paffage hence may be fortunate." So faying, he was filent for a moment, and then drank the poifon with an unaltered countenance. Mingling gentlenefs with authority, he ftilled the noify lamentations of his friends, faying, that in order to avoid fuch unmanly complaints, he had before difmiffed the women. As the poifon began to gain his vitals, he uncovered his face, and faid to Crito, "We owe a cock to Æfculapius, facrifice it, and neglect it not." Crito afked, if he had

CHAP. XXIV.

His prayer and death.

CHAP. XXIV.

any thing further to command? But he made no reply. A little after, he was in agony—Crito shut his eyes. Thus died Socrates; whom, his disciples declared, they could never cease to remember, nor remembering, cease to admire. "If any man," says Xenophon inimitably, "if any man, a lover of virtue, ever found a more profitable companion than Socrates, I deem that man the happiest of human kind[*]."

Transient persecution of his disciples.

The current of popular passions appears nowhere more uniform than in the history of Athens. The factitious resentment excited against Socrates by such improbable calumnies, as even those who were the readiest to receive and to disseminate, could never seriously believe, extended itself with rapidity to his numerous friends and adherents. But fortunately for the interest of letters and humanity, the endemic contagion was confined within the Athenian frontiers. Plato, Antisthenes, Æschines, Critobulus, and other Athenians, wisely eluded a storm which they had not strength to resist. Some took refuge in Thebes with their fellow-disciples, Simmias, Cebes, and Phædondas; others found protection in Megara from Euclid and Terpsion. This persecution of philosophy, however, was accidental and transient.

The Athenians repent, and honor the memory of Socrates.

Mingled sentiments of pity, shame, and resentment, soon gave a new direction to the popular

[*] Plato speaks with equal feeling, or rather enthusiasm. Καὶ γὰρ τὸ μιμνῆσθαι, καὶ αὐτὸν λέγοντα, καὶ ἄλλου ἀκουοντα, ἐμοίγε ἀεὶ πάντων ἥδιστον. Phæd. s. ii.

fury, which raged with more destructive, yet far juster cruelty, against the accusers and judges of Socrates¹⁵. Many were driven into exile; many were put to death; several perished in despair, by their own hands. The illustrious sage was honored by signal monuments of public admiration¹⁶; his fame, like the hardy oak, derived vigor from years¹⁷; and increased from age to age, till the superstition of the Athenians at length worshipped, as a god¹⁸, him whom their injustice had condemned as a criminal.

CHAP. XXIV.

The persecution, the death, and the honors of Socrates, all conspired to animate the affection, and to increase the zeal, of his disciples. Their number had been great in his lifetime: it became greater after his death; since those who followed, and those who rejected his doctrines, alike styled themselves Socratic philosophers. His name was thus adopted and profaned by many sects, who, while they differed widely from each other, universally changed, exaggerated, or perverted the tenets of their common master. Among the genuine followers of Socrates, Xenophon, as will appear hereafter, unquestionably merits the first place. Plato comes next, yet separated by a long

The writings of his disciples.

---

¹⁵ Plutarch. de Invid. p. 538.

¹⁶ Statues, altars, even a chapel, called Socrateion. Vide Diogen. in Socrat.

¹⁷ Crescit occulto, velut arbor, ævo
   Fama Marcelli — HORACE.

¹⁸ Or rather as a demi-god; but the boundaries were not very accurately ascertained, though that is attempted by Arrian, in Expedit. Alexand. l. iv. p. 66.

interval. In the same class may be ranked Cebes the Theban, Æschines, Crito, and Simon, Athenians. The table of Cebes, which has been transmitted to modern times, contains a beautiful and affecting picture of human life, delineated with accuracy of judgment, and illuminated by the splendor of sentiment. Three remaining dialogues of Æschines breathe the same sublime spirit, and abound in irresistible persuasions to virtue: "That happiness is attained, not by gratifying, but by moderating the passions; that he alone is rich and powerful, whose faculties exceed his desires; that virtue is true wisdom, and being attended with the only secure happiness which can be enjoyed in the present life, must, according to the unalterable laws of Providence, be crowned with immortal felicity hereafter."

The remains of Cebes and Æschines, and far more, as will appear in the sequel, the copious writings of Plato and Xenophon, may enable us to discriminate the philosophy of Socrates, from that of the various sects who misrepresented or adulterated his opinions. The establishment of these sects belongs not to the period of history now under our review. But the foundation of their respective tenets, which had been laid in a former age, was confirmed by the philosophers who flourished in the time of Socrates. Of these, the most distinguished were Euclid of Megara, Phædo of Elis, Aristippus of Cyrené, Antisthenes of Athens. The two first restored the captious logic of the sophists; Aristippus embraced their licentious morality. While the schools of Elis and Megara studied to confound the understanding, that of Cyrené labored to corrupt the heart. Antisthenes set himself to oppose these pernicious sects, deriding the refined subtilties of the sceptics, and disdaining the mean pleasures of the Epicureans[19]. To prefer the mind to the body, duty to interest, and virtue to pleasure, were the great lessons of Antisthenes. Yet this sublime philosophy he carried to extravagance[20], affecting not only to moderate and govern, but to silence and extirpate the passions, and declaring bodily pleasure not only unworthy of pursuit, but a thing carefully to be avoided, as the greatest and most dangerous of evils. His rigid severity of life deceived not the penetration of Socrates. The sage could discern, that no small share of spiritual pride lurked under the tattered cloak of Antisthenes.

While philosophy, true or false, thus flourished in Greece, a propitious destiny watched over the imitative arts, which continued, during half a

[19] I anticipate these names. The *scepticism* of Pyrrho, as will be explained hereafter, arose from the quibbling sophisms of the schools of Elis and Megara. *Epicurus*, having adopted and refined the fifth philosophy of Aristippos, had the honor of distinguishing by his name, the *Epicurean* sect.

[20] His follower, *Diogenes*, as will appear in the sequel, pushed this extravagance still further. They both taught in the suburb of Athens called the *Cynosarges*, from which they and their disciples were called *Cynics*. In a subsequent part of this work, it will be explained how the *Cynical philosophy* gave rise to *Stoicism*, so called, because Zeno and his followers taught at Athens in the "*Stoa pœcile*," the painted portico.

CHAP.
XXIV.
A.C 431.
— 404.

century of perpetual wars and revolutions, to be cultivated with equal assiduity and success. The most distinguished scholars of Phidias were Alcamenes of Athens, and Agoracritus of the isle of Paros. They contended for the prize of sculpture in their respective statues of Venus; and the Athenians, it is said, too partially decided in favor of their countryman. Agoracritus, unwilling that his work should remain in a city where it had met with so little justice, sold it to the borough of Rhamnus. There it was beheld with admiration, and soon passed for a production of Phidias[53] himself. The sculptor Ctesclaus excelled in heroes. He chose noble subjects, and still farther ennobled them by his art[54]. His contemporary Patrocles distinguished himself by his statues of Olympic victors, and particularly of celebrated wrestlers. Assisted by Canachus, he made the greatest work mentioned during the period now under our review, thirty-one figures of bronze, representing the respective commanders of the several cities or republics, who, under the conduct of Lysander, obtained the memorable victory of Ægos Potamos. They were erected in the temple of Delphian Apollo, together with the statue of Lysander himself, crowned by Neptune. Inferior artists[55] were employed to copy the statues of various divinities, dedicated at the same time, and in the same place, by the Lacedæmonian conqueror.

[53] Vid. Suid. et Hesych. voc. Paωμοτ.   [54] Plin. l. xxxv.
[55] See their names in Pausan. l. x. p. 621. et seqq.

THE HISTORY OF GREECE. 297

It appears not however that, during the Peloponnesian war, any new style was attempted either in sculpture or painting. The artists of that period contented themselves with walking in the footsteps of their great predecessors. The same observation applies to music and poetry; but eloquence, on the contrary, received a new form, and flourishing amidst the tumults of war and the contentions of active life, produced that concise, rapid, and manly character of composition which thenceforth distinguished the Attic writers. The works of Homer, Sophocles, and Pindar, left few laurels to be gained by their successors. It was impossible to excel, it was dangerous to rival them. Great genius was required to start, without disgrace, in a career where such candidates had run. But great genius is rare, and commonly disdains imitation, and the first poetical prizes being already carried off, men who felt the animation and vigor of their own powers, naturally directed them to objects which possessed the charms of novelty, and promised the hope of excellence.

Even in prosaic composition the merit and fame of Herodotus and Democritus[14] (not to mention authors more ancient) opposed very formidable

CHAP.
XXIV.
Of literature.

Principal authors in prose preceding this period.

[14] Itaque video visum esse nonnullis Platonis et Democriti locutionem, etsi absit a versu, tamen quod incitatius feratur, et clarissimis verborum luminibus utatur, potius poema putandum, quam comicorum poëtarum. Cicero ad M. Brutum Orator. c. xx. See also de Orator. l. I. c. xl. It is impossible to read Lucretius, without fancying, if we recollect Cicero's criticisms on Democritus, that we are perusing the long lost works of that great philosopher.

CHAP.
XXIV.
Character
of Herodotus as an historian.

obstacles to the ambition of their successors. In a work no less splendid than important, the father of profane history had deduced the transactions between the Greeks and Barbarians, from the earliest accounts till the conclusion of the Persian war; a work including the history of many centuries, and comprehending the greatest kingdoms and empires of the ancient world. This extensive subject was handled with order and dignity. The episodes were ingeniously interwoven with the principal action. The various parts of the narrative were so skilfully combined, that they mutually reflected light on each other. Geography, manners, religion, laws, and arts, entered into the plan of his work; and it is remarkable that the earliest of historians agrees more nearly, as to the design and form of his undertaking, with the enlightened writers of the present century, than any historical author in the long series of intervening ages.

His language was the picture of his mind; natural, flowing, persuasive; lofty on great occasions [19], affecting in scenes of distress [20], perspicuous in narration, animated in description. Yet this admired writer has sometimes inserted reports romantic and incredible. Of many, indeed, of the fables of Herodotus, as ignorance conceited of its knowledge long affected to call them, subsequent experience has proved the reality;

[19] Longinus cites as an example of the sublime, Herodot. l. vii. c. i0. The whole expedition of Xerxes is written with an elevation becoming the subject.
[20] See the affecting story of Adrastus, l. i. c. xxxv.

THE HISTORY OF GREECE. 299

modern discoveries and voyages seem purposely directed to vindicate the fame of a writer, whom Cicero [17] dignifies with the appellation of Prince of Historians. Of other wondrous tales which he relates, his own discernment showed him the futility. Whatever is contrary to the analogy of nature he rejects with scorn. He speaks with contempt of the Ægepodes, and of the one-eyed Arimaspi, and of other ridiculous and absurd fictions which have been adopted, however, by some credulous writers even in the eighteenth century. But Herodotus thought himself bound in duty to relate what he had heard, not always to believe what he related [18]. Having travelled into Egypt and the East, he recounts, with fidelity, the reports current in those remote countries. And his mind being opened and enlarged by an extensive view of men and manners, he had learned to set bounds to his disbelief, as well as to his credulity. Yet it must not be dissembled that the fabulous traditions, in which he too much abounds, give the air of romance to his history. Though forming, comparatively, but a small part of the work, they assume magnitude and importance, when invidiously detached from it [19]. It thus seems as if

CHAP.
XXIV.

---

[17] L. II. de Orator.

[18] Ἐγὼ δὲ ὀφείλω λέγειν τὰ λεγόμενα, πείθεσθαί γε μὲν οὐ παντάπασιν ὀφείλω. Herodot. l. vii. c. clii. p. 433.

[19] The reproaches which Juvenal (Satyr. x.) and Plutarch (in his treatise entitled the Malignity of Herodotus) make to this great historian, are fully answered by Aldus Manutius, Camerarius, and Stephanus. Plutarch, forsooth, was offended that his countrymen

CHAP.
XXIV.

this most instructive author had written with a view rather to amuse the fancy than to inform the understanding. The lively graces of his diction tend to confirm this supposition. His mode of composition may be regarded as the intermediate shade between epic poetry and history. Neither concise nor vehement, the general character of his style is natural, copious, and flowing[*]; and his manner throughout breathes the softness of Ionia, rather than the active contention of Athens.

Of Thucydides.

In this light Herodotus appeared to the Athenians in the age immediately succeeding his own. At the Olympic games he had read his work with universal applause. Thucydides, then a youth, wept mixed tears of wonder and emulation[**]. His father was complimented on the generous ardor

---

made so bad a figure in the history of Herodotus. The criticism of Dionysius of Halicarnassus, a writer of more taste and discernment than Plutarch, does ample justice to the father of history.

[*] Aristotle, in his Rhetoric, l. III. c. ix. distinguishes two kinds of style; the continuous and the periodic. The former flows on without interruption, until the sense is complete. The latter is divided, by stops, into due proportions of duration, which are easily felt by the ear, and measured by the mind. The former style is irksome, because in every thing men delight to see the end; even racers, when they pass the goal, are quickly out of breath. Herodotus is the most remarkable instance of the continuous style. In his time scarcely any other was in use; but it is now entirely laid aside. So far Aristotle, who seems rather unjust to Herodotus, since many parts of his work are sufficiently adorned by periods, although the loose style in general prevails. But the partiality of his countryman Dionysius completely avenges the wrongs of Herodotus.

[**] Suidas, Photius, Marcellinus.

of a son, whose early inquietude at another's fame announced a character formed for great designs and illustrious exertions. But Herodotus had preoccupied the subjects best adapted to historical composition; and it was not till the commencement of the memorable war of twenty-seven years, that Thucydides, amidst the dangers which threatened his country, rejoiced in a theme worthy to exercise the genius, and call forth the whole vigor of an historian. From the breaking out of this war, in which he proved an unfortunate actor, he judged that it would be the greatest, the most obstinate, and important that had ever been carried on. He began therefore to collect, and treasure up, such materials as were necessary for describing it; in the selection, as well as in the distribution of which, he afterwards discovered an evident purpose to rival and surpass Herodotus. Too much indulgence for fiction had disgraced the narrative of the latter: Thucydides professed to be animated purely by the love of truth. "His relation was not intended to delight the ears of an Olympic audience. By a faithful account of the past, he hoped to assist his readers in conjecturing the future. While human nature remained the same, his work would have its use, being built on such principles as rendered it an everlasting possession, not a contentious instrument of temporary applause[b]." The execution corresponded with this noble design. In his introductory discourse

---

[b] Thucydid. in proem.

CHAP. XXIV.

he runs over the fabulous ages of Greece, carefully separating the ore from the dross. In speaking of Thrace, he touches, with proper brevity, on the fable of Tereus and Progne[1]; and in describing Sicily, glances at the Cyclops and Lestrigons. But he recedes, as it were, with disgust, from such monstrous phantoms, and immediately returns to the main purpose of history. In order to render it a faithful picture of the times, he professes to relate not only what was done, but what was said, by inserting such speeches of statesmen and generals as he had himself heard, or as had been reported to him by others. This valuable part of his work was imitated by all future historians, till the improvement of military discipline on the one hand, and the corruption of manners on the other, rendered such speeches superfluous. Eloquence once served as an incentive to courage, and an instrument of government. But the time was to arrive, when the dead principles of fear and interest should alone predominate. In most countries of Europe, despotism had rendered public assemblies a dramatic representation, and in the few, where men are not enslaved by a master, they are the slaves of pride, of avarice, and of faction.

Comparison between them.

Thucydides, doubtless, had his model in the short and oblique speeches of Herodotus; but in this particular he must be acknowledged far to surpass his patron. In the distribution of his subject,

[1] Ovid. Metam. l. vi.

however, he fell short of that writer. Thucydides, aspiring at extraordinary accuracy, divides his work by summers and winters, relating apart the events comprehended in each period of six months. But this space of time is commonly too short for events deserving the notice of history, to be begun, carried on, and completed. His narrative, therefore, is continually broken and interrupted: curiosity is raised without being satisfied, and the reader is transported, as by magic, from Athens to Corcyra, from Lesbos to Peloponnesus, from the coast of Asia to Sicily. Thucydides follows the order of time; Herodotus the connexion of events: in the language of a great critic, the skill and taste of Herodotus have reduced a very complicated argument into one harmonious whole; the preposterous industry of Thucydides has divided a very simple subject into many detached parts and scattered limbs of history, which it is difficult again to reduce into one regular body ". The same critic observes, that Herodotus's history not only possesses more art and variety, but displays more gaiety and splendor. A settled gloom, doubtless, hangs over the events of the Peloponnesian war; but what is the history of all wars, but a description of crimes and calamities? The austere gravity of Thucydides admirably corresponds with his subject. His majesty is worthy of Athens, when she commanded a thousand tributary republics. His concise, nervous, and energetic style, his

*] Dionys. Halicarn. de Herodot. et Thucydid.

CHAP. XXIV.

Transition to the military transactions of Greece.

abrupt brevity, and elaborate plainness, admirably represent the contentions of active life, and the tumult of democratical assemblies. Demosthenes, whom Dionysius himself extols above all orators, transcribed eight times, not the elegant flowing smoothness of Herodotus, but the sententious, harsh, and often obscure annals of Thucydides[11].

Thucydides left his work unfinished in the twenty-first year of the Peloponnesian war. It was continued by Xenophon, who deduced the revolutions of Greece through a series of forty-eight years to the battle of Mantinæa; a work which enables us to pursue the important series of Grecian history.

To a reader accustomed to contemplate the uniform and consistent operations of modern policy, it must appear extraordinary that, at the distance of less than two years from the subversion of the Athenian democracy by a Spartan general, the same turbulent form of government should have been re-established with new splendor, by the approbation, and even the assistance, of a Spartan king. The reasons explained in the preceding chapter may lessen, but cannot altogether remove, his surprise; and, in order fully to comprehend the causes of this event, it is necessary to consider not only the internal factions which distracted the councils of Sparta, but the external objects of ambition or revenge which solicited and employed her arms.

[11] Dionys. Halicarnass. de Herodot. et Thucydid.

While

While the fortune of the Peloponnesian war still hung in doubtful suspense, the peaceful inhabitants of Elis often testified an inclination to preserve an inoffensive neutrality, that they might apply, with undivided attention, to their happy rural labors, to the administration of the Olympian festival, and to the indispensable worship of those gods and heroes to whom their territory was peculiarly consecrated. The continual solicitation of Sparta, and the unprovoked violence of Athens, determined the Elians to declare for the former republic; but of all the Spartan allies they were the most lukewarm and indifferent. In time of action their assistance was languid and ineffectual, and when the regular return of the Olympic solemnity suspended the course of hostilities, they showed little partiality or respect for their powerful confederates, whose warlike and ambitious spirit seemed incompatible with the enjoyment of their own contemplative tranquillity. This omission of duty was followed by the actual transgression of the Elians. In conjunction with the Mantinæans and Argives they deserted the alliance of Sparta; defended themselves by arms against the usurpations of that republic; and excluded its members from consulting the oracle, and from partaking of the games and sacrifices celebrated at Olympia[a]. These injuries passed with impunity until the successful issue of the war of Peloponnesus disposed the Spartans to feel with sensibility, and enabled them severely to chastise every insult that had been

[a] Thucydid. l. r.

CHAP.
XXIV.

The Spartans invade Elis.
Olymp. xciv. 2.
A. C. 403.

offered them during the less prosperous current of their fortune.

While Pausanias and Lysander settled the affairs of Athens and of Asia, Agis the most warlike of their princes, levied a powerful army, to inflict a late, but terrible, vengeance on the Elians. That he might attack the enemy unprepared, he led his forces through the countries of Argolis and Achaia, entering the Elian territory by the way of Larissa, and intending to march by the shortest road to the devoted capital. But he had scarcely passed the river Larissus, which gives name to the town and separates the adjoining provinces of Elis and Achaia, when the invaders were admonished, by repeated shocks of an earthquake, to abstain from ravaging a country which enjoyed the immediate protection of Heaven. Into such a menace, at least, this terrible phænomenon was interpreted by the superstition of the Spartan king, who immediately repassed the river, and, returning home, disbanded his army. But the hostility of the Spartans was restrained, not extinguished. Having offered due supplications and sacrifices to sanctify their impious invasion, the ephori, next year, commanded Agis again to levy troops, and to enter the Elian territory. No unfavorable sign checked the progress of his arms. During two summers and autumns, the country was desolated; the villages burned or demolished; their inhabitants dragged into captivity; the sacred edifices were despoiled of their most valued ornaments; the porticoes, gymnasia, and temples, which adorned the city of Jupiter, were many of them reduced to ruins.

CHAP.
XXIV.

The Spartans neither alone incurred the guilt, nor exclusively enjoyed the profits of this cruel devastation. The Elian invasion furnished a rich harvest of plunder to the Arcadians and other communities of Peloponnesus, whose rapacious lust was enflamed by the virgin bloom of a country which had long been protected by religion against the ravages of war. When the principal property of the Elians was destroyed or plundered, the Spartans at length granted them a peace, on condition that they surrendered their fleet, acknowledged the independence of the inferior towns and villages, which were scattered along the delightful banks of the Peneus and the Alpheus, and modelled their internal government according to the plan prescribed by their conquerors[17].

The war of Elis occupied, but did not engross, the attention of the Spartans; nor did the punishment of that unfortunate republic divert them from other projects of revenge. The Messenians were not their accidental and temporary, but their natural and inveterate, foes; and might justly expect to feel the unhappy consequences of their triumph. After the destruction of Messené, and the long wanderings and misery of its persecuted citizens, the town of Naupactus, situate on the northern shore of the Corinthian gulph, furnished a safe retreat to a feeble remnant of that ancient

The Spartans drive the Messenians from Greece. Olymp. xcv. 4. A. C. 401.

[17] Xenophon Hellen. L. III. c. 2. Diodor. l. xiv. p. 404.

CHAP.
XXIV.

community; which, flourishing under the protection of Athens, spread along the western coast, and planted a confiderable colony in the neighbouring island of Cephalenia. We have already described the memorable gratitude of the Meffenians, who were the moft active, zealous, and, according to their ability, the moft ufeful, allies of Athens in the Peloponnefian war. But *their* affiftance (and affiftance far more powerful than theirs) proved ineffectual; and the time was now arrived when they were to fuffer a fevere punifhment for their recent as well as ancient injuries. The refentment of Sparta drove them from Naupactus and Cephalenia. The greater part efcaped to Sicily; above three thousand failed to Cyrenaica, the only countries inhabited by the Hellenic race, which lay beyond the reach of the Lacedæmonian power[u].

Caufes which withdrew Cyrenaica and Sicily from the fphere of Grecian politics.

From the æra of this important migration, the names of Sicily and Cyrenaica will feldom occur in the prefent hiftory; on which account it may not be improper briefly to explain the caufes which withdrew from the general fphere of Grecian politics a fruitful and extenfive coaft, and an ifland not lefs fruitful and extenfive, and far more populous and powerful. The infulated fituation of thofe remote provinces, while it rendered it extremely inconvenient for Greece to interfere in their affairs, peculiarly expofed them to two evils, which rendered it ftill more inconvenient for them to interfere in the affairs of Greece. Removed from the

[u] Diodor. l. xiv. p. 415.

protection of their Peloponnesian ancestors, both the Cyreneans and Sicilians often endured the oppression of domestic tyrants, and often suffered the ravages of foreign barbarians.

The inhabitants of Cyrenaica alternately carried on war against the Libyans and Carthaginians[49]. They were actually oppressed by the tyrant Ariston. Soon afterwards they recovered their civil liberty[50]; but were compelled frequently to struggle for their national independence. Though often invaded, their country was never subdued by any barbarian enemy; and their liberties survived the republics of their European brethren, since they reluctantly submitted, for the first time, to the fortunate general of Alexander, who, in the division of his master's conquests, obtained the fertile and wealthy kingdom of Egypt[51].

The revolutions of Sicily are far better known than those of Cyrené, and still more worthy to be remembered. During the latter years of the Peloponnesian war, the assistance given by Syracuse to the Lacedæmonians became gradually more faint and imperceptible, and at length it was totally withdrawn. This was occasioned by the necessity of defending the safety of the whole island, in which that of the capital was involved, against the formidable descents of the Carthaginians; whom the invitation of Segesta and several inferior cities at

CHAP. XXIV.

Subsequent history of Cyrenaica.

Of Sicily.

[49] Aristot. Polit. Sallust. de Bell. Jugurth.
[50] Diodor. l. xiv. p. 411.
[51] Diodor. l. xix. p. 715. et Strabo. l. xvii. p. 836.

CHAP.
XXIV.

variance with their powerful neighbours, the hopes of acquiring at once those valuable commodities, the annual purchase of which drained Africa of such immense treasures, and, above all, the desire of revenging the death of Hamilcar, and the dishonor of the Carthaginian name in the unfortunate siege of Himera, encouraged to undertake and carry on various expeditions for the entire subjugation of Sicily.

which is long harassed by the Carthaginians;
Olymp. xcii. 3.
Olymp. xciv. 1.
A. C. 410.
—404.

Hannibal, the grandson of Hamilcar, was intrusted with the conduct of the war, which commenced the four hundred and tenth, and continued, with little intermission, till the four hundred and fourth year before the Christian æra. The domestic troops of Carthage were reinforced by their African allies. Considerable levies were made among the native Spaniards and Italians, who had long envied the splendor, and dreaded the power of the Greeks, to whose conquests and colonies they saw no bounds. The united army exceeded an hundred thousand men, and was conveyed to the southern shore of Sicily in a proportionable number of transports and gallies[11].

whose conquests are interrupted by pestilence.
A. C. 409.

The design of Hannibal, as far it appears from his measures, was to conquer successively the smaller and more defenceless towns, before he laid siege to Syracuse, whose natural strength, recently improved by art, bidding defiance to assault, could only be taken by blockade. The first campaign was rendered memorable by the conquest of

[11] Diodor. Sicul. l. xiii. c. 43, et seqq.

THE HISTORY OF GREECE. 311

Selinus and Himera; the second by the demolition of Agrigentum; the third by the taking of Gela. The inferior cities of Solas, Egesta, Motya, Ancyra, Entelta, and Panormus, either invited the Carthaginian arms, or surrendered without resistance. The invaders might have proceeded to the siege of Syracuse, the main object of their expedition; but pestilence followed the bloody havoc of war, and swept off, in undistinguished ruin, the victors and the vanquished. Not only the general, but the most numerous portion of his troops, had fallen a prey to this calamity; and Hamilcar, who succeeded to the command, contented himself with leaving garrisons in the towns which had been conquered, and returned to Africa with the enfeebled remains of his armament, which communicated the pestilential infection to Carthage; where it long raged with destructive fury[11].

According to the genius of Grecian superstition, it was natural to ascribe the sufferings of the Carthaginians to the unexampled cruelty and impiety with which, in their successive ravages, they had deformed the fair face of Sicily. It would be useless and disgustful to describe the horrid scenes of bloodshed and slaughter transacted in the several places which presumed to resist their power. Whatever atrocities could be invented by the unprincipled licence of the Italians, approved by the stern insensibility of the Spaniards, and inflicted by the implacable revenge of the Africans, were com-

CHAP. XXIV.
A. C. 406.
A. C. 405.

Excessive cruelty of the Carthaginians.

[11] Diodor. L. xiii. c. 70, et seqq.

CHAP.
XXIV.

mitted in the miserable cities of Selinus, Himera, Gela, and Agrigentum. After the taking of Himera, Hannibal sacrificed in one day, three thousand of its inhabitants to the manes of his grandfather, who, in the first Carthaginian invasion, had perished before its walls; and the lot of these unhappy victims, dreadful as it was, might justly be an object of envy to the long tormented natives of Gela and Selinus.

Ancient magnificence of Agrigentum.

Yet of all Sicilian cities, the fate of Agrigentum seemed the most worthy to be deplored, from the striking contrast of its fallen state with its recent splendor and prosperity. The natural beauties [10] of Agrigentum were secured by strength, and adorned with elegance; and whoever considered, either the innumerable advantages of the city itself, or the gay cultivation of the surrounding territory, which abounded in every luxury of the sea and land, was ready to pronounce the Agrigentines the most favored inhabitants of the earth. The exuberant fertility of the soil, particularly the rich luxuriance of the vines and olives [11], exceeded every thing that is related of the happiest climates, and furnished the materials of a lucrative commerce with the populous coast of Africa; which was very sparingly provided in those valuable plants. The

---

[10] The following particulars in the text, concerning Agrigentum, we learn from Diodorus Siculus, p. 316—378. Valer. Maxim. l. iv. 8. Athenæus, l. I. c. 2.

[11] Diodorus celebrates the height of the vines, which we are not used to consider as a proper subject of panegyric.

THE HISTORY OF GREECE. 313

extraordinary wealth of the Agrigentines was displayed in the magnificence of public edifices, and in the splendid enjoyment of private fortunes. They had begun, and almost completed, the celebrated temple of Jupiter, built in the grandest style of architecture employed by the Greeks on the greatest and most solemn occasions. Its walls were encompassed by pillars without, and adorned by pilasters within; and its magnitude far exceeded the ordinary dimensions of ancient temples, as it extended three hundred and forty feet in length, sixty in breadth, and an hundred and twenty in height, without including the lofty and spacious dome. The grandeur of the doors and vestibule corresponded with the simple majesty of the whole edifice, whose sculptured ornaments represented, with finished elegance, and with a laborious accuracy that distinguished each particular figure, the defeat of the Giants, and the taking of Troy; respectively, the most illustrious exploits of Grecian gods, and Grecian heroes.

This noble monument, consecrated to piety and patriotism, might be contrasted, by a philosophic mind, with others destined to a very different purpose. Without the walls of Agrigentum an artificial pond, or rather lake, thirty feet deep and near a mile in circumference, was continually replenished with a rare variety of the most delicate fishes, to furnish a sure supply to the sumptuous extravagance of public entertainments. But nothing could rival the elegance and beauty of the tombs and sepulchres erected by the Agrigentines, to perpetuate the fame of their coursers which had obtained the Olympic prize; and, if we believe the testimony of an eye-witness[16], to commemorate the quails and other delicate birds, which were cherished with an affectionate and partial fondness by the effeminate youth of both sexes. Such capricious and absurd abuses of opulence and the arts might be expected amidst the mortifying discrimination of ranks, and the enormous superabundance of private riches, which distinguished the Agrigentines. The labor of numerous and active slaves cultivated agriculture and manufactures with extraordinary success. From the profit of these servile hands many citizens attained, and exceeded, the measure not only of Grecian, but of modern wealth. A short time before the siege of the town, Hexenitus returned in triumph from Olympia, with three hundred chariots, each drawn by two milk-white horses of Sicilian blood. Antisthenes had eclipsed this magnificence in celebrating the marriage of his daughter. But every native of Agrigentum yielded the fame of splendor to the hospitable Gellias, whose palace could entertain and lodge five hundred guests, who had been clothed from his wardrobe, and whose cellars, consisting of three hundred spacious reservoirs, cut in the solid rock, daily invited the joyous festivity of strangers and citizens.

[16] Timæus apud Diodor. l. xlii.

Before the second Carthaginian invasion, the Agrigentines, warned by the fate of Selinus and Himera, had prepared whatever seemed most necessary for their own defence. Their magazines were stored with provisions, their arsenals with arms. Elevated by the confidence of prosperity, they had courage to resist the first impressions of their enemies; but, corrupted by the vices of wealth and luxury, they wanted fortitude to persevere. Their allies in Sicily and Italy showed not that degree of ardor which might have been expected in a war which so deeply concerned them all: yet, by the partial assistance of Syracuse, Gela, and Camerina, as well as several Grecian allies in Italy, the Agrigentines stood the siege eight months, during which, the Carthaginians employed every resource of strength and ingenuity. At length the place was reduced to great difficulties by means of immense wooden machines, drawn on wheels, which enabled the besiegers to fight on equal ground with those who defended the walls. But before any breach was effected, the greater part of the inhabitants determined to abandon the city.

CHAP. XXIV. Siege of Agrigentum.

In the obscurity of night, they departed with their wives and families, and many of them fortunately escaped to Gela, Syracuse, and Leontium. Others, wanting courage for this dangerous resolution, or unwilling to survive the fate of their country, perished by their own hands. A third class, more timid, or more superstitious, shut themselves up in the temples, expecting to be saved by the

Unhappy fate of the inhabitants.

protection of the gods, or by the religious awe of the enemy. But the Barbarians no more respected what was sacred, than what was profane. The consecrated statues, and altars, and offerings, were confounded with things the most vile, and plundered or destroyed in the promiscuous ruin. One memorable act of despair may represent the general horror of this dreadful scene. With his numerous friends, and most valued treasure, the humane and hospitable Gellias had taken refuge in the temple of Minerva; but when he understood the universal desolation of his country, he set fire to that sacred edifice, chusing to perish by the flames rather than by the rage of the Carthaginians [97].

Near fourscore years before the demolition of Agrigentum, Sicily had acquired immortal glory, by defeating more numerous invaders; but, at that time, the efforts of the whole island were united and animated by the virtues and abilities of Gelon; whereas, amidst the actual dangers and trepidation of the Carthaginian war, the Sicilians were distracted by domestic factions. Syracuse had banished the only man whose consummate wisdom, and approved valor and fidelity, seemed worthy to direct the helm in the present tempestuous juncture: In the interval between the siege of Himera and that of Agrigentum, the patriotic Hermocrates had returned to Sicily; and, at the head of his numerous adherents, had attempted to gain

[97] Diodorus, p. 379.

THE HISTORY OF GREECE. 317

admission into the capital. But the attempt was immediately fatal to himself; and, in its consequences, destructive of the public freedom. His partisans, though discomfited and banished, soon found a leader qualified to avenge their cause, and to punish the ingratitude of Syracuse.

This was the celebrated Dionysius, a youth of twenty-two years; of mean parentage, but unbounded ambition; destitute (if we believe historians) of almost every virtue, and possessed of every talent; and whose fortune it was, to live and flourish amidst those perturbed circumstances of foreign war and civil dissension, which are favorable to the elevation of superior minds. Though esteemed and intrusted by Hermocrates, who could more easily discern the merit of his abilities, than discover the danger of his ambition, Dionysius had gained friends in the opposite faction, by whose interest he was recalled from exile. His services in the Carthaginian war raised him to eminence. He excelled in valor; he was unrivalled in eloquence; his ends were pursued with steady perseverance; his means were varied with convenient flexibility; the appearance of patriotism rendered him popular, and he employed his popularity to restore his banished friends.

The gratitude of one party, and the admiration of both, enabled him to attain the command of the mercenaries, and the conduct of the war. But he was less solicitous to conquer the Carthaginians than to enslave his fellow-citizens, whose factious turbulence rendered them unworthy of liberty.

CHAP. XXIV.

His character.

Means by which he usurped the government of Syracuse.
Olymp. xciii. 4.
A. C. 405.

318 THE HISTORY OF GREECE.

CHAP.
XXIV.

By the affected dread of violence from his enemies, he obtained a guard for his person, which his artful generosity easily attached to his interest; and the arms of his troops, the influence and wealth of Philistus, the historian of Sicily, who was honored with the appellation of the second Thucydides[n], above all his own crafty and daring ambition, enabled him, at the age of twenty-five, to usurp the government of Syracuse, which he held for thirty-eight years.

His successful reign.
Olymp. xciii. 4.
A. C. 405.
Olymp. cii. 2.
B. C. 367.

During his long and active reign he was generally engaged in war; sometimes with the Carthaginians, sometimes with his revolted subjects. Yet in both contests he finally prevailed, having reduced the Carthaginian power in Sicily, and appeased, or intimidated, domestic rebellion. His actual condition, however splendid, he regarded only as a preparation for higher grandeur. He besieged and took Rhegium, the key of Italy: nor could the feeble confederacy of the Italian Greeks have prevented the conquest of that country, had not the renewed hostilities of the Carthaginians, and fresh discontents at home, interrupted the progress of his arms. This growing storm he resisted as successfully as before, and transmitted, to a degenerate son, the peaceful inheritance of the greatest part of Sicily; after having strengthened, with wonderful art, the fortifications of the capital; enlarged the size, and improved the form of the

[n] Cicero de Orator. l. 3l.

Syracusan gallies; invented the military catapults, an engine of war which he employed, with great advantage, in the siege of Motya and Rhegium; and not only defended his native island against foreign invasion, but rendered its power formidable to the neighbouring countries.

His poetical labors were the least uniformly successful of all his undertakings. His verses, though rehearsed by the most skilful *rhapsodists* of the age, were treated with signal contempt at the Olympic games. A second time he renewed his pretension to literary fame in that illustrious assembly; but his ambassador was insulted by the most humiliating indignities; and the orator Lysias pronounced a discourse, in which he maintained the impropriety of admitting the representative of an impious tyrant to assist at a solemnity consecrated to religion, virtue, and liberty[19]. The oration of Lysias leaves room to suspect that the plenitude of Dionysius's power, rather than the defect of his poetry, exposed him to the censure and derision of the Olympic spectators; and this suspicion receives strong confirmation by considering, that, in the last year of his reign, he deserved and obtained the poetic crown at Athens; a city renowned for the impartiality of its literary decisions[20].

It is remarkable, that, with such an active, vigorous, and comprehensive mind; with such a variety of talents, and such an accumulation of

[19] Life of Lysias, p. 117. Dionys. Halicar. de Demosth.
[20] Isocrat. Panegyr.

CHAP.
XXIV.
peared so
odious to
ancient
historians.

glory, Dionysius should be universally held out and branded, as the most conspicuous example of an odious and miserable tyrant, the object of terror in his own, and of detestation in succeeding ages. Yet the uncorrupted evidence of history will prove, that the character of Dionysius was not decisively flagitious. His situation rendered it artificial; and he is acknowledged often to have assumed the semblance of virtue. Always crafty and cautious; but by turns, and as it suited his interest, mild, affable, and condescending; or cruel, arrogant, and imperious: nor did the Syracusans feel the rigor of his tyranny, until they had justly provoked it by an insurrection, during which they treated his wife and children with the most barbarous and brutal fury. But there are two circumstances in the character of Dionysius which peculiarly excited the indignation of the moralists of Greece and Rome, and which the moderation or the softness of modern times will be disposed to consider with less severity. He had usurped the government of a free republic; a crime necessarily heinous in the sight of those who held the assassination of a tyrant to be the most meritorious exertion of human virtue; and he professed an open contempt for the religion of his country; a crime of which the bare suspicion had brought to death the most amiable and respected of men. Yet the impiety of Dionysius was only the child of his interest, and sometimes the parent of his wit. He stripped a celebrated statue of Jupiter of a golden robe, observing, that it was too heavy

in

THE HISTORY OF GREECE. 321

in summer; and too cold in winter. For a reason equally ingenious he deprived Æsculapius of his golden beard; asserting, that such a venerable ornament ill became the son of the beardless Apollo. But if he despoiled the altars and statues, he increased and improved the fleets and armies, of Syracuse, which were successfully employed against the public enemy. And to the general current of satire and declamation against this extraordinary man [u], may be opposed the opinion of Polybius and Scipio Africanus, the most illustrious characters of the most illustrious age of Rome: "That none ever concerted his schemes with more prudence, or executed them with more boldness, than Dionysius the Elder."

C H A P. XLIV.

His son, Dionysius the Younger, exceeded his vices without possessing his abilities. The reign of this second tyrant was distracted and inglorious. His kinsman Dion, the amiable disciple of Plato, endeavoured to correct the disorders of his ungoverned mind. But the task was too heavy for Dion, and even for Plato himself. The former, unable to restrain the excesses of the prince, undertook the defence of the people. His patriotism interrupted, but did not destroy, the tyranny of Dionysius, which was finally abolished, twenty-two

Inglorious reign of Dionysius the Younger. Olymp. civ. 3. A.C 362. Olymp. cx. 1. A. C. 340.

[u] The authentic history of the reign of Dionysius is copiously recorded by Diodorus Siculus, l. xiv. et xv. To relate the numerous and improbable stories told of him by Cicero, Plutarch, Seneca, and other moralists, would be to transcribe what it is not easy to believe. The reader may consult, particularly, Plut. ex edit. Paris, le Moral. pp. 78 et 8). De Garrul. p. 505. In Dion. p. 561; and various passages of Cicero de Officiis, et Tusculan. Quæst.

VOL. III.   Y

CHAP.
XXIV.

years after he first mounted the throne, by the magnanimity of Timoleon [a]. This revolution happened only two years before Corinth, the country of Timoleon, as well as the other republics of Greece, submitted to the arms of Philip of Macedon; and, having lost their own independence, became incapable of asserting the freedom of their colonies.

Sicily becomes a province of Rome.
Olymp. cxlii. 1.
A.C. 212.

New tyrants started up in Syracuse, and almost in every city of Sicily, and held a precarious sway under the alternate protection of the Carthaginians and Romans. The citizens of Syracuse, mindful of their ancient fame, dethroned their usurpers, and enjoyed considerable intervals of liberty. But at length the Romans gained possession of the place; the persevering valor of Marcellus, assisted by the treachery of the garrison, prevailing, after a siege of three years, over the bold efforts of mechanical power, directed by the inventive genius of Archimedes [b]. The reduction of the capital was immediately followed by the conquest of the adjoining territory; and Sicily came thus to be regarded as the eldest province of Rome, and the first country, without the limits of Italy, which had taught that victorious republic to taste and enjoy the sweets of foreign dominion [c].

[a] Corn. Nepos. Diodorus Sicul. Plut. Dion.
[b] Polyb. Excerpt. l. VIII. Plut. in Marcell.
[c] Livy, L. xxiv, et Cicero in Verrem in few words — Omnium earundem gentium princeps Sicilia ad amicitiam fidemque, P. R. applicuit; primaque omnium, id quod ornamentum imperii est, provincia est appellata: prima docuit majores nostros, quàm præclarum esset exteris gentibus imperitare.

CHAP. XXV.

Death of Darius Nothus. — Cyrus disputes the Succession with his elder Brother Artaxerxes. — Character of Cyrus. — State of Lower Asia under his administration. — His Strength and Resources. — His Expedition into Upper Asia. — Describes the vast army of his Brother. — Battle of Cunaxa. — Death of Cyrus. — His Grecian Auxiliaries victorious. — Their Treaty with Tissaphernes. — Perfidious Assassination of the Grecian Generals. — Artaxerxes sends to the Greeks to demand their Arms. — Conference on that Subject.

WHILE the operations of war conspired with the revolutions of government, to detach the Grecian colonies in Italy, Sicily, and Cyrené, from the general interests and politics of the mother-country, a series of events, not less curious than important, connected, in the closest intimacy, the history of Greece with the annals of the Persian empire. The same memorable year which terminated the destructive war of Peloponnesus brought to a conclusion the active and prosperous reign of Darius Nothus. He named as his successor Artaxerxes, styled Mnemon, from the strength of his memory; and persisted in this choice, notwithstanding the opposition of the artful

CHAP.
XXV.

and ambitious Paryſatis, who employed her extenſive influence over the mind of an old and uxorious huſband, to obtain the kingdom for Cyrus, the younger brother of Artaxerxes, and the peculiar favorite of his mother. The rivalſhip of the young princes, both of whom were at court during the laſt illneſs of Darius, unhappily degenerated into enmity; and a circumſtance, which would be thought immaterial in the preſent age, increaſed the indignation of Cyrus. The birth of Artaxerxes had happened before the acceſſion of his father to the throne, but Cyrus was born the ſon of a king; a diſtinction which, however frivolous it may appear in modern times, had engaged Darius Hyſtaſpes to prefer Xerxes, the younger of his ſons, to his elder brother Artabazanes[1].

Cauſe of his reſentment againſt Artaxerxes.

The precedent eſtabliſhed by ſuch an illuſtrious monarch might have enforced the partial arguments of Paryſatis, and both might have been confirmed by the ſtrong claim of merit, ſince Cyrus early diſcovered ſuch talents and virtues, as fitted him to fill the moſt difficult, and to adorn the moſt exalted, ſtation. At the age of ſeventeen, he had obtained the government of Lydia, Phrygia, and Cappadocia; and the ſame mandate of Darius, which deſtroyed his hopes of ſucceſſion to the Perſian throne, rendered him hereditary ſatrap of thoſe valuable provinces. On the demiſe of that monarch, Cyrus prepared to return to Aſia

[1] Herodot. l. vii. c. ii.

THE HISTORY OF GREECE. 325

Minor, attended by the same escort with which he had come to Susa; a faithful body of three hundred heavy-armed Greeks, commanded by Xenias, an Arcadian. But when he prepared to leave the court, a very criminal and unfortunate incident retarded his departure. The selfish and perfidious Tissaphernes, who expected to divide the spoils of the young prince, accused him of treason. He was apprehended by order of Artaxerxes; but the powerful protection of Parysatis, who, though she loved only one, was beloved, or at least feared, by both of her sons, defended his life, vindicated his honor, and restored him in safety to his government.

The danger that had threatened his person could not much affect the heroic fortitude of Cyrus; but the affront offered to his dignity sunk deep into his heart; and from the moment that he recovered his freedom, he determined to revenge his injuries[1], or to perish in the attempt. In the despotic countries of the East, as there is scarcely any intermediate gradation between the prince and people, and scarcely any alternative but that of dominion or servitude, a discontented or rebellious subject must either stifle his animosity, submit to die, or aspire to reign[2]. The magnanimity of Cyrus

CHAP. XXV.

Circumstances favorable to his ambition.

---

[1] Xenoph. Anabas. L. I. c. 1. This was the origin of his resentment, which Xenophon expresses with great delicacy; ὁ δὲ ἀναλαβὼν καὶ ἀτιμασθεὶς, ἐβουλεύετο ὅπως μήποτε ἔτι ἔσται ἐπὶ τῷ ἀδελφῷ, etc. He asserted independence, the first wish of every great mind.

[2] "Cyrus determined no longer," says Xenophon, "to depend on his brother; ἀλλὰ ω δυνατὸν Βασιλευειν ἀντ' αυτου, but, if possible, to reign in his stead."

Y 3

CHAP.
XXV.

naturally preferred the road of danger and glory; he prepared not only to punish the injustice, but to usurp the throne of Artaxerxes, defended as it was by a million of armed men, and protected both by the power of superstition, and by the splendor of hereditary renown. This design would have been great, but romantic, if the young prince had not enjoyed very extraordinary resources in the powers of his own mind, in the affectionate attachment of his Barbarian subjects, and, above all, in the fidelity and valor of his Lacedæmonian allies.

Character of Cyrus;

Whether we consider what he said, or what he did, the testimony of his contemporaries, or the more unerring testimony of his life and actions, Cyrus appears to have been born for the honor of human nature, and particularly for the honor of Asia, which, though the richest and most populous quarter of the globe, has never, in any age, abounded in great characters. From the age of seven years, he had been trained, at the gate of the palace, to shoot with the bow, to manage the horse and to speak truth; according to the discipline instituted by the great founder of the monarchy, and well adapted, in an age of simplicity, to form the princes and nobles of Persia. But in the course of two centuries, the progress of refinement and luxury, the infectious example of a corrupt court, and the perfidious lessons of the world, had perverted, or rendered ineffectual, a very salutary system of education; and the grandees of Persia, whatever proficiency they made in their exercises,

contrasted with that of the Persian nobles.

felt so little regard for veracity, that (as will abundantly appear in the sequel) they seldom spoke but with a view to deceive, and rarely made a promise which they did not break, or took an oath which they did not violate. The behaviour of Cyrus was totally the reverse. He equalled, and surpassed his companions in all exterior accomplishments. But while his manly beauty, his bodily activity and address, and the superior courage, as well as skill, which he displayed in hunting, horsemanship, and every military exercise, commanded the admiration of the multitude, he himself seems not to have estimated such superficial advantages beyond their real worth. He regarded integrity of heart as the only solid basis of a great character. His probity was uniform, his word sacred, his friendship inviolable. In the giddy season of youth, he yielded, with uncommon docility, to the admonitions of experience. Neither wealth, nor birth, nor rank, but age and virtue, were the objects of his respect: and his behaviour, equally meritorious and singular, was justly and universally admired.

His subjects in Lesser Asia, in particular, were seized with the most pleasing astonishment, when, instead of a greedy and voluptuous satrap, eager only to squeeze, to amass, and to enjoy, they beheld a prince who preferred the public interest to his own; who alleviated the weight of taxes, that he might encourage the operations of industry; whose own hands gave the useful example of rural

State of Lower Asia during his administration.

328   THE HISTORY OF GREECE.

CHAP. XXV.

labor*; whose decisions united justice and mercy; and whose active vigilance introduced (what neither before nor since the government of Cyrus has been known in the Asiatic peninsula) such regularity of police, as rendered intercourse safe, and property secure.

His popular acts.

The virtues of justice and integrity, when accompanied with diligence and abilities, must procure such a degree of respect for the administration, as will naturally be extended to the person, of a prince. But something farther is required, not to obtain the public gratitude and esteem, but to excite the affectionate ardor of select and devoted friends; without the assistance of whom, it is seldom possible to accomplish any great and memorable design. Cyrus excelled all his contemporaries in the art both of acquiring and of preserving the most valuable friendships. His gratitude overpaid every favor; his liberality was large, yet discerning; and his donatives were always enhanced by the handsome and affectionate manner in which they were bestowed. When he discovered a man really worthy of his confidence and esteem, he was not satisfied with giving him a partial share of his affections; he gave his heart entire; and it was his constant prayer to the gods, that he might live to requite and surpass the good offices of his friends, and the injuries of his enemies.

* Xenoph. ibid. Cic. in Senect. Plut. in Lysand. have all celebrated this part of his character.

With such sentiments and character, Cyrus acquired the firm attachment of a few, and the willing obedience of all his Barbarian subjects, in the populous provinces which he commanded, whose united strength exceeded a hundred thousand fighting men; who, unwarlike as they were, yet excelled, both in bravery and in skill, the effeminate troops of Upper Asia.

Among his barbarian troops.

They were probably indebted for this advantage to their intercourse with the Greeks, whose disciplined valor, far more than the numbers of his Barbarians, encouraged Cyrus to undertake an expedition for acquiring the empire of the East. By the most important services he had deserved the gratitude of the Lacedæmonian republic; which had been raised, chiefly by his assistance, to the head of Greece, and to the command of the sea. In return for that favor, so inestimable in the sight of an ambitious people, the Spartans readily complied with his request, by sending into Asia eight hundred heavy-armed men, under the command of the intrepid Cheirisophus; and they charged their admiral, Samius, who had succeeded Lysander in the government of the Ionian coast, faithfully to co-operate with Cyrus, by employing his powerful fleet in whatever service the Persian prince might think proper to recommend[1]. Had they done nothing more than this, Cyrus might well have approved their useful gratitude; especially as their alliance, securing him on the

His chief confidence in the gratitude and valor of the Greeks.

---

[1] Xenoph. Hellen. l. iii.

CHAP.
XXV.

Amount of his Grecian troops.

side of Europe, enabled him, without danger, to drain his western garrisons, and to augment the strength of his army. But the friendship of the Spartans carried them still farther. They allowed him to recruit his forces in every part of their dominions; and the generous munificence of Cyrus had acquired numerous partisans well qualified to raise and to command those valuable levies. Clearchus the Spartan, Menon the Thessalian, Proxenus the Bœotian, Agias the Arcadian, and Socrates the Achæan, all alike devoted to the interest and glory of the Persian prince, collected, chiefly from their respective republics, above ten thousand heavy-armed men, and near three thousand archers and targeteers.

Secrecy of his preparations.

These preparations, which were carried on with silence and celerity, deceived the haughty indolence of the Persians; but they could not escape the vigilance of Alcibiades, who then resided at Grypium, a town of Phrygia, under the protection of Pharnabazus. Moved by resentment against the Lacedæmonians, or ambitious of gaining merit with the great king, he desired an escort from the satrap, that he might undertake with safety a journey to Susa, in order to acquaint Artaxerxes with the hostile designs of his brother. Pharnabazus, who possessed not the merit, desired the reward of the discovery; and therefore (as we formerly had occasion to relate*) readily gratified the request of Lysander, by the destruction of Alcibiades.

* See above, p. 248.

But neither the intelligence conveyed by the
Persian governor, nor the repeated solicitations of
Tissaphernes, nor the consciousness of his own injustice and cruelty, could rouse Artaxerxes from
the profound security of his repose. Cyrus completed his levies without molestation, and almost
without suspicion; and prepared, in the beginning
of the year four hundred before Christ, to march
from the Ionian coast into Upper Asia, at the
head of a hundred thousand Barbarians, and
above thirteen thousand Greeks. His journey towards Babylon, his defeat and death in the plain of
Cynaxa, the retreat and dispersion of his followers,
and the memorable return of the Greeks to their
native country, have been related by the admired
disciple of Socrates (whom the friendship of Proxenus, the Bœotian, recommended to the service
and esteem of Cyrus), with such descriptive beauty,
with such profound knowledge of war and of human nature, and with such inimitable eloquence,
as never were re-united in the work of any one
man but that of Xenophon the Athenian. The
retreat was principally conducted by Xenophon
himself; which has enabled him to adorn his narrative with such an affecting variety of incidents
and characters, as will always serve to prove that
the force of truth and nature is far superior to the
powers of the most fertile fancy. It would be an undertaking not only hardy, but presumptuous, to invade the province of such an accomplished writer, if
the design of the present work did not oblige us to
select the principal circumstances which illustrate

CHAP.
XXV.

Cyrus un-
dertakes
his expe-
dition into
Upper
Asia.
Olymp.
xcv. 1.
A. C. 400.

Xeno-
phon's ac-
count of
the expe-
dition.

CHAP. XXV.

Rapidity of his march.

the condition of the times, and connect the expedition of Cyrus with the subsequent history of Greece.

Having assembled his forces at Sardis, the Persian prince was carried, by the activity of his resentment or ambition, with the utmost celerity, towards Upper Asia. In ninety-three marches he travelled through the central provinces of Lydia, Phrygia, Cappadocia; traversed the mountains of Cilicia; passed unresisted through Syria; crossed the Euphrates at Thapsacus; and after penetrating the desert, entered the confines of Babylonia. In a journey of above twelve hundred miles, his numerous army experienced fewer difficulties than might naturally be expected. The fertile territory of Asia Minor supplying them abundantly with provisions, enabled them to proceed commonly at the rate of fifteen or sixteen miles a-day; and almost every second day brought them to a large and populous city. The dependent satraps or viceroys of Lycaonia and Cilicia were less solicitous to defend the throne of Artaxerxes, than anxious to protect their respective provinces from plunder and devastation. But the former experienced the severity of an invader whom he had the weakness to oppose, without the strength or courage to resist[7].

Cilicia defended by the beauty of Epyaxa.

Syennesis, governor of Cilicia, had reason to fear that his country might be plundered with equal rapacity. He endeavoured, therefore, to avail

[7] Xenoph. Anabas. l. i. p. 248.

himself of the natural strength of a province whose southern boundaries are washed by the sea, and which is defended on other sides by the winding branches of Mount Taurus[9]. Towards the west there is but one pass, called by Arrian the Gates of Cilicia[9]; sufficient to admit only one chariot at a time, and rendered dark and difficult by steep and almost inaccessible mountains. These were occupied by the troops of Syennesis, who, had he maintained his post, might have easily prevented the passage of an army. But the timid Cilician had not trusted in arms alone for the defence of his country. By the order, or at least with the permission of her husband, his queen, the beautiful Epyaxa, had met Cyrus at Cylenæ, on the frontiers of Phrygia; and, according to the custom of the East, presented her acknowledged liege-lord and superior with gold, silver, and other costly gifts. But the greatest gift was her youth and beauty, which she submitted, it is said, to the enamoured prince, who, after entertaining her with the utmost magnificence and distinction[10], restored

---

[9] Xenoph. p. 248.
[9] Arrian. exped. Alexand. L. II. p. 37.
[10] She requested Cyrus to show her his troops. He complied; and attended her coach, in an open car. But the curiosity of Epyaxa had almost cost her dear. "When the Barbarians were reviewed, the Greeks were ordered to their arms, and commanded to advance, as to a charge; after which, the soldiers, of their own accord, ran with shouts to their tents. The Barbarians were thrown into consternation; Epyaxa quitted her coach; the Greeks returned laughing to their tents; and Cyrus rejoiced at seeing the terror with which the Greeks had inspired the Barbarians." Xenoph. Anabas. l. I. p. 247.

her to Cilicia by a near, but difficult road, which led across the mountains.

The Greeks plunder Tarsus.

To the escort which accompanied her, Cyrus added a considerable body of Greeks commanded by Menon the Thessalian. The greater part arrived at Tarsus, the capital, before the army of Cyrus reached the gates of Cilicia; but two companies, amounting together to a hundred men, were missing, and supposed to have been destroyed by the mountaineers, while they wandered in quest of booty. Syennesis was mortified at hearing that the enemy had already entered his province. But when he likewise received intelligence that the Peloponnesian fleet had sailed round from Ionia, in order to co-operate with the army, the disagreeable news totally disconcerted the measures of his defence. He fled in precipitation, abandoning his tents and baggage to the invaders. Cyrus crossed the mountains without opposition, and traversed the beautiful irriguous plains of Cilicia, which were adorned with trees and vines, and abounded in sesame, panic, millet, wheat, and barley. In four days he arrived at the large and rich city of Tarsus, which was plundered by the resentment of the Greeks, for the loss of their companions.

Cyrus exchanges presents with Syennesis of Cilicia.

Cyrus immediately sent for the governor, who had removed from his palace, and, attended by the greater part of the inhabitants, had taken refuge among the fastnesses in the neighbouring mountains. By the assurances of Epyaxa, her

THE HISTORY OF GREECE. 335

timorous" husband was with much difficulty perfuaded to put himfelf in the power of a fuperior, to whom, as the price of his fafety, he carried large fums of money. Cyrus courteoufly accepted the welcome fupply, which the demands of his troops rendered peculiarly feafonable; and, in return, honored Syenneſis with fuch prefents as were deemed of great value by the kings of the Eaſt. They confifted in a Perfian robe, a horfe with a golden bit, a chain, bracelets, and fcimitar of gold, the reſtoration of prifoners, and the exemption of Cilicia from farther plunder ".

During their luxurious refidence at Tarfus, the Greeks were corrupted by profperity. They difdained to obey their commanders, and refufed to continue their journey. The defign of marching to Babylon, though it was not unknown to Clearchus, or to the Spartan fenate, had been concealed from the foldiers, left their impatience or their fears might be alarmed by the profpect of fuch a long and dangerous undertaking. At Tarfus they firft difcovered their fufpicions of the deceit, which immediately broke out into licentious clamors. They infulted the majeſty of Cyrus; they reproached the perfidy of their generals; and their

CHAP.
XXV.

Mutiny in the Grecian camp.

" Pride, as well as fear, feems to have actuated Syenneſis; ὁ δὲ μὴ πρότερον φάναι τοῦ κρείττονι ἑαυτῷ εἰς χεῖρας ἐλθεῖν ἰέναι, οὐδὲ τότε Κύρῳ ἰέναι φάναι, πρὶν ἡ γυνὴ αὐτὸν ἔπεισε; "Syenneſis declared that he had never formerly put himſelf in the power of a man in any reſpect fuperior to himſelf; nor would he then go to Cyrus, till his wife perfuaded him," etc. A true picture of oriental manners, meanneſs varniſhed with pride!

" Xenophon. Anabaſ. p. 249.

CHAP.
XXV.

Appeased by the address of Clearchus.

anger was ready to vent itself in open sedition, when the ferment was appeased by the address and prudence of Clearchus. While he privately assured Cyrus of his best endeavours to make the affair take a favorable turn, he openly embraced the cause of the soldiers, affected deeply to feel their grievances, and eagerly concurred with every measure that seemed proper to remove them. His eloquence and his tears diverted the design of immediate hostility. An assembly was summoned to deliberate on the actual posture of affairs. Several, of their own accord, offered their opinion; others spoke as they had been directed by Clearchus. One counsellor, who was heard with applause, advised them to pack up their baggage, and to demand guides or ships from Cyrus, to facilitate their return. Another showed the folly of this request from a man whose measures they had traversed, and whose purpose they had endeavoured to defeat[1]. They surely could not trust in guides

---

[1] This passage is translated as follows by Mr. Spelman: "After him another got up, showing the folly of the man who advised to demand the ships, as if Cyrus would not resume his expedition. He showed also how weak a thing it was to apply for a guide to that person whose undertaking we had defeated." If Cyrus refumed his expedition, it could not be said that his undertaking was defeated, nor is this the proper meaning of the word λυμαινεσθαι, which signifies to hurt or weaken. I am sensible that by an easy transition, it sometimes signifies to corrupt, to destroy, to defeat; but in the passage before us, if a translator should chuse to explain it by any of those words, he must say, "whose undertaking we had begun, endeavoured, or purposed, to defeat; an explanation of λυμαινεσθαι, which is justified by the analogy of the Greek language, and which the

given

THE HISTORY OF GREECE. 337

given them by an enemy; nor could it be expected that Cyrus should part with his ships, which were evidently so necessary to the success of his expedition. At length it was determined to send commissioners to treat with Cyrus, that he might either, by granting the demands of the Greeks, prevail on them to follow him, or be himself prevailed on to allow them to return home; and the difference was thus finally adjusted, by promising each soldier a darick and a half, instead of a darick, of monthly pay [1].

When this storm was happily appeased, the enemy left Tarsus, and marched five days through the fertile plains of Cilicia, till they arrived at Issus, the last town of the province; large, rich, and populous; and only fifteen miles distant from the frontier of Syria. This wealthy province was defended by two fortresses, called the Gates of Syria and Cilicia. They extended from the mountains to the sea. The interval of three furlongs between them contained several passes, narrow and intricate, besides the rapid Kersas, which flowed in the middle, one hundred feet in breadth. It was on this occasion that Cyrus experienced the full advantage of the Lacedæmonian assistance. A fleet of sixty sail, conducted by Pythagoras the Spartan, who had succeeded Samius in the naval command, prepared to land the Greeks on the

CHAP. XXV.

Cyrus passes the Syrian gates.

Base absolutely requires. "This is one of the few minute mistakes which I have discovered in Mr. Spelman's most accurate translation."
[1] Xenoph. ibid. p. 150, et seqq.

VOL. III.   Z

CHAP.
XXV.

eastern side of the Gates, which must have exposed the Syrian works to a double assault; but the cowardice of Abrocomas, who commanded the numerous forces of Syria and Phœnicia, rendered the execution of this measure unnecessary. The design, alone, was sufficient to terrify him. He abandoned his forts, and fled with precipitation before the approach of an enemy".

The army wade the Euphrates.

Cyrus thenceforth proceeded without meeting with any appearance of opposition, and in fifteen days march, reached the banks of the Euphrates. At Thapsacus, which in some eastern languages signifies the ford ", this noble river is above half a mile in breadth, but so shoaly that the navigation is reckoned dangerous even for boats which draw very little water.. The shallowness increases in the autumnal season, which happened to be the time that the army passed the Euphrates, which no where reached above the breast. This favorable circumstance furnished an opportunity to the inhabitants of Thapsacus to flatter Cyrus, that the great river had visibly submitted to him as its future king". Elevated by this auspicious prediction, he pursued his journey through Mesopotamia, part of which was anciently comprehended under the name of Syria ". While he proceeded through this fertile country he did not forget that a laborious march of seventeen days, through a barren

---

" Xenoph. p. 213.
" Foster's Geographical Dissertation on Xenophon's Retreat.
" Xenoph. p. 214.
" So it is called by Xenoph. Ibid.

desert, must conduct him to the cultivated plains of Babylon.

Having amply provided for this dangerous undertaking, he performed it with uncommon celerity, both in order to avoid risking the want of provisions, and, if possible, to take his enemy unprepared. For several days the army marched, without interruption, through the province of Babylonia; and, on the fifth, came to a deep and broad ditch, which had been recently dug to intercept, or retard, their passage. But as this defence was left altogether unguarded, and the great king had taken no measures to protect the most valuable portion of his dominions, it was generally believed that he had laid aside the design of venturing an engagement. The troops of Cyrus, therefore, who had hitherto maintained their ranks with circumspection, no longer observed any order of march; their arms were carried in waggons, or on sumpter-horses; and their general, in his car, rode in the van with few armed attendants. While they proceeded in this fearless contempt of the enemy, and approached the plain of Cynaxa, which is within a day's journey of Babylon [18], Patagyas, a Persian, and confidential friend of Cyrus, came riding towards

CHAP. XXV.

Traverse the desert, and reach Babylonia.

---

[18] I have used an indeterminate expression to denote the uncertain situation of those places as described by Strabo, l. ii. et Plut. in Artaxerx. Mr. Spelman justly observes, that the error of Xenophon (unnoticed by any former translator), who makes the distance between Babylon three thousand and sixty stadia, is so enormous, that it can only be owing to a mistake of the transcriber.

CHAP.
XXV.

Cyrus descries the immense army of his brother.

them in full speed, his horse all in a foam, calling aloud succeffively in his own language, and in Greek, that the king was at hand with a vast army [10].

The experienced Greeks, who beft knew the danger of being attacked in diforder, were moft fenfibly alarmed by this fudden furprife. Cyrus, leaping from his car, put on his corflet, mounted his horfe, feized his javelin, commanded the troops to arm, and ordered every man to his poft. His orders were readily obeyed; and the army advanced, feveral hours, in order of battle. It was now mid-day; yet no enemy appeared: but in the afternoon they perceived a duft like a white cloud, which gradual'y thickened into darknefs, and overfpread the plain. At length the brazen armor flafhed; the motion, the ranks, and fpears, were diftinctly feen. In the front were innumerable chariots, armed with fcythes in a downward, and in an oblique direction. The cavalry, commanded by Tiffaphernes, were diftinguifhed by white corflets; the Perfians by wicker bucklers; the Egyptians by wooden fhields reaching down to their feet. Thefe formed the chief ftrength of Artaxerxes; but the various multitude of nations, marching in feparate columns according to their refpective countries, had fcarcely any armor of defence, and could annoy the enemy only at a diftance, with their flings, darts, and arrows [11].

[10] Xenoph. p. 263.
[11] Xenoph. p. 263, et feqq.

THE HISTORY OF GREECE. 341

While the hostile battalions approached, Cyrus, accompanied by Pigres the interpreter, and a few chosen attendants, all mounted on horses of extraordinary swiftness, rode through the intermediate space, observing the numbers and disposition of the enemy. He had learned from deserters, that the troops of the great king amounted to twelve hundred thousand, divided into four equal bodies of men, respectively commanded by the four generals Tissaphernes, Gobrias, Arbaces, and Abracomas. The last, however, had not yet joined; nor did he reach Babylonia till five days after the battle. But, notwithstanding this defect, the numbers of Artaxerxes were still sufficient to perform whatever numbers can accomplish. According to the custom of the East, the king, surrounded by a chosen body of cavalry, occupied the centre of the army, as the place of greatest security, and most convenient for issuing his orders with promptitude and effect. But such was the extent of ground covered by the various nations whom he commanded, that even his centre reached beyond the left wing of the army of Cyrus; who, therefore, called aloud to Clearchus to advance opposite to the king's guard, because, if that should be broken, the work would be done. But Clearchus was unwilling to withdraw the Greeks from the Euphrates, lest they should be surrounded by the enemy; he therefore kept his post, assuring Cyrus of his utmost care to make all go well.

The disobedience of Clearchus, and the distrust of Cyrus, threw away the fortune of the day,

CHAP. XXV.

Its numbers and disposition.

The battle of Cyaxa.

CHAP.
XXV.
Olymp.
xcv. 1.
A. C. 400.

which involved the fate of Persia, and the renown of Greece. For although, by skilful evolutions, Clearchus eluded the armed chariots and cavalry of the enemy; though the Greeks, by their countenance and shouts alone, put to flight the opposing crowd, who could not endure the sight of their regular array, their burnished arms, or hear without terror the martial sounds of their harmonious Pæans, intermixed with the clanging of their spears against their brazen bucklers; yet the great king, perceiving the rapid pursuit of the Greeks, and that nothing opposed him in front, commanded his men to wheel to the left, and advanced with celerity in order to attack the rear of the enemy. If this design had been carried into execution, it is probable that the Greeks, having prevailed on the first onset, would immediately have faced about, and, animated by the joy of victory, and their native ardor, have repelled and routed the troops of Artaxerxes.

Rash Impetuosity of Cyrus.

But the impatience of Cyrus defeated this favorable prospect. He observed the movement of his brother, and eagerly rode to meet him, at the head of only six hundred horse. Such was the rapid violence of his assault, that the advanced guards of the king were thrown into disorder, and their leader Artagerses fell by the hand of Cyrus, who, with all his great qualities, had not learned to distinguish between the duties of a soldier and a general. By a seasonable retreat he might still, perhaps, have saved his life, and gained a crown. But his eye darting along the ranks, met that of

THE HISTORY OF GREECE. 343

his brother. He rushed forward, with a blind
instinctive fury, crying out, "I see the man!"
and, penetrating the thick globe of attendants,
aimed his javelin at the king, pierced his corslet,
and wounded his breast. His eagerness to destroy
the enemy prevented proper attention to save
himself. From an uncertain hand he received a
severe wound in the face, which, however, only
increased the fury with which he assaulted his
brother. Various and inconsistent accounts were
given of the death of Cyrus, even by those who
assisted in this memorable engagement. The
crowd of historians thought it incumbent on them
to make him die like the hero of a tragedy,
after many vicissitudes of fortune, and many
variations of misery. Dinon and Ctesias[10], the
longer to suspend the curiosity of their readers,
kill him as with a blunted weapon; but Xenophon is contented with saying, that he fell in the
tumultuary conflict of his attendants with the guards
of Artaxerxes, who zealously defended their respective masters; and that eight of his most confidential friends lay dead upon him, thus sealing
with their blood their inviolable affection and
fidelity[11].

CHAP.
XXV.

His death.

Such was the catastrophe of this audacious and
fatal enterprise; after which the troops of Artaxerxes advanced, in the ardor of success, and proceeded, without encountering any resistance, to the
hostile camp; Ariæus leading off the forces of

The Persian troops plunder the camp of Cyrus.

[10] Apud Plutarch. in Artaxerx.   [11] Xenoph. p. 266.

Z 4

CHAP.
XXV.

Lesser Asia, dejected and dismayed by the loss of their prince and general. Among the valuable plunder in the tents of Cyrus, the Barbarians found two Grecian women, his favorite mistresses, the elder of Phocæa, the younger of Miletus. The former, whose wit and accomplishments heightened the charms of her beauty, received and deserved the name of Aspasia, from the celebrated mistress of Pericles, whose talents she rivalled, and whose character she too faithfully resembled. The young Milesian likewise fell into the hands of the enemy; but while carelessly guarded by the Barbarians, intent on more useful plunder, escaped unobserved, and arrived naked in the quarter of the Greeks, where a small guard had been left to defend the baggage.

The Greeks, victorious in their quarter of the field, pursue the enemy.

Meanwhile Clearchus, at the head of the Grecian phalanx, pursuing the fugitives, had been carried above the distance of three miles from Artaxerxes. But when he heard that the Barbarians were in his tent; and perceived, that, tired with plunder, they advanced to attack his rear, he faced about in order to receive them. The time was spent, till sun-set, in various dispositions made by the cavalry of Artaxerxes; but neither the soldiers, nor their commanders, had courage to come within the reach of the Grecian spear. They fled in scattered disorder, wherever the Grecians advanced; who, wearied with marching against an enemy that seemed incapable to fight, at length determined to return to their camp; wondering that neither Cyrus himself appeared, nor any of

THE HISTORY OF GREECE. 345

his meſſengers ²⁰. They arrived in the beginning of the night, but found their tents in diſorder, their baggage plundered, their proviſions deſtroyed or ſpent. They chiefly regretted the loſs of four hundred carriages filled with wine and flour, which had been provided by the foreſight of Cyrus, as a reſource in time of want. Even theſe were rifled by the king's troops; and the Greeks, whom the ſudden appearance of the enemy had not allowed to dine, were obliged to paſs the night without ſupper; their bodies exhauſted by the fatigue of a laborious day, and their minds perplexed by the uncertain fate of their allies ²¹.

At the approach of light, they prepared to move their camp, when the meſſengers of Ariæus arrived, acquainting them with the death of Cyrus. The new commander, they ſaid, had aſſembled the troops of Leſſer Aſia in their former encampment, about twelve miles from the field of battle; where he intended to continue that day, that the Greeks might have time to join him; but if they delayed, he would next day proceed, without them, towards Ionia, with the utmoſt expedition. When

CHAP. XXV.

Behaviour of the Greeks when informed of Cyrus's death.

---

[20] In relating this battle, I have followed the advice of Plutarch in Artaxerxes, who ſays, " that Xenophon has deſcribed it with ſuch perſpicuity, elegance, and force, as ſets the action before the eyes of his reader, and makes him aſſiſt with emotion at every incident, not as paſt, but as preſent. A man of ſenſe, therefore, will deſpair to rival Xenophon; and, inſtead of relating the action in detail, will ſelect ſuch circumſtances only as are moſt worthy of notice."

[21] Xenoph. p. 270, et ſeqq.

CHAP.
XXV.

the Greeks recovered from the confternation into which they were thrown by thefe unexpected and melancholy tidings, Clearchus replied, "Would to God Cyrus were alive! but fince he is dead, let Ariæus know, that we have conquered the king; that his troops have every where fled before us; and that now no enemy appears to refift our arms. You may, therefore, affure Ariæus, that if he will come hither, we will place him on the Perfian throne, which is the juft reward of our victory." With this propofal the meffengers departed, and Clearchus led his troops to the field of battle, to collect provifions, which were prepared by ufing for fuel the wooden bucklers, fhields, and arrows, of the Barbarians[11].

Their anfwer to the heralds of Artaxerxes, who demanded their armor.

Next morning heralds arrived from Artaxerxes, who entertained a very different opinion from that expreffed by Clearchus, concerning the iffue of the battle. Among thefe refpected minifters was Philinus, a fugitive Greek, a man efteemed by Tiffaphernes, both as a fkilful captain and as an able negociator When the chiefs were affembled, Philinus, fpeaking for his colleagues, declared it to be the will of the great king, who had defeated and killed Cyrus, "That the Greeks, who had now become the flaves of the conqueror, fhould furrender their arms." The demand was heard with univerfal indignation. One defired him to tell the king "to come and take them;" another, "that it was better to die, than to deliver up their arms."

[11] Xenoph. p. 272.

Xenophon spoke to the following purpose: "We have nothing, as you see, O Philinus! but our arms, and our valor. While we keep possession of the one, we can avail ourselves of the other: but, if we deliver up our arms, we also surrender our persons. Do not therefore expect that we shall throw away the only advantages which we still enjoy; on the contrary, be assured, that, relying on our arms and our valor, we will dispute with you those advantages which you possess." Clearchus enforced the sentiments of Xenophon, which were confirmed by the army; and Philinus, after a fruitless attempt to discover the immediate designs of the Greeks, returned with his colleagues to the Persian camp [17].

Meanwhile, Ariæus replied to the honorable embassy which had been sent him, "That there were many Persians of greater consideration than himself, who would never permit him to be their king; he repeated his desire that the Greeks should join him; but, if they declined to come, persisted in his resolution of returning with all haste to Ionia." This proposal was approved by the propitious indications of the victims: the army marched in order of battle to the encampment of Ariæus; who, with the most distinguished of his captains, entered into treaty with the Grecian commanders, binding themselves by mutual oaths to perform to each other the duties of faithful and affectionate allies. Having ratified this engagement by a

[17] Xenoph. p. 273.

CHAP. XXV.

solemn sacrifice, they proceeded to deliberate concerning their intended journey. It was determined, that instead of traversing the desolated country by which they had arrived at the field of battle, they should direct their course towards the north, by which means they would avoid the desert, acquire provisions in greater plenty, and cross the great rivers, which commonly diminish near their source, with less difficulty and danger. They resolved also to perform their first marches with all possible expedition, in order to anticipate the king's approach; since with a small force he would not dare to follow, and with a great army he would not be able to overtake them [11].

They accept a truce from Artaxerxes.

This plan of retreat proposed by Ariæus, had the dishonorable appearance of flight; but fortune proved a more glorious conductor. Such was the effect of the Grecian courage and firmness on the counsels of Artaxerxes, that he, who had so lately commanded the soldiers to surrender their arms, sent heralds to them the day following to treat of a truce. This memorable agreement, the consequences of which were so calamitous, yet so honorable to the Greeks, was concluded by the intervention of Tissaphernes; who engaged, on the part of his master, to furnish them with a market, to cause them to be treated as friends in the countries through which they marched, and to conduct them without guile into Greece. For the Greeks, on the other hand, Clearchus and the generals swore,

[11] Xenoph. p. 276.

that they should abstain from ravaging the king's territories; that they should supply themselves with meat and drink only, when, by any accident, the market was not provided; but when it was, that they should purchase whatever they wanted for a reasonable price [19].

CHAP. XXV.

When this business was transacted, Tissaphernes returned to the king, promising to come back as soon as possible. But on various pretences, he delayed twenty days; during which the Persians had an opportunity to practise with Ariæus. By the dread of punishment, if he persisted in rebellion; by the promise of pardon, if he returned to his allegiance; and, above all, by the warm solicitation of his kinsmen and friends, that unsteady Barbarian was totally detached from the interest of his Grecian allies. His conduct gave just ground to suspect this disposition, which became fully evident after the return of Tissaphernes. From that moment Ariæus no longer encamped with the Greeks, but preferred the neighbourhood of that perfidious satrap. Yet, for three weeks, no open hostility was committed; the armies, fearing, and feared by each other, pursued the same line of march; Tissaphernes led the way; and, according to agreement, furnished the Greeks with a market; but treacherously increased the difficulty of their journey, by conducting them by many windings through the canals and marshes between the Tigris and Euphrates. When they had crossed the

Treachery of Tissaphernes and Ariæus.

[19] Xenoph. p. 281, et seqq.

former river, they continued to march northward along its eastern banks, always encamping at the distance of two or three miles from the Barbarians. Yet this precaution was unable to prevent the parties sent out to provide wood or forage from quarrelling with each other. From reproachful words, they soon proceeded to hostile actions; and these partial encounters were likely to produce the worst consequences, by inflaming the latent, but general animosity, which it had been so difficult to stifle or conceal [10].

At length they arrived at the fatal scene, where the river Zabatus, flowing westward from the mountains of Media, pours its tributary waters into the broad stream of the Tigris. The Grecian generals, and particularly Clearchus, who had long seen and lamented the unfortunate jealousies prevailing among those who had sworn mutual fidelity, proposed a conference between the commanders, in order amicably to explain and remove every ground of hatred and complaint. Tissaphernes and Ariæus, as well as their colleague Orontes, eagerly desired the conference, though their motives were very different from those which actuated Clearchus. A measure so agreeable to both parties was, without difficulty, carried into execution; and the Greeks, on this occasion alone, forsook that prudence and caution, which, both before and after, uniformly governed their conduct. Five generals, and twenty captains, repaired to the

[10] Xenoph. p. 282.

tent of Tissaphernes; only two hundred soldiers followed them, under pretence of going to market. Clearchus, with his colleagues, Menon, Proxenus, Agias, and Socrates, were conducted into the satrap's apartment; the rest, whether captains or soldiers, were not allowed to enter. This separation occasioned fear and distrust. The appearance of armed Barbarians increased the terror. A gloomy silence prevailed; when, on a given signal, those within the tent were apprehended, and those without cut to pieces. At the same time the Persian cavalry scoured the plain, destroying whomever they encountered. The Greeks were astonished at this mad excursion, which they beheld from their camp; until Nicarchus, an Arcadian, came, miserably mangled, and informed them of the dreadful tragedy that had been acted [11].

Upon this intelligence they ran to their arms; expecting an immediate assault. But the cowardly Barbarians, not daring to engage in open and honorable war, endeavoured to accomplish their designs by the same impious treachery with which they had begun them. Instead of advancing in a body to attack the Grecian camp, they sent Ariæus, Arteazus, and Mithridates, persons whose great credit with Cyrus might prevent their intentions from being suspected by the enemy. They were attended by three hundred Persians, clad in complete armor. When they drew near to the Greeks, a herald called out, " 'That, if any of

CHAP. XXV.

Artaxerxes sends to the Greeks to demand their arms.

[11] Xenoph. p. 286, et seqq.

CHAP. XXV.

Conference on that subject.

the generals or captains were present, they should advance, in order to be made acquainted with the king's pleasure." Cheirisophus the Lacedæmonian, who, next to Clearchus, had hitherto maintained the greatest influence over the army, happened to be absent with a party of foragers. But the remaining generals, Cleanor the Orchomenian, and Sophonetus the Stymphalian, proceeded with caution from the camp, accompanied by Xenophon the Athenian, who (though only a volunteer) followed the commanders, that he might learn what was become of his friend Proxenus[15]. When they came within hearing of the Barbarians, Ariæus said, "Clearchus, O Greeks! having violated his oath, and the articles of peace, is punished with just death; but Proxenus and Menon, who gave information of his crimes, are rewarded with the king's favor. Of you the king demands your arms, which, he says, are now his property, because they belonged to Cyrus, who was his slave." Cleanor the Orchomenian, speaking in the name of the rest, replied to this demand with the utmost indignation, reproaching the perfidy of Ariæus, who had betrayed the friends and benefactors of his master Cyrus; and who co-operated with the enemy of that master, the deceitful and impious Tissaphernes. The Persian endeavoured to justify himself, by repeating his accusation of Clearchus. Upon which Xenophon observed, "That Clearchus, if guilty of perjury, had been justly punished;

[15] Xenoph. p. 286, et seqq.

but

but where are Proxenus and Menon, who are *your* benefactors, and *our* commanders? Let them, at least, be sent to us, since it is evident that their friendship for both parties will make them advise what is best for both." This reasonable request it was impossible to elude; and the Barbarians, after long conferring together, departed without attempting an answer [11]. Their mean duplicity in this interview sufficiently indicated the unhappy treatment of the Grecian commanders, who were kept in close captivity, and afterwards sent to Artaxerxes, by whose order they were put to death.

[11] Xenoph. p. 287.

CHAP. XXVI.

Consternation of the Greeks. — Manly Advice of Xenophon. — Their Retreat. — Difficulties attending it — Surmounted by their Skill and Perseverance. — Their Sufferings among the Carduchian Mountains. — They traverse Armenia. — First behold the Sea from Mount Thecbes. — Defeat the Colchians. — Description of the southern Shore of the Euxine. — Transactions with the Greek Colonies there. — The Greeks arrive at Byzantium. — Enter into the Service of Seuthes. — His History. — Conjunct Expeditions of the Greeks and Thracians. — The Greeks return to the Service of their Country.

THE perfidious assassination of their commanders converted the alarm and terror, that had hitherto reigned in the Grecian camp, into consternation and despair. This dreadful catastrophe completed the afflictions of men distant above twelve hundred miles from their native land; surrounded by craggy mountains, deep and rapid rivers; by famine, war, and the treachery of their allies, still more formidable than the resentment of their enemies. The soldiers reflected, that it was dangerous to depart, yet more dangerous to remain; provisions could be acquired only by the point of the sword; every country was hostile;

although they conquered one enemy, another would be still ready to receive them; they wanted cavalry to pursue the Barbarians, or to elude their pursuit; victory itself would be fruitless; defeat, certain ruin.

Amidst these melancholy reflections they had spent the greater part of the night; when Xenophon the Athenian, inspired, as he acknowledges, by a favorable dream, and animated, as his conduct proves, by the native vigor of a virtuous mind, roused and emboldened by adversity, undertook, amidst the general dejection and dismay, the care of his own and of the public safety. Having assembled the captains belonging to the division of his beloved Proxenus, he faithfully represented to them their situation, which dangerous as it was, ought not to sink brave men to despair. Even in the worst circumstances, fortitude, and fortitude alone, could afford relief. They had been deceived, but not conquered, by the Barbarians; whose perfidious violation of faith, friendship, and hospitality, rendered them odious and contemptible to men and gods; the gods, who were the umpires of the contest, and whose assistance could make the cause of justice and valor prevail over every superiority of strength and numbers [1].

The manly piety of Xenophon was communicated, by a generous sympathy, to the breasts of his hearers; who, dispersing through the various quarters of the camp, summoned together the

[1] Xenoph. p. 291.

CHAP
XXVI.
raised to
the chief
command.

principal officers in the army. To them Xenophon addressed a similar discourse, encouraging them by every argument that religion, philosophy, experience, and particularly their own experience, and that of the Grecian history, could afford, to expect success from their own bravery, and the favor of Heaven, and to disdain the offers of accommodation (if such should be made) from their impious foes, whose insidious friendship had always proved more hurtful than their open enmity. The hearty approbation of the Spartan Cheirisophus added weight and authority to the persuasive eloquence of the Athenian; who farther exhorted them to substitute commanders in the room of those whom they had lost; to disentangle themselves from every superfluous encumberance that might obstruct the progress of their march, and to advance with all expedition towards the sources of the Tigris and Euphrates, in the form of a hollow square, having the baggage and those who attended it in the middle, and presenting the valor of their battalions on every side to the enemy. These resolutions were unanimously approved by the council, after which they were referred to the assembled troops, by whom they were readily confirmed, and carried into immediate execution *. Timasion, Xanthicles, Cleanor, Philysias, succeeded to the late commanders; Xenophon supplied the place of Proxenus: and so ably was the ascendant of Spartan and Athenian virtue maintained

* Xenoph. p. 299.

THE HISTORY OF GREECE.

by him and Cheirisophus, that the names of their unequal colleagues will seldom occur in the following narrative of their retreat.

CHAP. XXVI.

The greater part of the day had been employed in these necessary measures; and in the afternoon, the troops having passed the Zabatus, pursued their march in the disposition recommended by Xenophon. But they had not proceeded far, before their rear was harassed by the Persian archers and cavalry, which afforded them a very inauspicious presage of the hardships to which they must be continually exposed in eighteen days journey along the level frontiers of Media. It was difficult to repel these light skirmishers, and impossible to attack them without being exposed to considerable loss; because a detachment of heavy-armed men, or even of targeteers, could not overtake them in a short space, nor could they continue the pursuit without being cut off from the rest of the army. Xenophon, with more valor than prudence, tried the unfortunate experiment; but was obliged to retreat fighting, and brought back his men wounded, disheartened, and disgraced [1].

The Greeks harassed in their retreat by the Persian archers and cavalry.

But this unfortunate event neither disheartened nor disgraced the commander. He ingenuously acknowledged his error, which, pernicious as it was, had taught the Greeks their wants. They wanted cavalry and light-armed troops; the former of which might be obtained by equipping for war the baggage-horses which had been taken from

They equip their sumpter-horses for war, and furnish the Rhodians with slings.

[1] Xenoph. p. 305, et seqq.

CHAP. XXVI.

the enemy; and the latter might be supplied by the Rhodians (well skilled in the sling), of whom there were great numbers in the army. This advice was approved; a company of fifty horsemen was soon raised, the men vying with each other to obtain the honor of this distinguished service; and two hundred Rhodians were drawn from the ranks, who furnished themselves with slings and leaden balls, which they threw twice as far as the stones employed by the Barbarians. The horsemen wore buff coats and corslets; they were commanded by Lycius the Athenian [*].

Their success in consequence of these measures.

The utility of these preparations was discovered as soon as the enemy renewed their assaults, with a thousand horse, and four thousand slingers and archers. The newly-raised troops advanced with boldness and celerity, being assured that their unequal attack would be sustained by the targeteers and heavy-armed men. But the Persians, not waiting to receive them, fled in scattered disorder; the Greeks pursued, took many prisoners, made great slaughter, and mangled the bodies of the slain, in order to terrify, by such a dreadful spectacle of revenge, their cowardly and perfidious enemies [†].

New difficulties with which they had to struggle.

After this advantage, the army continued to march along the banks of the Tigris, and the western boundaries of Media, meeting with many rich and populous villages, from which they were supplied with provisions; and admiring, as they

[*] Xenoph. p. 307.   [†] Ibid. p. 308.

THE HISTORY OF GREECE. 359

passed along, the immense walls, the lofty and durable pyramids, the spacious but deserted cities, which testified the ancient greatness of that flourishing kingdom, before the Medes reluctantly submitted to the oppressive government of Persia. The Barbarians still endeavoured to annoy them, but with very little success, unless when they passed a bridge, or any narrow defile. On such occasions, the square form, in which they had hitherto marched, was found doubly inconvenient[c]. In order to traverse such a passage, the soldiers were obliged to close the wings, and to crowd into a narrow space, which disordered the ranks, and made them obstruct each other. When they had crossed the bridge or defile, they were again obliged to run with all haste, in order to extend the wings, and resume their ranks, which occasioned a void in the centre, and much disheartened the men, thus exposed to the sudden attack of the pursuers.

To obviate both inconveniences, the Greeks separated from the army six companies, each consisting of an hundred men. These were subdivided into smaller bodies, of fifty and twenty-five, each division of the company, as well as the whole, commanded by proper officers. When it became necessary to close the wings, in order to pass a defile, these troops staid behind, thus disburdening the army of a superfluous mass, and thereby enabling them to proceed without confusion

[c] Xenoph. p. 310.

CHAP.
XXVI.

The Greeks approach the country of the Carduchians.

in their ranks. After the passage was effected, the army might again extend the wings, and assume the same loose arrangement as before, without exposing the centre to danger; because the vacuity left there was immediately supplied by the detached companies; the opening, if small, being filled up by the six divisions of an hundred men each; if larger, by the twelve divisions of fifty, and if very large, by the twenty-four divisions of twenty-five'; as the same number of men, in proportion to the number of columns into which they were divided, would occupy a wider extent of ground'.

With this useful precaution the Greeks performed a succesful march to the mountains of the Carduchians, where the enemy's cavalry could no longer annoy them. But here they found new difficulties, far more formidable than those with which they had hitherto been obliged to contend. The Tigris, on their left, was so deep and rapid, that the passage appeared absolutely impracticable. Before them rose the high and craggy mountains, which overshadowed the river, inhabited by a

---

' Xenoph. p. 310.

' I have explained this matter minutely, because the words of Xenophon are mistaken by great military writers. Major Meusvillon, a skilful engineer and excellent scholar, proposes a transposition of the words of Xenophon, that the greater gaps may be filled up by the greater divisions. He justly observes, that no translator or commentator has taken notice of the difficulty that naturally presents itself on reading the passage, which however, I hope is sufficiently perspicuous in the text. See l'Essai sur l'Influence de la Poudre à Canon, etc. a work which, I believe, no military man can read without receiving from it instruction and entertainment.

THE HISTORY OF GREECE. 361

warlike race of men, whose barbarous independence had always defied the hostilities [9] of Persia, as that of their successors, the modern Curdes, does the arms of the Turk, to whom they are but nominally subject [10]. While the Greeks doubted what course to pursue, a certain Rhodian undertook to deliver them from their perplexity, provided they gave him a talent, to reward his labor. "I shall want, besides," continued he, "two thousand leather bags, which may be obtained by flaying the sheep, goats, oxen, and asses, which the country affords in such numbers as we see around us. The skins may be blown, tied at the ends, and fastened together by the girts belonging to the sumpter-horses, then covered with fascines, and lastly with earth. I shall use large stones instead of anchors; every bag will bear two men, whom the fascines and earth will prevent from slipping, and whom, with very little labor on their part, the rapidity of the current will waft across the river [11]."

This ingenious contrivance was commended, but not carried into execution; the Grecians having learned from some prisoners recently taken, that the road through the country of the Carduchians would soon conduct them to the spacious and plentiful province of Armenia. Thither they fearlessly penetrated, regardless of the report, that under a former reign, a Persian army of a hundred

CHAP. XXVI.

Ingenious contrivance of a Rhodian for passing the Tigris.

The sufferings of the Greeks among the mountains of the Carduchians.

[9] Xenoph. p. 315. [10] Rauwolf's Travels.
[11] Xenoph. p. 314.

CHAP. XXVI.

and twenty thousand men had been cut off by those fierce barbarians, whose manners were more rude and inhospitable than the mountains which they inhabited. At the approach of the Greeks, the Carduchians retired to their fastnesses, leaving the villages in the plain at the mercy of the invaders. The troops were restrained from injury; but their inoffensive behaviour, and kind invitations to peace, were regarded with contempt by the common enemies of the Greeks, of the Persians, and of human kind. They seized every opportunity to obstruct the march of the army; and though unprepared for a close engagement, used with extraordinary effect their bows, three cubits long, which they bent by pressing the lower part with their left foot. The arrows were near as long as the bows; and their irresistible points pierced the firmest shields and corslets. The Greeks employed their skill in tactics, and their valor, to elude, or to repel, the assault of these dangerous foes, from whom they suffered more in seven days than they had done in as many weeks from the bravest troops of Artaxerxes [13]. At length they arrived at the river Centrites, two hundred feet broad, which forms the southern boundary of Armenia, having just reason to rejoice that they had escaped the weapons of the Carduchians, whose posterity, the Parthians [14], with the same arms and address, became formidable to Rome, when Rome was formidable to the world [15].

[13] Xenoph. p. 218—226.   [14] Strabo, l. xvi. p. 115.
[15] Plut. in Crasso et Marc. Anton.

THE HISTORY OF GREECE. 363

The month of January was employed in traversing the fruitful plains of Armenia [15], which are beautifully diversified by hills of easy ascent. Teribazus, the Persian governor of the province, entered into an agreement with the generals, that if they abstained from hostilities, he would not obstruct their march, but furnish them plentifully with provisions. But this league was perfidiously violated. The Greeks had recourse to arms; pursued Teribazus; assaulted and plundered his camp [16]. Next day they were exposed to a more dangerous contest, in which neither skill nor valor could avail. The snow fell in such quantities during the night, as completely covered the men with their arms. Their bodies were benumbed and parched with the piercing coldness of the north-wind. Many slaves and sumpter-horses perished, with about thirty soldiers. The rest could scarcely be persuaded by Xenophon to put themselves in motion, which was known to be the only remedy for their distress; and as the severity of the weather still continued during the remainder of their march through Armenia, several soldiers lost their sight by the glare of the snow, and their toes and fingers by the intenseness of the cold [17]. The eyes were best defended by wearing something black before

CHAP.
XXVI.
They traverse Armenia.

In danger of perishing by the intense cold of that country.

[15] There the Greeks found παντα τα επιτηδεια, οιτος ητο αγαθα, εμπιον, σιτον, οινους παλαιους ευωδεις, αςαβιδας, οσπρια παντοδαπα} " all kinds of necessaries, and even luxuries, victims, corn, old fragrant wines, dried grapes, and all sorts of pulse. "
[16] Xenoph. p. 328.   [17] Ibid. p. 329, et seqq.

CHAP.
XXVI.
Proceed
through
the territories of
the Taochians.

them; the feet were preserved by constant motion in the day, and by stripping bare in the night.

From Armenia they proceeded to the country of the Taochians, who, alarmed by the approach of an unknown enemy, had abandoned the vallies, and taken refuge on the mountains, with their wives, children, and cattle. Hither also they had conveyed all their provisions; so that the Greeks were obliged to attack these fastnesses, otherwise the army must have been starved. The Barbarians boldly defended them, by letting fly innumerable vollies of stones down the precipices. But this artillery was at length exhausted; the Greeks became masters of the heights; and a dreadful scene followed. The women first threw their children down the rocks, and then themselves. The men imitated this frantic example of despair; so that the assailants made few prisoners; but took a considerable quantity of sheep, oxen, and asses [19].

The fierce
and fearless character of
the Chalybeans.

From thence the army proceeded with uncommon celerity through the bleak and rocky country of the Chalybeans; marching, in seven days, about an hundred and fifty miles. The Chalybeans were the fiercest nation in all those parts. They wore, for their defence, linen corslets, greaves, and helmets; they carried a short falchion at their girdles; and attacked with pikes fifteen cubits long. Instead of discovering any symptoms of flight or fear, they sang, danced, and rejoiced, at the approach of an enemy. They boldly defended

[19] Xenoph. p. 338.

their villages; not declining even a close engagement with the Greeks; who could supply themselves with nothing from this inhospitable and warlike country, but, in their dangerous march through it, subsisted entirely on the cattle lately taken from the Taochians [19].

The river Harpasus, four hundred feet broad, separated the territories of the Chalybeans and Scythinians. From the latter the Greeks met with little resistance, in a march of thirteen days, which brought them to the lofty mount Theches, a place held in particular devotion by the inhabitants of the neighbouring territory. The vanguard had no sooner ascended this sacred mountain, than the army were alarmed by loud shouts, which continued to redouble with increasing violence. It was imagined that some new form of danger had appeared, or that some new enemy was ready to assail them. The rear advanced with all possible expedition to the assistance of their companions; but having arrived within hearing, were seized with the most pleasing astonishment, when their ears were saluted from every quarter with the repetition, "The sea! the sea!" the sight of which, a sight so long wished in vain, at first filled them with transports of tumultuous joy, and afterwards recalled more distinctly the remembrance of their parents, their friends, their country, and every object of their most tender concern [20]. The soldiers, with tears in their eyes, embraced

[19] Xenoph. p. 318.   [20] Ibid. p. 319.

CHAP. XXVI.

each other, and embraced their commanders; and then, as by a hidden consent of sympathy (for it was never known by whose orders), heaped up a mount of stones, which they covered with barbaric arms, as a trophy of their memorable journey through so many fierce and hostile nations.

They pass through the country of the Macronians.

The distant prospect of the Euxine made them forget that they had not yet attained the end of their labors. A space, indeed, of less than sixty miles' intervened; but it was covered by the trackless forests of the Macronians, and by the abrupt and intricate windings of the Colchian mountains. A fortunate circumstance enabled them without difficulty to surmount the first of those obstacles. Among the Grecian targeteers was a man who understood the language of the Barbarians. He had been carried to Athens in his youth, where he had served as a slave. At the sight of the Macronians, he recognised his long-forgotten countrymen; and having addressed them in terms of friendship and respect, engaged them to exchange presents, and to enter into alliance with the Greeks[11], whom they plentifully supplied with provisions, and having cut down the trees that interrupted their passage, conducted them in three days to the western frontier of Colchos.

Enter Colchos.

This country, so famous in the fables of antiquity[12], was inhabited by an ancient colony of Egyptians, who long preserved pure from any foreign admixture, not only their original language,

[11] Xenoph. p. 340.   [12] See Vol. I. p. 19, et seqq.

but the singular manners; and the more singular rites and ceremonies, of their mother-country[1]. Though diftinguifhed in other refpects from the neighbouring nations, whom they detefted, and to whom they feemed deteftable, they agreed with them in their jealoufy of the Greeks, whofe flourifhing colonies along the fouthern fhores of the Euxine threatened the fafety of their dominions. They affembled therefore from all quarters, occupied the heights, and prepared to difpute the paffage with obftinacy. Their numbers, their difcipline, their arms, but, ftill more, their fituation, rendered them formidable. If the Greeks advanced in a phalanx, or full line, their ranks would be broken by the inequalities of the ground, the centre would be difordered, and the fuperior numbers of the enemy would outreach either wing[2]. Thefe inconveniences might partly be remedied by making fuch parts of the line, as had an eafy afcent, wait for the flow and difficult progrefs of their companions through more abrupt and inacceffible mountains; and, by extending the phalanx in length, and leaving very few men in file, their front might be rendered equal to that of the Colchians But the firft of thefe operations would have too long expofed the army to the darts and arrows of the Barbarians, and the fecond would have fo much enfeebled the line, as muft have rendered it liable to be penetrated. Amidft this choice of difficulties,

[1] Herodot. l. 4. c. 217. [2] Idem, p. 301.

CHAP.
XXVI.

Xenophon propofed, and the propofal was readily approved by his colleagues, that the heavy-armed men fhould be divided into companies of an hundred each, and that each divifion fhould be thrown into a feparate column. The wide intervals between the columns might thus enable the fmaller army to extend on the right and left beyond the enemy's line; each company or divifion might afcend the mountain wherever they found it moft convenient; the braveft men might be led firft to the charge; the depth of the columns [51] could not poffibly be penetrated; nor could the enemy fall into the intervals between them, without being cut off by the divifions on either fide, which might be arranged in fuch a manner as to relieve, encourage, and fupport each other.

Defeat the Colchians.

This judicious difpofition was attended with the expected fuccefs. The heavy-armed men formed eighty companies; the targeteers and archers, divided into three bodies, each of about fix hundred men, flanked the army on the right and left. Their third divifion, confifting chiefly of Arcadians, occupied a diftinguifhed place in the centre. Thus difpofed for battle, the wings of the Grecian army, and particularly the targeteers and archers, who were moft capable of expedition, advanced with

[51] The λοχος ορθιος is defined by Arrian to be a body of men, with the files longer than the ranks; that is, with more men in depth than in front. The φαλαγξ, without any epithet, means the contrary. But the φαλαγξ ορθια is an army, as the fame author tells us, εχων τα μερη τεταγμενα, that is, having more men in depth than in front, and employing, for fome extraordinary reafon, what is naturally the line of march as an order of battle.

celerity

THE HISTORY OF GREECE. 369

celerity to the attack. The enemy, who saw them approach, and who perceived that on either hand they outreached their line, filed to the right and left in order to receive them. By this movement they left a void in their centre, towards which the Arcadian targeteers, supported by the nearest columns, advanced with rapidity, and soon gained the summit. They could thus fight on equal terms with the Barbarians, who, thinking they had lost all when they lost the advantage of the ground, no longer offered resistance, but fled on every side with disordered trepidation, leaving the Greeks masters of the field of battle, as well as of the numerous villages in that neighbourhood ⁶⁶, and within two days march of the Euxine sea, without any other enemy to oppose their long-disputed passage thither.

CHAP. XXVL

The southern shore of the Euxine, which actually presents one uniform scene of effeminate indolence and sullen tyranny, anciently contained many barbarous but warlike tribes, totally independent on each other, and scarcely acknowledging any dependance on the king of Persia. That part which extends towards the east and the borders of Mount Caucasus, and which afterwards formed the kingdom of the great Mithridates, was inhabited by the Colchians, Drillians, Mysonæcians, and Tybarenians; the middle division was possessed by the Paphlagonians, who gloried in the irresistible prowess of their numerous cavalry; and the western parts, extending two hundred miles from Heraclea

Description of the southern shore of the Euxine.

⁶⁶ Xenoph. p. 342.

VOL. III. B b

CHAP. XXVI.

The Greek colony of Sinopè.

to the Thracian Bosphorus, were occupied by the inhospitable Bithynians; a colony of Thrace, who excelled and delighted in war, which, like their ancestors in Europe, they carried on with a savage fury[97].

Amidst the formidable hostility of those numerous nations arose, at wide intervals, several Grecian cities, which enlivened the barbaric gloom, and displayed the peculiar glory of their arts and arms. Sinopè, the mother and the queen of those cities, was advantageously situated on a narrow isthmus which joined its territory, consisting in a small but fertile peninsula[98], to the province of Paphlagonia. The foundation of Sinopè remounted to the highest antiquity, and was ascribed to Antolycus, one of the Argonauts[99]. The city was afterwards increased by a powerful accession of Milesians. It possessed convenient harbours on either side of the isthmus. The peninsula was surrounded by sharp rocks, which rendered it inaccessible to an enemy; and the sea abounded with the tunny-fish, which flow in shoals from the Palus Mæotis, where they are supposed to be bred[100], to the Euxine and Propontis.

[97] See Dionysius Periegetes, and Arrian's Periplus.

[98] Tournefort, v. iii. p. 46. says it is about six miles in circumference.

[99] See the account of the Argonautic expedition, vol. I. p. 89. et seqq. Strabo, l. xii. p. 546. who gives us this information, says farther, that Lucullus, when he took the town, carried away the statue of Antolycus.

[100] Tournefort, Voyage au Levant.

Such multiplied advantages rendered the Sinopians populous and powerful. They diffused their colonies to the east and west. It is not improbable that they founded Heraclea[16], on the frontier of Bithynia; and it is certain that they built Cotyora in the territory of the Tybarenians, Cerasus in that of the Mysonæcians, and Trapezus in that of the Drillians.

CHAP. XXVI.
The Sinopians found new colonies on that coast.

Trapezus, or Trebizond, was the first friendly city at which the Grecians arrived, after spending more than a twelvemonth in almost continual travelling and war. The numerous inhabitants of this flourishing sea-port, which has now decayed into the much-neglected harbour of Platana[17], received them with open arms, generously supplied their wants, and treated them with all that endearing yet respectful hospitality of kinsmen, who commiserated their sufferings and admired their virtue. The Grecians, on their part, displayed a very just and becoming sense of the evils which they had escaped, and of their actual security. In the fervor of religious gratitude they paid the solemn vows and sacrifices which they had promised to

The Greeks are hospitably received at Trebisond, one of these colonies.

[16] Strabo, l. xii. p. 542. calls Heraclea a colony of the Milesians, by whom we may understand the Sinopians, who were themselves a colony of that people. Xenophon, however, called Heraclea a colony of Megareans. Xenoph. Anabas. p. 358.

[17] Tournefort, l. xvii. This place, however, is still large, but depopulated; containing more woods and gardens than houses, and those only of one story; yet the town retains the form of an oblong square; the modern walls being built on the ruins of the ancient; the shape of which occasioned the name of Trapezus, from the Greek word signifying a table. Tournefort, ibid.

Bb 2

CHAP.
XXVI.
Jupiter the preserver, and the other gods and heroes, whose bountiful protection had hitherto conducted them through so many known, and so many concealed dangers. They afterwards celebrated, with much pomp and festivity, the gymnastic games and exercises; an entertainment equally agreeable to themselves, to the citizens of Trebizond, and to the divinities whom they both adored. When these essential duties, for such the Greeks deemed them, had been performed with universal satisfaction, the soldiers, who were unwilling to be burdensome to their Trebizontian friends, found sufficient employment in providing for their own subsistence, and that of their numerous attendants. For several days they ravaged the neighbouring villages of the Colchians and Drillians; and while they cruelly harassed the enemies, they carefully respected the allies of Trebizond. Their repeated devastations at length desolated the country immediately around them, so that the foraging parties could no longer set out and return on the same day; nor could they penetrate deep into the territory, without being endangered by the nocturnal assaults of the Barbarians. These circumstances rendered it necessary for them to think of leaving Trebizond; on which account an assembly was convened to fix the day of their departure, and to regulate the mode and plan of their future journey[11].

Chirisophus calls to the

In this important deliberation the soldiers very generally embraced the opinion of Anaxileon of

[11] Xenoph. 343, et seq.

Thuria, who told them that, for his part, he was already tired with packing up his baggage, marching, running, mounting guard, and fighting, and now wished, after all his labors, to perform the remainder of the journey like Ulysses, and, stretched out at his ease, to be carried asleep[10] into Greece. That this pleasing proposal might be put in execution, Cheirisophus sailed to the Hellespont, hoping to obtain ships from Anaxibius, who commanded the Spartan fleet in that sea. But in case such a request could not be conveniently granted, the soldiers determined to demand a few ships of war from the inhabitants of Trebizond, with which they intended to put to sea, and to capture whatever merchantmen they could meet with in the Euxine; in order to employ them as transports[11].

Several weeks elapsed without bringing any news of Cheirisophus, or promising any hope of assistance

CHAP. XXVI.
Hellespont to demand transports from the Spartan admiral.

Meanwhile the Greeks

[10] Thus was Ulysses transported by the Phæacians, who placed him sleeping on the shore of Ithaca:

Ὃι δε ενδον' εν τω ιδη επι τουτο αγοντες

Κατθεσαν εν ιδμη, etc. Odyss. xiii. 133.

The beautiful images which the poet, in the same book, gives of the pleasures of rest, after immoderate labor, played about the fancy of Anacreon:

Και την νηδυμος υπνος επι βλεφαροισι επιπτε

Νηγρετος ηδιστος θανατω αγχιστα εοικως. v. 80.

And again, " The ship cut the waves with a rapidity, which the flight of the swiftest hawk could not accompany, carrying a man.

Ὃς πριν μεν μαλα πολλα παθ' αλγεα ον κατα θυμον

Ανδρων τε πτολεμους, αλεγεινα τε κυματα πειρων.

Δη τοτε γ'ατρεμας ευδε, λελασμενος ὁσσ' επεπονθει."

[11] Xenoph. p. 346.

from the Spartan admiral. Meanwhile the Grecian pirates, for they deserve no better name, infested the Euxine sea. Dexippus, the Lacedæmonian, with a degree of perfidy worthy of his commission, betrayed his companions, and sailed off with the galley which he commanded[16]. But Polycrates, the Athenian, behaved with an ardor and fidelity which even robbers sometimes display in their transactions with each other; and his successful diligence soon collected such a number of vessels as served to transport to Cerasus the aged, the infirm, the women and baggage; while the strength of the army, consisting of men below forty years of age, reached the same place in three days march[17].

The colony of Cerasus, or Cerazont, was delightfully situated near the sea, among hills of easy ascent, covered in every age[18] with whole woods of cherry-trees, from which, in all probability, the place derived its name[19]. From thence the voluptuous Lucullus, in the six hundred and eightieth year of Rome, first brought into Italy this delicious fruit, which ancient naturalists scarcely believed capable of thriving in an Italian sky; but which actually adorns the bleakest and most northern

---

[16] Xenoph. p. 345. [17] Xenoph. p. 349.
[18] Tournefort.
[19] Κερασος, cerasus, cerise, cherry. For a similar reason Tadmor in the desert was called Palmyra, à *palmis*, the palm-tree. Tournefort mentions it as the opinion of St. Jerom, that the place gave name to the fruit. The difference is not material.

regions of our own island. At Cerasus the Greeks remained ten days, disposing of their booty, supplying their wants, and reviewing the army, which still amounted to eight thousand six hundred men, the rest having perished by fatigue, war, cold, and sickness[40].

After this necessary delay, the less active portion again embarked, while the vigorous youth pursued their journey through the romantic country of the Mosynæcians; a barbarous, yet powerful tribe, who received their singular denomination from the wooden houses, or rather towers, which they inhabited[41]; and which, either by chance or design, were scattered in such a manner among the hills and vallies, that at the distance of eight miles, the villages could hear and alarm each other[42]. The army next proceeded through the dark and narrow district of the Chalybians, who subsisted by the working of iron; and whose toilsome labors, rugged mountains, and more rugged manners[43], must have formed a striking contrast with the smiling plains, the pastoral life[44], the innocent and hospitable character of their Tybarenian neighbours; who treated the Greeks with every mark of friendship and respect, and conducted them, with attentive civility, to the city of Cotyora.

It might be expected, that the army, having reached the country of their friends and kinsmen,

[40] Xenoph. p. 349.
[41] Xenoph. p. 351.
[42] Μόγις ετ αντες.
[43] Idem, p. 353.
[44] Dionysius Periegetes qualifies them by the epithet πολυμηλοι; abounding in sheep.

CHAP.
XXVI.
Soon after
their ar-
rival in
Cotyora.

should have been disposed peaceably to enjoy the fruits of their past labors and dangers. If they were unwilling to expose themselves to fresh hostilities from the warlike inhabitants of Paphlagonia and Bithynia, they might have waited the arrival of ships from Sinopé and Heraclea, or from the Spartan admiral in the Hellespont, who would either retain them in his own service, or transport them to the Chersonesus, to Byzantium, and to other cities and territories, which, being lately conquered by Sparta, required the vigilant protection of brave and numerous garrisons. But it is more easy for men to repel the assaults of external violence, than to elude the effects of their own ungovernable passions. The Greeks were involved in real danger, in proportion as they attained apparent security. During the long course of their laborious journey, the terror of unknown Barbarians hanging over them, preserved their discipline and their union. But the air of a Grecian colony at once dissolved both. They, who in the remote regions of the East had acted with one soul, and regarded each other as brethren, again felt the unhappy influence of their provincial distinctions. The army was divided by separate interests, as well as by partial attachments. Those who had acquired wealth, desired to return home to enjoy it. Those who were destitute of fortune, longed to plunder friends and foes, Greeks and Barbarians. The commanders despised and deceived the troops; the troops clamored against, and insulted the commanders. Both were really in the wrong;

THE HISTORY OF GREECE:

and both suspected and accused each other of imaginary crimes, of which none were guilty.

Xenophon, who, with wonderful address, has justified himself from every reproach[41] that can reflect either on his understanding or his heart, does not deny an imputation to which he was exposed by discovering (somewhat, perhaps, unseasonably) the just and extensive views of a philosopher. When he surveyed the southern shores of the Euxine, covered in ancient times, as well as they are at present, with tall and majestic forest-trees, admirably adapted to ship-building; when he considered the convenience of the harbours, and the productions of the neighbouring territory, consisting in flax, iron, and every commodity most necessary in raising a naval power, he was ambitious of establishing a new settlement, which the numbers, the valor, and the activity of his followers, must soon render superior to the other Grecian colonies on the Euxine, or perhaps in any part of Asia. But this noble design, which might have proved so useful and honorable to the army, was blasted by the mean jealousy of his enemies. Xenophon was reproached with forming projects equally romantic and dangerous; and accused of an intention to keep the soldiers from home, that they might continue dependent on himself, and that he might increase his own fame and fortune at the risk of the public safety[42].

Xenophon's great views defeated by the mean jealousy of his enemies.

[41] Xenoph. p. 367.   [42] Idem, p. 369, et seqq.

CHAP.
XXVI.
Sufferings
of the
Greeks in
their
march
through
Bithynia.

The mutinous and distracted spirit of the troops rendered all their future measures weak and wavering. The terror which they inspired, and their wants, which it was necessary to supply, made them very unwelcome guests at Cotyora, Sinopé, and Heraclea, at which places they continued several months, under pretence of waiting for transports, but meanwhile plundering the neigbouring country, laying the cities under contribution, and threatening them with burdens that exceeded their faculties. The inhabitants of Heraclea, while they affected to consider those unreasonable demands, removed their effects from the villages, shut the gates of their city, and placed armed men on the walls. Cheirisophus had by this time returned with vessels from Anaxibius, the Spartan admiral, but not sufficiently numerous to transport so great an army. The soldiers thus disappointed of their hopes, and discontented with their commanders, and with each other, rashly undertook, in separate bodies, the dangerous journey through Bithynia, a country extending two hundred miles from Heraclea to Byzantium, and totally inhabited, or rather wasted, by the Thynians, a Thracian tribe, the most cruel and inhospitable of the human race. In this expedition they lost above a thousand men; and the destruction must have been much greater, had not the generous activity of Xenophon seasonably led his own division to the assistance of those who had deserted his standard. Cheirisophus was soon afterwards killed by a medicine which he had taken in a fever. The sole command devolved on Xenophon; not by appointment, but by the voluntary submission of the troops to his superior mind. He at length taught them to defeat the irregular fury of the Thynians; and, after taking many slaves, and much useful booty, conducted them in safety to Chrysopolis[47], which is now known by the name of Scutari, and considered as the Asiatic suburb of Constantinople.

The neighbourhood of a Grecian colony seemed infectious to the temper of the troops. At Byzantium their mutinous spirits were again thrown into fermentation. Cleander, the governor of that city, who had come to meet them, narrowly escaped death during the fury of a military sedition. Their behaviour rendered them the objects of terror to all the inhabitants of those parts. The Lacedæmonians dreaded the assistance of such dangerous allies; and the satrap Pharnabazus, alarmed for the safety of his province, practised with Anaxibius, who commanded in the Hellespont, to allure them, by fair promises, into Europe. Gained by the bribes of the Persian, not only Anaxibius, but his successor Aristarchus, made proposals of advantage to the army, which he had not any intention to fulfil. The troops, enraged at this disappointment, and still more at the treachery of the Spartan commanders, would have attacked and plundered Byzantium, had they not been restrained by the wisdom and authority of Xenophon, who, struggling like a skilful pilot against the violence

[47] Xenoph. p. 277, et seqq.

CHAP. XXVI.

Xenophon dissuades them from plundering that place.

of a tempest, prevented the execution of a measure which must have exposed them to immediate danger, and covered them with eternal infamy[1].

With tears and prayers, he conjured them "not to tarnish, by the destruction of a Grecian city, the glory of a campaign signalized by so many illustrious victories over the Barbarians. What hopes of safety could they entertain, if, after unsuccessfully attempting to dethrone the king of Persia, they should provoke the resentment of Sparta? Destitute as they were of friends, of money, of subsistence; and reduced by their misconduct to a handful of men, could they expect to insult, with impunity the two greatest powers in the world? The experience of late years ought to correct their folly. They had seen that even Athens, in the zenith of her greatness, possessed of four hundred gallies, an annual revenue of a thousand talents, and ten times that sum in her treasury; Athens, who commanded all the islands, and occupied many cities both in Asia and Europe, among which was Byzantium itself, the present object of their frantic ambition, had yielded to the arms of Sparta, whose authority was actually acknowledged in every part of Greece. What madness, then, for men in their friendless condition, a mixed assemblage of different nations, to attack the dominions of a people whose valor was irresistible, and from whose vengeance it was impossible for them to fly, without flying from their country, and taking refuge

[1] Xenoph. p. 399, et seqq.

THE HISTORY OF GREECE.

among those hostile Barbarians, from whom, for near two years past, they had met with nothing but cruelty, injustice, persecution, and treachery?"

The judicious representations of Xenophon saved Byzantium; but it is probable that neither the weight of argument, nor the power of eloquence, would have long restrained the discontented and needy troops from attempting other enterprises of a similar nature, if an opportunity had not fortunately presented itself of employing their dangerous activity in the service of Seuthes, a bold and successful adventurer of Lower Thrace. Mæsades, the father of Seuthes, reigned over the Melandeptans, the Thynians, and the Thranipsans, who inhabited the European shores of the Propontis and Euxine sea. The licentious turbulence of his subjects compelled him to fly from his dominions. He took refuge with Medocus, king of the Odrysians, the most powerful tribe in Upper Thrace, with whose family his own had long been connected by the sacred ties of hospitality. Medocus kindly received, and generously entertained, the father; and, after his decease, continued the same protection and bounty to his son, Seuthes. But the independent spirit of the young prince disdained, as he expresses it, to live like a dog at another man's table. He desired horses and soldiers from Medocus, that he might acquire subsistence for himself. His request was granted; his incursions were successful; the terror of his name filled all the maritime parts of Thrace; and there was

CHAP.
XXVI.

The Greeks invited into the service of Seuthes.

his history.

CHAP.
XXVI.

Their agreement with that prince.

reason to believe that if he could join the Grecian forces to his own, he might easily regain possession of his hereditary dominions [9].

For this purpose he sent to Xenophon Medosades, a Thracian, who, understanding the Greek language, usually served him as ambassador. The terms of the treaty were soon agreed on. Seuthes promised each soldier a Cyzicene (about eighteen shillings sterling), the captains two Cyzicenes, and the generals four, of monthly pay. The money, it was observed, would be clear gain, as they might subsist by plundering the country; yet such of the booty as was not of a perishable nature, Seuthes reserved for himself, that by selling it in the maritime towns, he might provide for the pay of his new auxiliaries [10].

The Grecian commanders entertained in the camp of Seuthes.

Having communicated their designs to the army, the Grecian commanders followed Medosades to the camp of Seuthes, which was distant about six miles from the coast of Perinthus, a city of considerable note in the neighbourhood of Byzantium. They arrived after sun-set, but found the Barbarians awake and watchful. Seuthes himself was posted in a strong tower; horses ready bridled stood at the gate; large fires blazed at a distance, while the camp itself was concealed in darkness; precautions, however singular, yet necessary against the Thynians, who were deemed, of all men, the most dangerous enemies in the

[9] Xenoph. p. 353, et seqq. [10] Idem ibid.

night. The Greeks were permitted to enter. Seuthes received them with rustic hospitality; before entering on business, challenged them to drink in large horns full of wine; then confirmed the promises of his ambassadors; and still farther allured Xenophon by the hopes of receiving, besides the stipulated pay, lands and cattle, and an advantageous establishment on the sea-shore.

Next day the Grecian army joined the camp of their new master. The commanders were again entertained with a copious feast, in which Seuthes displayed all his magnificence. After supper, the buffoons and dancers were introduced, the cup went briskly round, and the whole assembly were dissolved in merriment. But Seuthes knew how far to indulge, and when to restrain, the joys of festivity. Without allowing his revels to disturb the stillness of the night, he rose with a martial shout, imitating a man who avoided a javelin; and then addressing the Grecian captains without any sign of intoxication, desired them to have their men ready to march in a few hours, that the enemy, who were as yet unacquainted with the powerful reinforcement which he had received, might be taken unprepared, and conquered by surprise[11].

The camp was in motion at midnight; it was the middle of winter, and the ground was in many parts covered with a deep snow. But the Thracians, clothed in skins of foxes, were well prepared for such nocturnal expeditions. The Greeks

[11] Xenoph. p. 606. et seqq.

CHAP.
XXVI.

By the af-
sistance
of the
Greeks,
Seuthes
recovers
his heredi-
tary do-
minions.

suffered much [11] by the cold; but the rapidity of their march, animated by the certain prospect of success, made them forget their sufferings. Where-ever they arrived, the villages were attacked and plundered, the houses were burned, many captives and cattle were taken, and the ravages of that bloody night sufficiently represent the uniform scene of cruelty, by which, in the course of a few weeks, Seuthes compelled into submission the inhabitants of that fertile and populous slip of land that lies between the Euxine and Propontis. But the possession of this territory, which formed the most valuable portion of his hereditary dominions, could not satisfy his ambition. He turned his arms northwards, and over-ran the country about Salmydessus, a maritime city situate at the mouth of a river of the same name, which flows from the southern branch of mount Hæmus into a spacious bay of the Euxine. There the allied army repeated the same destructive havoc which they had already made in the south; and avenged, by their cruel incursions, the cause of violated hospitality; for the Barbarians of those parts were so much accustomed to plunder the vessels which were often shipwrecked on their shoaly coast, that they had distinguished it by pillars, in the nature of

[11] Ἦν δὲ χιὼν πολλὴ, καὶ ψύχη οὕτως ὥστε τὸ ὕδωρ, ὁ ἐφέροντο ἐπὶ δεῖπνον, ἐπήγνυτο, καὶ ὁ οἶνος ὁ ἐν τοῖς ἀγγείοις. καὶ τῶν Ἑλλήνων πολλῶν καὶ ῥῖνες ἀπεκαίοντο καὶ ὦτα. There was much snow, and the cold so intense, that the water froze as they were carrying it to supper, and the wine in the vessels. Many of the Greeks also lost their ears and noses. Xenoph. p. 408.

land-marks

land-marks, to prevent inteſtine quarrels, by aſcertaining the property of the ſpoil[51].

In the ſpace of two months after his junction with the Greeks, Seuthes extended his poſſeſſions ſeveral days march from the ſea; his numerous, but unſkilful enemies, fighting ſingly, were ſucceſſively ſubdued; each vanquiſhed tribe increaſed the ſtrength of his army; the Odryſians, allured by the hopes of plunder, flocked to his ſtandard, and the growing proſperity of his fortune, no longer requiring the ſupport, diſpoſed him to neglect the ſervices, of his Grecian auxiliaries[16]. The ungrateful levity of the Barbarian was encouraged by the perfidious counſels of his favorite Heraclides of Maronea, one of thoſe fugitive Greeks, who having merited puniſhment at home for their wickedneſs, obtained diſtinction abroad by their talents; men ſullied with every vice, prepared alike to die or to deceive, and who having provoked the reſentment of their own countrymen by their intrigues and their audacity, often acquired the eſteem of foreigners by their valor and eloquence, their ſkill in war, and dexterity in negociation. Heraclides ſtrongly exhorted his maſter to defraud the Greeks of their pay, and to deliver himſelf from their troubleſome importunities, by diſmiſſing them from his ſervice. But the fears, rather than the delicacy of Seuthes, prevented him from complying with this advice; he loſt his honor

CHAP. XXVI.

His figural ingratitude.

[51] Xenoph. p. 408. [16] Idem, p. 414 et ſeqq.

CHAP.
XXVI.
The Greeks return to the service of their country.

without saving his money; and the Grecian generals had an early opportunity to reproach his perfidy and ingratitude, being soon called to engage in a more honorable war[1], kindled by the resentment of Artaxerxes against the presumption of the Spartans, who had so strenuously supported the unfortunate rebellion of Cyrus.

[1] Xenoph. p. 427.

END OF THE THIRD VOLUME.

www.ingramcontent.com/pod-product-compliance
Lightning Source LLC
Chambersburg PA
CBHW032020220426
43664CB00006B/307